MILITARY HISTORY IN THE NORTH WEST

MILITARY HISTORY IN THE NORTH WEST

*Compiled and Edited
by
Terry Wyke
and
Nigel Rudyard*

Bibliography of North West England
Manchester
1994

Bibliography of North West England

This work forms Volume 15 of the former Lancashire Bibliography series.

© 1994
Bibliography of North West England,
North Western Regional Library System,
Manchester Central Library,
St. Peter's Square,
Manchester M2 5PD

Registered Charity No. 519720

ISBN 0 947969 13 6

All rights reserved. No part of this publication may be reproduced, stored in a retrieval system, or transmitted, in any form or by any means, electronic, mechanical, photocopying, recording and/or otherwise without the prior written permission of the publishers. This book may not be lent, resold, hired out or otherwise disposed of by way of trade in any form of binding or cover other than that in which it is published, without the prior consent of the publishers.

Computer processing and typesetting by the Bibliography of North West England.

Printed in England by
Manchester Free Press,
Unit E3,
Longford Trading Estate,
Thomas Street,
Stretford,
Manchester M32 0JT.

CONTENTS

	Page
Section I: General Reference Works	1
Section II: Regiments and Major Units	
Cheshire Regiment	6
East Lancashire Regiment	14
King's (Liverpool) Regiment	20
King's Own Royal Border Regiment	28
King's Own Royal Regiment (Lancaster)	32
Lancashire Fusiliers	37
Loyal North Lancashire Regiment	45
Manchester Regiment	50
Queen's Lancashire Regiment	59
Royal Artillery	61
Royal Engineers	64
South Lancashire Regiment (Prince of Wales' Volunteers)	65
Section III: Militia, Volunteers, Yeomanry, Rifle Volunteers and Territorials	
Militia	70
Volunteers	74
Yeomanry	82
Rifle Volunteers	85
Territorial Forces	90
Section IV: Royal Air Force and Associated Units	93
Section V: Royal and Merchant Navies	97
Section VI: 1750-1914	100
Section VII: World War I	106
Section VIII: World War II	122
Addresses	142
Author Index	147
Subject Index	159

A man who wishes to seek out good instruction and who is suddenly placed in a vast historical library finds himself thrown into a veritable labyrinth. To know what remains of the ancient historians, to know what has been lost, to distinguish the original fragments from the supplements written by good and bad commentators, this alone is almost a science, or at least an important field of study. Thus the knowledge and choice of the good historians, the good memoirs, the true chronicles of a period is a real and useful knowledge. If...there were a special school of history, and if the first course given there were in bibliography, a young man, instead of wasting months getting lost in unimportant reading, or reading material in which little confidence might be placed would be directed toward the best works and more easily and quickly attain a better education.
Napoleon, 1807

That war is an evil is something that we all know, and it would be pointless to go on cataloguing all the disadvantages involved in it. No one is forced into war by ignorance, nor, if he thinks he will gain from it, is he kept out of it by fear. The fact is that one side thinks that the profits to be won outweigh the risks to be incurred, and the other side is ready to face danger rather than accept an immediate loss.
Thucydides, History IV

Only those who know what it is to spend several months on end in the atmosphere of an army on active service can appreciate how blissfully happy Nikolai felt when he got beyond the region overrun by troops and their foraging parties, provision-trains and field hospitals - when, instead of soldiers, army wagons and the filth which betrays the presence of a military camp, he found himself among villagers of peasant men and women, gentlemen's country houses, fields with grazing cattle, and post-houses with their sleepy masters. He was so happy that he might have been seeing everything for the first time.
Leo Tolstoy, War and Peace

My argument is that War makes rattling good history; but peace is poor reading.
Thomas Hardy

...we lost at Stoney Hill Barracks, Jamaica, 7 officers, 4 doctors, 21 sergeants, 182 rank and file, 5 women, 4 children in six weeks. I thought the whole regiment was going to die.
William Mansfield, Quarter Master, of the 22nd Regiment of Foot, 1798-1834, Diary, Cheshire Military Museum

...if we have not been born again, we have entered a new life- a new life not without hope for the future- and not without hope that the past has at least taught us one thing transcending all others - the utter absurdity of war-the folly-the futility and the idiocy of it all...what better example than the Gallipoli Campaign?
L. Carr, A Sergeant's Log of Gallipoli, 1915-1916, Lancashire Fusiliers Regimental Museum

Introduction

For a number of years subscribers to the former *Lancashire Bibliography* have asked for a publication dealing with military history. This volume meets these requests. It covers military history in the north west from the middle of the eighteenth century to the present day. We have defined military history in a broad manner. At the heart of the bibliography is the identification of printed and published works relating to land forces in the north west. This covers not only those Lancashire and Cheshire regiments, whose connection with the region, in some cases, existed long before the territorial focus initiated by the army reforms of the late nineteenth century, but it also encompasses the various volunteer and militia organisations that have been such a vital part of the nation's armed forces. Whilst, understandably, the bulk of the references are concerned with the army sufficient entries were identified to justify separate, if shorter, sections on the navy and the air force. Although we had originally decided to use the seventeenth century as the starting point for collecting material, it soon became clear that most military references dealing with the seventeenth and first half of the eighteenth century related to the Civil War and the Jacobite rebellions. As the majority of these entries had been identified in Volumes 8 and 9 of the *Lancashire Bibliography*[1] it was decided not to repeat them. Thus in this volume, the starting point for the majority of the references is the 1750s, a key decade in the history of the army, with the reorganisation of regiments and the passing of the Militia Act in 1757.

As in a number of respects this work differs from previous volumes, a word about how the material was collected will help the user appreciate the boundaries of the project. Initially, we followed the standard procedure of the *Lancashire Bibliography* by concentrating on identifying published and printed material and its location in the main libraries in the region, though, of course, that geographical area has now been expanded to include Cheshire and the Isle of Man. Only material that dealt specifically or extensively with the region's military history was considered for inclusion. No attempt was made to trace monographs and articles in which the military history of the north west was mentioned in passing. However, from an early stage of the project we recognised that to identify only published material would produce a narrow reference work, in a subject area where much information was unpublished, and which, moreover, was held in repositories outside of record offices. A more broadly constructed reference work would prove more useful to the researcher. Thus it was decided to locate and include brief surveys of the holdings of the main public archives and museums in the north west. In addition specialist libraries and museums outside of the area administered by the North Western Region Library System were contacted for information on holdings relevant to the north west. If the tendency of local military historians to neglect material located in national and specialist collections in other parts of the country is no longer as great as it was when Atkinson drew attention to it some fifty years ago,[2] it still exists and researchers will appreciate information on the existence of relevant material in such collections. By extending the coverage of the bibliography in this way we believe that we have increased its usefulness.

Having determined these boundaries, the task of collecting the entries was started. We began by extracting relevant titles from the catalogue of local history references held in the office of the Bibliography of North West England in Manchester Central Library. Member libraries were then contacted and asked to submit their holdings on military history. These were added to the appropriate section of the list and in the case of conflicting references checks were carried out against BNB and information held on the regional database. At the same time record offices and museums, inside and outside of the region, were contacted for information on their holdings. Within the time available, the project was started in the spring of 1993, visits were arranged to examine those collections inside the region where the holdings were clearly sizeable.

The bibliography is arranged in the following way. The first section is a select list of general reference works which will assist the researcher in locating information on a wide range of military topics. This is followed by sections devoted to those regiments and militia forces associated with the region. Entries which did not easily fit into the sections on regiments have been organised in three sections: 1750-1914, First World War, and the Second World War. Separate sections are included on the Royal Navy and the Royal Air Force. The addresses for libraries, record offices and museums used in the project follow the bibliographical sections.

In each section published entries are arranged alphabetically by author's name or where no author is cited by the title of the work, excluding the definite and indefinite article. The standard entry for books and pamphlets identifies author, title, place of publication, publisher, and year of publication. For an article in a periodical or magazine, information on author, title of article, journal title, volume number and pages is provided. Considerations of space and time decided us against providing a fuller reference though for many of the entries the Bibliography's database contains additional information. Following the practise of the *Lancashire Bibliography* locations are identified for each entry except for those with ten or more locations, when an asterisk appears. A key to the libraries and other repositories appears at the beginning of the volume. As in most bibliographies certain works could have been located in more than one section. In order to avoid duplicating references we have placed references in only one category, the one that we judged best corresponded to the main theme of the work.

In each of the major sections the listing of published works is followed by a survey of the principal holdings of archive materials. This covers holdings in record offices and museums, and archival material in the possession of regiments and military museums. It is not a comprehensive listing of all archival holdings but rather a listing of the main groups of records. Each section is prefaced with a short introduction which in the case of the regiments also includes a simplified family tree to help understand their often complex lineage.[3]

We are indebted to all of the librarians, archivists and museum curators who have supplied us with information, answered queries and spent time showing us their collections. Without their assistance this would have been a far slimmer and less useful volume, and one that would not have appeared so quickly. We hope that they will find it a valuable reference tool when dealing with enquiries from all types of library user. We are also grateful for the considerable encouragement and advice provided by the members of the Bibliography's advisory committee. A special thanks to Major Tony Astle, Dr. Stephen Bull, Mr. Peter Donnelly, Major John Ellis, Major John Hallam, Dr. Michael Powell and Diana Winterbotham, who took the time to read and comment on an earlier draft of the work. I would also like to thank the Manchester Metropolitan University for providing me with the time to work on this project.

Although this volume captures many more references and provides much greater information on the region's military history than can be found in the standard military history reference works,[4] we would not wish to suggest that it approaches completeness or that it is free of errors. We would be pleased to hear from users of omissions and corrections. However in spite of its limitations we do believe that it will prove an essential and time-saving guide to all types of researcher interested in military history. Above all we hope that it will play a part in encouraging research into this important but much neglected aspect of the region's history. Recent general social and economic histories of Lancashire and Cheshire have had little to say about the role of the military.[5] The yeomanry that has attracted the historian has tended to be spelt, except in the year 1819, in the lower case. As with the teachers, so with the students. Military history is not one of the fashionable areas which occupy the attention of that ever increasing band of undergraduates and postgraduates researching local history dissertations. Yet, at a national level, the writing of military history has been radically reformed and re-directed in recent years by Brian Bond, Edward Spiers and other historians. Sufficient work has been published to indicate that military history should no longer be viewed as some backwater of history, populated only by militaria buffs. The impact of this scholarship has still to reverberate in this region. In drawing attention to the extraordinarily rich printed and manuscript resources available to the local and regional researcher studying military history we hope that this volume will stimulate interest, and the researching and writing of more substantial and considered studies of the role of the military in the north west. The bibliographies of a later generation will testify to the realisation of this hope.

Terry Wyke
Editor

Notes

[1] P.M. Turner (comp). *Lancashire History. Historical Period Stuart.* Vol. 8 (Manchester 1976); P.M. Turner (comp). *Lancashire History. Historical Period Hanover.* Vol. 9 (Manchester 1978).

[2] C.T. Atkinson, "Material for Military History in the Reports of the Historical Manuscripts Commission", *Journal of the Society for Army Historical Research,* 21 (1942) 17-34.

[3] These are largely derived from John B.M. Frederick. *Lineage Book of the British Army:Mounted Corps and Infantry 1660-1968.* (New York, 1969

[4] For example, A. Bruce, *A Bibliography of British Military History 1660-1914* (London, 1985) 2nd edition. Other titles are listed in Section I.

[5] J.K. Walton, *Lancashire A Social History, 1558-1939* (Manchester, 1987); C.B. Phillips and J.H. Smith, *Lancashire and Cheshire from AD 1540* (Harlow, 1994).

Bibliography of North West England: Location Codes

Locations in brackets refer to the main authority to which the library belongs. Locations in bold are headquarters or main libraries.

1	**Manchester**	43	Farnworth (Bolton)
2	**Liverpool**	44	Fleetwood (Lancashire)
3	**Lancashire**	45	Crosby (Sefton)
4	**Cheshire**	46	Hindley (Wigan)
5	Cumbria	47	Warrington Collegiate Institute
6	Blackburn (Lancashire)	48	Newton-le-Willows (St. Helens)
7	**Bolton**	50	Radcliffe (Bury)
8	**Sefton**	51	Royton (Oldham)
9	Burnley (Lancashire)	52	**Trafford**
10	**Bury**	53	Swinton & Pendlebury (Salford)
11	**Oldham**	54	Edge Hill College (Ormskirk)
12	Preston (Lancashire)	55	Douglas Public Library
13	**Rochdale**	56	Westhoughton Library (Bolton)
14	**St. Helens**	57	**Wirral**
15	**Salford**	58	Chester (Cheshire)
16	Southport (Sefton)	59	**Stockport**
17	Warrington (Cheshire)	60	Wallasey (Wirral)
18	**Wigan**	61	Dukinfield (Tameside)
18A	Wigan Archives	62	Hyde (Tameside)
18B	Wigan History Shop	63	Macclesfield (Cheshire)
19	Accrington (Lancashire)	64	Bebington (Wirral)
20	**Tameside**	65	Ellesmere Port (Cheshire)
21	Bacup (Lancashire)	66	Hale (Trafford)
22	Chorley (Lancashire)	67	Southport College
23	Colne (Lancashire)	68	Joint Services Central Library
24	Darwen (Lancashire)	69	Northwich (Cheshire)
25	Eccles (Salford)	70	Sale (Trafford Local Studies Lib.)
26	Haslingden (Lancashire)	72	Bury Metropolitan College
27	Heywood (Rochdale)	74	Bolton Metropolitan College
28	Lancaster (Lancashire)	75	University of Central Lancashire
29	Leigh (Wigan)	76	Crewe (Cheshire)
30	Lytham (Lancashire)	77	University College Salford
31	Middleton (Rochdale)	79	Liverpool University
32	Nelson (Lancashire)	79A	" Archives
33	Rawtenstall (Lancashire)	79B	" Sydney Jones Library
34	Widnes (Cheshire)	79C	" Harold Cohen Library
35	Ashton-in-Makerfield (Wigan)	80	Edge Hill College (Chorley)
36	Atherton (Wigan)	83	Winstanley College
37	Chadderton (Oldham)	85	Manchester University
39	Crompton (Oldham)	86	Neston (Cheshire)
40	**Knowsley**	88	Clitheroe (Lancashire)
41	Denton (Tameside)	89	B.B.C. Library, Manchester
42	Failsworth (Oldham)	90	Oldham College

91	U.M.I.S.T.	114	Hollings College
92	Blackpool (Lancashire)	115	Manchester Metropolitan University
93	Runcorn (Cheshire)	116	Stockport College
94	Altrincham (Trafford)	120	Macclesfield College
98	Hopwood Hall College	121	South Trafford College
100	Salford College	124	Granada Television
101	St. John Rigby 6th Form College		
102	Stalybridge (Tameside)		
105	Bolton Institute (Chadwick)	200	Wilmslow (Cheshire)
106	Bolton Institute (Deane)	201	Winsford (Cheshire)
110	Crewe & Alsager College	202	Runcorn New Town (Cheshire)
111	Salford University	203	Congleton (Cheshire)
112	Lancaster University	204	Nantwich (Cheshire)
113	Crewe & Alsager College	205	Uppermill Library

Special Libraries, Museums and Archives

BA	Bury Archives
BM	Blackburn Museum
BOM	Bolton Museum and Art Gallery
CCRO	Chester City Record Office
CL	Chetham's Library
CMM	Cheshire Military Museum
CRO	Cheshire Record Office
CURO (B)	Cumbria Record Office (Barrow)
CURO (C)	Cumbria Record Office (Carlisle)
CURO (K)	Cumbria Record Office (Kendal)
GM	Grosvenor Museum, Chester
GMCRO	Greater Manchester County Record Office
KORM	King's Own (Royal Lancaster Regiment) Museum
KRMA	King's Regiment Museum Archives, Liverpool (National Museums and Galleries on Merseyside)
LCRM	Lancashire County and Regimental Museum
LFRM	Lancashire Fusiliers Regimental Museum
LRO	Lancashire Record Office
LSM	Liverpool Scottish Museum
MMM	Merseyside Maritime Museum, (National Museums and Galleries on Merseyside)
MNH	Manx National Heritage
MRO	Merseyside Record Office
NAM	National Army Museum, London
RAFM	Royal Air Force Museum, Hendon
RAHT	Royal Artillery Historical Trust, London
RMP	Regimental Museum, Preston (Fulwood Barracks)
SAC	Salford Archives Centre

Important Note: All entries marked * have ten or more locations. It can be reasonably assumed that some, if not all, of the main libraries will hold these titles.

I. GENERAL REFERENCE WORKS

This section identifies basic reference works on modern British military history. Its primary purpose is to draw to the attention of researchers some of the key specialist military bibliographies and research aids that will open up paths into the general secondary literature. Fortunately, the production of bibliographies and other research aids on military history has taken off in recent years. These range from general bibliographical guides such as Bruce [5, 6,] to more specialist, though equally indispensable, works such as that compiled by White on regiments [50]. Apart from studies covering long periods of times considerable effort has been put into controlling the mountains of publications concerned with the two world wars [3, 15, 16, 41]. Complementing these enumerative and annotated bibliographies, the academic researcher is in the fortunate position of being able consult two collections of bibliographical essays assessing the secondary literature [28, 31]. Other literature surveys have appeared in specialist periodicals [45, 46]. Researchers can also turn to a number of encyclopedias and dictionaries offering succinct overviews and definition of terms [10, 12]. The puzzles surrounding the ancestry, amalgamations and name-changes of regiments have been unpicked by a number of authors [20, 27]. The sensational increase in the number of individuals researching family history has also reverberated through military history resulting in the publication of various specialist guides covering, for example, the important collections of War Office documents at the Public Record Office [19, 29]. Non-genealogists will also find these guides valuable.

[1] Ascoli, David. *Companion to the British Army, 1660-1983.* London: Harrap, 1983. **Locations: 1, 3, 4, 7, 8, 10, 11, 13, 14**

[2] Barnes, Robert Money. *A History of the Regiments and Uniforms of the British Army.* London: Seeley Service, 1950. **Locations: 1, 3, 4, 8, 13, 18, 20, 57, 68**

[3] Bayliss, Gwyn M. *Bibliographic Guide to the Two World Wars. An Annotated Survey of English- Language Reference Materials.* London: Bowker, 1977. **Locations: 10, 14, 40, 79, 111**

[4] Brereton, J.M. *A Guide to the Regiments and Corps of the British Army on the Regular Establishment.* London: Bodley Head, 1985. **Locations: 1, 2, 3, 4, 7, 8**

[5] Bruce, Anthony. *A Bibliography of the British Army, 1660-1914.* London: K. G. Saur, 1985. (2nd edition). **Locations: 1, 3, 4, 7, 18**

[6] Bruce, Anthony. *A Bibliography of British Military History from the Roman Invasions to the Restoration, 1660.* Munich: K. G. Saur, 1981. **Locations: 1, 2, 112**

[7] Cantwell, John D. *The Second World War: a guide to documents in the Public Record Office.* London: H.M.S.O., 1993 (2nd edition). Public Record Office Handbook No. 15. **Locations: 3, 4, 7**

[8] Carew, Tim. *How the Regiments Got Their Nicknames.* London: Leo Cooper, 1974. **Locations: ***

[9] Chichester, Henry M. and Burges-Short, George. *The Records and Badges of every Regiment and Corps in the British Army.* London: Greenhill Books, 1986. (2nd edition) **Locations: 1, 3, 7, 57**

[10] Craig, Hardin. *A Bibliography of Encyclopedias and Dictionaries dealing with Military, Naval and Maritime Affairs, 1577-1971.* Houston, Texas. 1971 **Locations: 1**

[11] Davis, Brian L. *British Army Uniforms and Insignia of World War II.* London: Arms and Armour Press, 1983. **Locations: ***

[12] Dupuy, Richard E. and Dupuy, Trevor N. *The Encyclopedia of Military History from 3500 B.C. to the present.* London: Jane's Publishing Company, 1986 (2nd edition). **Locations: 1, 2, 3, 4, 8, 11**

[13] Edwards, Thomas J. *Regimental Badges.* London: Charles Knight, 1974 (6th edition) **Locations: ***

[14] Elliot, George H. *Cavalry Literature. A Bibliographical Record of Works on the History, Organisation, Tactics and Administration of the Cavalry.* Calcutta, 1893 **Locations: 1**

[15] Enser, A. G. S. *A Subject Bibliography of the First World War: Books in English 1914-1987.* Gower, 1990 (2nd edition). **Locations: 1, 2, 7, 13, 112**

[16] --- *A Subject Bibliography of the Second World War: Books in English 1939-1974.* London: Andre Deutsch, 1977 **Locations: ***

[17] ---- *A Subject Bibliography of the Second World War and aftermath: Books in English 1975-1987.* Aldershot: Gower, 1990 **Locations: 2, 3, 7, 111, 115**

[18] Falls, Cyril. *War Books: An Annotated Bibliography of Books About the Great War. With a New Introduction and additional entries by R.J. Wyatt.* London: Greenhill Books, 1989. **Locations: 1, 115**

[19] Fowler, Simon. *Army Records for Family Historians.* London: PRO Publications, 1992. Public Record Office Readers Guide, No.2. **Locations: ***

[20] Frederick, John B. M. *Lineage Book of the British Army:Mounted Corps and Infantry 1660-1968.* New York: Hope Farm Press, 1969 **Locations: 1**

[21] Funk, A.L. *The Second World War: a Select Bibliography of Books in English published since 1975.* California: Regina Books, 1985. **Locations: 1**

[22] Gander, Terry. *Encyclopedia of the Modern British Army.* Wellingborough, Northants: Patrick Stephens, 1986. (3rd edition) **Locations: 1, 2, 4, 7, 8, 11, 13, 20, 52**

[23] Gibson, Jeremy, and Medlycott, Mervyn. *Militia Lists and Musters, 1757-1876: a directory of holdings in the British Isles.* Birmingham: Federation of Family History Societies, 1990. (2nd edition) **Locations: 2, 3, 7, 10, 14, 19, 70, LRO**

[24] Gordon, L. L., et al. *British Battles and Medals: A Description of every campaign medal and bar awarded since the Armada, with the historical reasons for their awards.* London: Spink & Son, 1988 (6th edition). **Locations: 1, 2, 4, 7, 20, 52, 59**

[25] Green, Howard. *Guide to the Battlefields of Britain and Ireland.* London: Constable, 1973. **Locations: ***

[26] Griffin, David. *Encyclopedia of Modern British Army Regiments.* Wellingborough, Northants: Patrick Stephens, 1985. **Locations:** *

[27] Hallows, Ian S. *Regiments and Corps of the British Army.* London: Arms and Armour, 1991. **Locations: 1, 2, 3, 4, 10, 18, 57, 59, 70**

[28] Higham, Robin (ed.). *A Guide to the Sources of British Military History.* London: Routledge Kegan & Paul, 1972. **Locations: 1, 7, 11, 59, 85, 115**

[29] Holding, Norman. *The Location of British Army Records 1914-1918.* Birmingham: Federation of Family History Societies, 1991. (3rd edition) **Locations:** *

[30] Imperial War Museum. Department of Printed Books. *Subject Guide to Booklists and Information Sheets.* London: Imperial War Museum, 1976. **Locations: 1**

[31] Jordan, Gerald, (ed.). *British Military History. A Supplement to Robin Higham's Guide to the Sources.* London: Garland Publishing, 1988. **Locations: 1**

[32] Kipling, Arthur Lawrence, and Hugh Lionel King. *Head-Dress Badges of the British Army.* Vol. 1: Up to the end of the Great War. London: Muller, 1972. **Locations: 1, 7, 15, 52, 59;** (2nd Revised edition) **1978: 7, 13, 52, 57**

[33] --- *Head-Dress Badges of the British Army.* Vol. 2: From the end of the Great War to the present day. London: Muller, 1979. **Locations: 1, 4, 7, 13, 18, 52**

[34] Kitzmiller, John M II. *In Search of the "Forlorn Hope": A Comprehensive Guide to Locating British Regiments and their Records 1640 to World War One.* 2 vols. Salt Lake City: Manuscript Pub. Foundation, 1988. **Locations: 1**

[35] Law, Derek G. *The Royal Navy in World War Two: An Annotated Bibliography.* London: Greenhill Books, 1988. **Locations: 85**

[36] Lawson, Cecil C. P. *A History of the Uniforms of the British Army from its beginnings to 1760.* 5 vols., London: Norman Military Publications, 1940-1967. **Locations: 1, 3, 4, 7, 18, 40**

[37] Leslie, J.H., Lt-Col. "Militia Regiments of Great Britain; A Calendar of their Records and Histories," *Journal of the Society for Army Historical Research,* 12 (1933) 45-49, 96-99 **Locations: 1**

[38] Lewis, Peter. *Squadron Histories: R.F.C., R.N.A.S. and R.A.F., 1912-59.* London, Putnam, 1959. **Locations: 4**

[39] Litchfield, Norman E. H. *The Territorial Artillery, 1908-1988: their lineage, uniforms and badges.* Nottingham: Sherwood Press, 1992. **Locations: 3, 4**

[40] Manwaring, George Ernest. *A Bibliography of British Naval History. A Bibliographical and Historical Guide to Printed and Manuscript Sources.* London: Conway Maritime Press, 1970. **Locations: 1, 13, 15**

[41] Mayer, S.L. and Koenig, W.J. *The Two World Wars. A Guide to Manuscript Collections*

in the United Kingdom. London: Bowker, 1976. **Locations: 1, 3, 14, 59, 79, 111, 115**

[42] Milne, Samuel M. *The Standards and Colours of the Army from the Restoration to the Introduction of the Territorial System, 1661 to 1881.* Leeds, 1893. **Locations: 1**

[43] Public Record Office. *Alphabetical Guide to War Office and other Military Records in the Public Records Office.* P.R.O. Lists and Indexes, LXIII, 1931, repr.1963. **Locations: 1**

[44] Smith, Myron J. *World War II: a Bibliography of Sources in English.* 4 vols. in 3. New Jersey: Scarecrow Press, 1976. **Locations: 1**

[45] Spiers, Edward M. "The British Army 1856-1914: recent writing reviewed", *Journal of the Society for Army Historical Research* 63 (1985) 194-207. **Locations: 1**

[46] Strachan, Hew. "The British Army, 1815-1856: recent writing reviewed", *Journal of the Society for Army Historical Research* 63 (1985) 68-79. **Locations: 1**

[47] Swinson, Arthur (ed.). *A Register of the Regiments and Corps of the British Army: The Ancestry of the Regiments and Corps of the Regular Establishment.* London: Archive Press, 1972. **Locations: 1, 14, 15, 40, 59**

[48] Thomas, Garth. *Records of the Militia from 1757 including records of the Volunteers, Rifle Volunteers, Yeomanry, Fencibles, Territorials and the Home Guard.* London: PRO Publications, 1993. Public Records Office Readers' Guide No 3. **Locations: ***

[49] Thorpe, Frances and Pronay, Nicholas. *British Official Films in the Second World War: an Descriptive Catalogue.* Oxford: Clio Press, 1980. **Locations: 1, 2, 3, 112**

[50] White, Arthur Sharpin. *A Bibliography of Regimental Histories of the British Army.* London, London Stamp Exchange, 1988 (Rev. edition). **Locations: 1, 4, 7, 8, 40**

[51] Whittaker, L. B. *Stand Down: Orders of Battle for the Units of the Home Guard of the United Kingdom, November 1944.* Newport: R. Westlake, 1990. **Locations: 1, 7, 18B**

[52] Wickes, H. L. *Regiments of Foot: a Historical Record of all the Foot Regiments of the British Army.* Reading: Osprey, 1974. **Locations: 1, 3, 4, 7, 8, 13, 14, 15, 18**

[53] Wilson, Eunice. *The Records of the Royal Air Force: how to find the few.* Birmingham: Federation of Family History Societies, 1991. **Locations: 3, 10, 18, 102**

[54] Wilson, Frank. *Regiments at a Glance.* London: Blackie, 1956. **Locations: 1**

[55] Wise, Terence. *A Guide to Military Museums* and other places of military interest. Knighton, Powys: T. Wise, 1992. (7th edition) **Locations: 1**

[56] Ziegler, Janet. *World War II: Books in English, 1945-1965.* Stanford: Hoover Institution Press, Stanford University, 1971. **Locations: 1**

II. REGIMENTS

The purpose of this section is to identify published and manuscript material relating to those regiments whose histories have been primarily associated with the old counties of Lancashire and Cheshire. After listing the printed and published material for each regiment, a brief survey of the relevant archives follows. We have focused on the *principal* regiments that have had a long association with the region though we have also included a briefer set of references on the Border Regiment given its connections with the County Palatine and, more recently, its amalgamation with the King's Own Royal Regiment (Lancaster). A difficulty that faces researchers entering this subject for the first time arises out of the many changes that have been made in the titles and structure of regiments. To assist the researcher we have provided a simplified genealogy, beginning with the first regiment to be raised, for each of the region's major regiments.

The writing of regimental histories dates back to the early Victorian period and, in particular, to Richard Cannon's heroic efforts to provide separate histories for each regiment. Some of Cannon's volumes dealt with regiments associated with the North West [65, 281, 328]. In this century the history of individual regiments has been continued by other writers. They are the obvious starting point for research into a regiment, though many, having been written on behalf of the regiment by members of the regiment for other members of the regiment, are characterised by a rather narrow historical focus. They range on the one hand from accounts that provide an overly detailed narrative, to infuriatingly brief chronologies which are all but silent on central areas of regimental life. There is an obvious need to broaden the agenda of themes examined in such histories. The over-concern with military engagements - the examination of 'great' (European) and 'small' (non-European) wars - needs to be re-focused; greater attention needs to be paid to the *normal* rhythms of regimental life, and how regiments interacted with the civilian communities in which they were situated. In spite of the growing interest shown by social historians into the history of ordinary people there is still a shortage of accounts of the life of the common soldier.

To help all types of researcher there now exists a number of general studies of the modern British army which should be read alongside the regimental histories with a view to extending the agenda of the more conventional military historian. Correlli Barnett, *Britain and Her Army, 1509-1970. A Military, Political and Social Survey* (London, 1970) remains one of the best single volume introductions to the historical role and development of the army. Other general studies cover shorter time periods. Students studying the army in the north west during the nineteenth century will find their perspectives widened by consulting the work of, for example, Gwyn Harries-Jenkins, *The Army in Victorian Society* (London, 1978) and Edward Spiers, *The Late Victorian Army, 1868-1902* (Manchester, 1992). Both of these studies open up themes of military life rarely explored in the older regimental histories.

Future research will also need to examine manuscript materials more systematically and critically than has been done in the past. As the following sections indicate there is a remarkably rich set of archives ranging from official records to personal letters and diaries, many of which appear not to have been used in the writing of existing regimental histories. Similarly, even some elementary published sources, such as the regimental magazines, appears to have been used sparingly by historians. It is worth emphasising that many of the key regimental archives remain in the possession of the regiments. However, extensive as these local archives are it should be remembered that significant and unique holdings of manuscript material relating to the region's regiments are located in the major national specialist libraries and record repositories outside of the region.

CHESHIRE REGIMENT: GENERAL LINEAGE

1688: Raised as the Duke of Norfolk's Regiment of Foot

Known by the names of the colonels until 1751:
1689: Henry, Duke of Norfolk
1689-1701: Lt. General Sir Henry Bellasis
1701-1702: Maj. General William Selwyn
1702-1712: Maj. General Thomas Handasyd
1712-1730: Maj. General Roger Handasyd
1730-1734: Lt. General William Barrell
1734-1737: General The Hon. James St. Clair
1737-1738: Maj. General John Moyle
1738-1741: General Thomas Pagett
1741-1757: General Richard O'Farrell

1747: Ranked as 22nd Regiment

1751: Designated by number

1782: Redesignated as 22nd (The Cheshire) Regiment of Foot

1881: Redesignated as The Cheshire Regiment

Cheshire Regiment

[57] Anderson, William Hastings, Major-General. *The History of the Twenty-Second Cheshire Regiment, 1689-1849.* London: Hugh Rees, 1921.
Locations: 1, 4, 57, 58

[58] Boyd, Violet. "A Mascot of the Cheshires." *Cheshire Life* 15 (January 1949) 12.
Locations: 4, 58

[59] Cheshire Regiment. *1st Battalion the 22nd (Cheshire) Regiment. Exercise Borneo Bough. Post Exercise Report 10th July-27th August 1985.* Cheshire: J.C. Advertising Co., 1985.
Locations: 70, 94, 102, 203

[60] --- *The Acorn: the Monthly Magazine of The 2nd Battalion, 22nd (Cheshire) Regiment.* Secunderabad: The Regiment, 1907-12. **Locations: CMM (1907-12)**

[61] --- *Cheshire Regiment. Distinguished Conduct Medal, 1914-20: Citations.* London: London Stamp Exchange, 1985. **Locations: 4**

[62] --- *Cheshire Regiment: the Old 22nd: a brochure distributed with a view to encouraging recruitment.* Cheshire: The Regiment, 1940. **Locations: 4, 70, 102**

[63] --- *Digest of Services of 1st Garrison Battalion The Cheshire Regiment, 1915-1919.* 1919.
Locations: 4

[64] --- *Do You Remember? The Adventures of the 7th Battalion the 22nd (Cheshire) Regiment during the World War 1939-45.* 1947. **Locations: 102**

[65] --- *Historical Record of the Twenty-Second, or The Cheshire Regiment of Foot; containing an Account of the Formation of the Regiment in 1689, and of its subsequent Services to 1849. Compiled by Richard Cannon, Esq., Adjutant-General's Office, Horse Guards.* London: Parker, Furnivall & Parker, 1849. Cannon's Historical Records Series. **Locations: 1, 57, 70, CMM**

[66] --- *The Oak Tree: the Journal of the Cheshire Regiment.* Chester: The Regiment, 1915-.
Locations: 1, 57 (1915-); 70 (1968-1970); 102 (1984-1986); CMM (1919-)

[67] --- *The Oakleaf: the Monthly Magazine of the 1st Battalion The Cheshire Regiment.* Bellary, Secunderabad: The Regiment, 1895-. **Locations: CMM (1895-)**

[68] --- *A Short History of the Twenty-Second or Cheshire Regiment.* 1936. **Locations: 70**

[69] --- *Soldiers Died in The Great War, 1914-19. Part 27: The Cheshire Regiment.* HMSO, 1921. **Locations: 4**

[70] --- *Soldiers Died in The Great War, 1914-19. Part 27: The Cheshire Regiment.* Polstead: J.B. Hayward, 1989. **Locations: 4, 57**

[71] --- "With The 1st Cheshires in Germany, by a Military Observer." *Cheshire Life* 12 (October 1945) 11. **Locations: 4, 58**

[72]	Cheshire Regiment. 4th Volunteer Battalion. *Record of active service members in South Africa, 1900-1902.* Cheshire: The Regiment, 1902. **Locations: 102**

[73]	Chester City Record Office. "Military records preserved at the Chester City Record Office." *Cheshire Sheaf, 5th series* (1976) 4. **Locations: 1, 58, 65**

[74]	Chester. Western Command. *Printed souvenir programme, Headquarters Western Command, Salute and Farewell to Chester, 8 July 1972.* 1972. **Locations: NAM**

[75]	Churton, William A. V., Lieutenant-Colonel. *The War Record of the 1/5th (Earl of Chester's) Battalion, The Cheshire Regiment, August 1914-June 1919.* Chester: Phillipson & Golder, 1920. **Locations: 4, 10, 58, 69, 70, 201, 202, NAM**

[76]	Congleton Borough Council. *The Conferment of the Freedom of the Borough upon the 22nd (Cheshire) Regiment to mark its Tercentenary 1689-1989.* 1989. **Locations: 52**

[77]	Crookenden, Arthur, Colonel. *The 22nd (Cheshire Regiment). A Pocket History.* Chester: W.H. Evans, Sons & Co., Ltd, 1958. **Locations: 102**

[78]	--- *The History of The Cheshire Regiment in the Great War.* Chester: W.H. Evans, Sons & Co., 1938; Second edition 1939. **Locations: ***

[79]	--- *The History of The Cheshire Regiment in the Second World War.* Chester: W.H. Evans, Sons & Co., 1949. **Locations: ***

[80]	--- *A Short History of The Twenty-Second or Cheshire Regiment.* Chester: The Regiment, 1958. **Locations: 4, 63, 70**

[81]	--- *Twenty-Second Footsteps, 1849-1914: An account of life in The 22nd (Cheshire) Regiment in those years.* Chester: W.H. Evans, Sons & Co. Ltd., printer, 1956. **Locations: 4, 63, 65, 70, 76, 102, 202**

[82]	Dorning, H. *The History of No.3, Hale Platoon, "A" Company, 1st Volunteer Battalion, The Cheshire Volunteer Regiment: A Humble Record of War Service 1914-1919.* Manchester: 1920. **Locations: 94**

[83]	Durtnell, C. S., Lieutenant-Colonel, *Do You Remember? The Adventures of the 7th Battalion The 22nd (Cheshire) Regiment during the World War, 1939-45.* Privately Printed, 1947. **Locations: 4, 58**

[84]	Fantom, William. "Cheshire Diarists: II William Fantom, peace-time soldier." *Cheshire Life* 47(December 1981)58-9. **Locations: 4, 58**

[85]	Fytton, Francis. "The Charge That Never Was." *Cheshire Life* 22(September 1956)73. **Locations: 4, 58**

[86]	Gleave, John. *The Jungle War. With the First Battalion The Cheshire Regiment in Malaya.* Chester: Chester Chronicle and Associated Newspapers, Ltd, 1958. **Locations: 70**

[87]	Hugh, James. "The Territorial Army in Cheshire-1: 4th Battalion, The Cheshire Regiment." *Cheshire Life* 17 (January 1951) 22-3. **Locations: 4, 58**

[88]   --- "The Territorial Army in Cheshire-IV: 7th Battalion, The Cheshire Regiment." *Cheshire Life* 17 (April 1951) 22-3. **Locations: 4, 58**

[89]   JHW. "Cheshire in Arabia." *Cheshire Life* 35 (March 1969) 92. **Locations: 4, 58**

[90]   Johnson, Barry. "The 13th Cheshires at Vimy Ridge, 1916 - an episode of the Great War." *Cheshire History* 31 (1993) 25-8. **Locations: 4**

[91]   Johnston, Harrison, Lieutenant-Colonel. *Extracts from an Officer's Diary, 1914-18, being the story of the 15th and 16th Service Battalions The Cheshire Regiment (originally Bantams)*. Manchester: George Falkner & Sons, 1919. **Locations: 4, 57**

[92]   Kellie, Harry Francis. *Memories and Musings*. Chester: Phillison & Golder, 1926. **Locations: 4, 58**

[93]   Kerslake, Major W. B. *Exercise Himalayan Acorn - Khumbu-Everest East Nepal. 11 March-23rd April 1983*. Chester: 1st Battalion 22nd (Cheshire) Regiment, 1985. **Locations: 57, 63, 70, 203, 205**

[94]   McGuinness, J. H., (ed.). *The First Hundred Years: the Story of the 4th Battalion, The Cheshire Regiment, 1859-1959*. Chester: W.H. Evans, 1959. **Locations: 58, 70, NAM**

[95]   "Meannee" (pseud.) "The Twenty-Second." *Cheshire Life* 20 (September,1954) 47. **Locations: 4, 58**

[96]   Miles (pseud.). "The Cheshire Regiment's Anniversary." *Cheshire Life* 5(January 1939)24-5. **Locations: 4, 58**

[97]   --- "Cheshire's Territorials. Number 1. The 4/5th (The Earl of Chester's) Battalion. The Cheshire Regiment." *Cheshire Life* 5 (September 1938) 36. **Locations: 4, 58**

[98]   --- "The County's Territorials. Number 2. The 60th (6th Cheshire and Shropshire) Medium Brigade, Royal Artillery." *Cheshire Life* 5 (October 1938). **Locations: 4, 58**

[99]   --- "The County's Territorials. Number 7. The 7th Battalion, The Cheshire Regiment." *Cheshire Life* 5 (April 1939) 34. **Locations: 4, 58**

[100] Rigby, Bernard. *The Cheshire Military Museum, Chester*. Derby: English Life Publications, 1972. **Locations: 1, 4, 70, CMM, NAM**

[101] --- *Ever Glorious: the Story of the 22nd (Cheshire) Regiment*. Vol. 1. Chester: W.H. Evans & Sons Ltd., 1982. **Locations: 4, 58, 63, 65, 70, 76, 102, 202, 203**

[102] Simpson, Frank. *The Cheshire Regiment, or 22nd Regiment of Foot*. Chester: G.R. Griffith, 1905. **Locations: 4, 57, GM**

[103] --- "The Cheshire Regiment or 22nd Regiment of Foot." *Journal of the Architectural, Archaeological and Historic Society of Chester* 11 (1905) 25-64. **Locations: 1, 4, 58**

[104] --- *The Cheshire Regiment or 22nd Regiment of Foot: the First Battalion at Mons and The Miniature Colour*. Chester: W.H. Evans, Sons & Co., 1929. (2nd edition.) **Locations: ***

[105]   --- *The Chester Volunteers, with special reference to "A" Company, 3rd Volunteer Battalion the Cheshire Regiment (1914-1920)* Chester: Courant Press, 1920. **Locations: 1, 4, 58, 63, GM, NAM**

[106]   --- *Short History of the Cheshire Regiment or 22nd Regiment of Foot.* 1917. **Locations: 102**

[107]   Skinner. "Our Glorious Cheshires." *Cheshire Life* 59 (1993) 32-3. **Locations: 4, 58**

[108]   Smith, Charles, (ed.). *War History of the 6th Battalion, The Cheshire Regiment (T.F.) compiled from the War Diaries of the Battalion.* Stockport: 6th Cheshire Old Comrades Association, 1932. **Locations: 1, 102, 202**

[109]   Spencer, Julie. "Arms and the Men." *Cheshire Life* 53 (March 1987) 28-35, 92. **Locations: 4, 58**

[110]   Wolff, Anne S. *Subalterns of the Foot: Three World War I Diaries of Officers of the Cheshire Regiment.* Worcester: Square One Publications, 1992. **Locations: 3, 8**

ARCHIVES

The main archive relating to the Cheshire Regiment is held at the Cheshire Military Museum sited in The Castle, Chester. The museum's holdings include collections of weapons, uniforms, artifacts and manuscript records relating to the history of the regiment. It also holds material relating to the Cheshire Yeomanry, 3rd Carabiniers and 5th Royal Inniskilling Dragoon Guards. Included in the archives is material concerning the regiment's activities in recent decades, and files dated after 1960 fall under the 30-year rule, and access is therefore restricted. A guide to the museum appeared in 1972, see [100] above. Researchers wishing to consult the collection should contact the curator.

Smaller collections of archive material relating to the Cheshire Regiment can be found at the Chester City Record Office and Cheshire Record Office. The Public Record Office, National Army Museum and Imperial War Museum also hold relevant manuscript material.

Chester City Record Office

[111]   *Welsh and Midland Command and Western Command: Specialist Sanitary Officer: Records.* correspondence; orders; reports; and returns, 1902-14.

[112]   *Cheshire Volunteer Regiment: Chester Company. Records.* Contents: the records of this company, which took part in the First World War, comprise a minute book (1914-1916) and a handbill of weekly orders, 27 September 1915.

Cheshire Military Museum Archives

[113]   Cheshire Regiment Files: containing various records, diaries and miscellaneous items relating to the regiment: Eighteenth Century, Pre-1900, 1900, 1900-2, 1903-7, 1908-13, 1914, 1915, 1916, 1917, 1918, 1919, 1939, 1940, 1941, 1942, 1943, 1944, 1945, 1946-50, 1951-60,

1961-70, 1971-80, 1981, 1982, 1983, 1984, 1985, 1986, 1987, 1988, 1989, 1990, 1991, 1992.

Regimental Orders, Records and War Diaries:

1st Cheshire Rifle Volunteers: camp orders, 1863-1881.

2nd Cheshire Rifle Volunteers: Attestations, 1859-1860-contains oaths of allegiance and overlaid letters of resignation from members of the company.

4th Volunteer Battalion: "B" Company, No.8 Platoon. List of men, 1916-18. Gives Regiment no., rank, section, name and address, religion, date of birth, date of enrolment, height, chest, trade, passed efficient drill, passed musketry.

6th Battalion War Diary: 1st August 1915-31st August 1919.

13th Battalion Operation Orders, compiled by Hugh Knightly Finch, Captain and Brevet Major. Vol.1: 1917-1919, Vol.2: 1907-1917. Contents: Battle plans, trench maps, field maps, operations relating to the 11th Battalion, Lancashire Fusiliers, press cuttings, correspondence, roll of officers and men, sports and social events, tickets, permits, interrogation of a German prisoner, 7th Infantry Brigade orders, telegraphs, memos, records of Finch's attempt to escape from P.o.W. camp and social events therein, award of his O.B.E.

Rules and Regulations:

Officer's Mess, framed in 1820, revised 1855; Sergeants' Mess, 1st Battalion, compiled 22nd April, 1882, revised 29th October 1890; 2nd Battalion Mess Rules, framed in 1820, revised 1855; Regimental standing orders of the Twenty-Second or Cheshire Regiment, 4th July 1829. Kingston-Jamaica. Printed at the Jamaica Courant and Public Advertiser Office, 1829; Mess Rules, 22nd Regiment, Newcastle-upon-Tyne, 17th day of June 1820.

Minute Books:

Finance Committee 1st Volunteer Battalion. March 1901-February 1908. Officers' Mess, 4th Battalion, November 1908 to November 1913. 1st and 2nd Battalions, 1948-1964; Sergeants' Mess, 1938-1966 (381p.); Mess, 1927-1940; 3rd Battalion C.R.V., 1888-1948; 4/5th (E of C) Battalion, 1925-1939; Mess Meetings, 1917-1930; 5th V.B.C.R., Macclesfield Detachment [n.d.]

Document Files: Files relating to the First World War contain documents, badges, cuttings books, medals, correspondence, sketch books, diaries, newspapers, postcards, menus, social events.

1st Battalion Records: 4th August 1914-3rd April 1917, 1st May 1917-20th April 1919.

2nd Battalion Records: 2nd February 1915-28th February 1919.

1st/4th Battalion Records: 8th August 1915-31st August 1919.

1st/7th Battalion Records: 9th August 1915-31st March 1919.

8th Battalion Records: 26th June 1915-28th February 1919.

9th Battalion Records: 19th July 1915-10th February 1919.

10th Battalion Records: 27th September 1915-30th June 1918.

11th Battalion Records: 25th September 1915-31st July 1918.

13th Battalion Records: 25th September 1915-31st January 1918.

15th Battalion Records: 1st March 1916-22nd April 1919.

16th Battalion Records: 30th January 1916-8th February 1918.

23rd Battalion Records: 20th May 1918-25th May 1919.

Charles Napier: Record Book of the Scinde Irregular Horse: Vol.1: From 8th August, 1839 to 1st October, 1851 (355 pages. Private printing 1902).

Vol.2: From 8th October, 1851 to 13th June, 1855 (283 pages. Sukkur: printed at the Victoria Printing Press, 1903).

Divisional Orders by General Sir Charles Napier, 1842-1847. Contains an account of the Battle of Meannee, 17th February 1843.

General Napier Newscuttings: Bath, 1837. Compiled by General Napier, and annotated with

his responses to criticisms made of him. Cuttings date from 1830-1875.
Visitors' Books:
22nd Cheshire Regiment, 1889-1985, 1953-55; Chester Castle, 1938-41; 4th Battalion, 1957-1961; Regimental Museum Depot, 1855-1881 and 1893-1926, also contains a list of honorary members, 1879-1902 (inverted at rear of book); 1st Volunteer Battalion, 1899-1956.
Personal Diaries:
Diary of William Mansfield, quarter master of the 22nd Regiment of Foot, 1798-1834.
Record of Private Edward Glenn, Cheshire Regiment of Foot, 1843-1854.
Scrapbooks and Newspaper Cuttings:
Scrapbook of Colour Sergeant William Hill, 2nd Battalion 22nd or Cheshire Regiment of Foot, 1841-1859.
Miscellaneous material:
Officers' Mess Depot, The 22nd Cheshire Regiment: Silver Book, 1935-54.
Officers' Mess, 1st Vol. Battalion: Library Book 1905-57.
Officers' Leave Book, 1957-1982.
No.7 Co. 1st V.B.C.R. Scoring Book.
Hunting Diary 22nd, 1923-36.
1st V.B.C.R. Clothing Sub-Committee Book, 1904-7.
Battalion Pilgrimage: France and Belgium, May 1990. (Contains a list of graves visited and photographs of the pilgrimage).
Sergeants' Mess, 2nd Battalion: Descriptive Record, mess silver 1912-c.1938 (with photographs).
Manuscript folders of "Ever Glorious"- The Story of the 22nd (Cheshire) Regiment.
Medal Rolls.
Photographic Files:
1. Pre-1900; 2. 1900-2; 3. 1903-7; 4. 1908-13; 5. 1914; 6. 1915; 7. 1916; 8. 1917; 9. 1918, 9A: France and Flanders, 9B: Gallipoli, 9C: Palestine 1917-18, 9D: Macedonia 1916-18, 9E: Mesopotamia 1916-18, 9F: POW's 1914-18; 10. UK 1919-39, 10A: Home Stations (including Malta) 1919-39; 11. India 1919-39; 12. 1939; 13. 1940; 14. 1941; 15. 1942; 16. 1943; 17. 1944; 18. 1945, 18A: Western Desert, 18B: France 1939-40, 18C: Malta 1941-3, 18D: Sicily and Italy 1943-5, 18E: North West Europe 2nd World War, 18F: 1939-45, 18G: POW's 1939-1945; 19. 1946-50; 20. 1951-60; 21. 1961-70; 22. 1971-80; 23. 1981; 24. 1982; 25. 1983; 26. 1984; 27. 1985; 28. 1986; 29. 1987. Also folders for post-1988.
Audio-Visual Material:
Sound recordings-Skins, Carabiniers, Cheshire Regiment.
Video and audio cassettes- band marches etc., and music of the regiment.

National Army Museum

[114]   Fantom, W., Pte. *MS Journal of Pte W Fantom, Cheshire Regiment.* 1904-14.

[115]   Grant, Robert, Captain. *Collection of documents collected by and relating to Captain Robert Grant, 1905-66, documenting his service with the Seaforth Highlanders, Scottish Horse, 3rd Cheshires, 35, 7 and 41 Indian Cavalry, 1915-21, and Sutherland TAFA 1949-51.* 1905-66.

[116]   *Two documents of the Antrobus Family.* 1855-60.

[117]   Warre, William, Lt-Gen Sir. *Papers of Lt Gen Sir William Warre (1784-1853).* 1807-49.

Trafford Local Studies Library
[118]   ---   *Extracts from newspapers giving an account of the recruiting march of a detachment of the Cheshire Regiment (Depot and band 1st Battalion) through Cheshire, March to April 1914.*

Wirral Libraries
[119]   ---   *Photograph Albums of the Cheshire Regiment in Camp. 1904, 1904, 1906, 1908, 1909, 1910, 1911, 1912, 1913.*   1904-13.

EAST LANCASHIRE REGIMENT: GENERAL LINEAGE

1689: Raised as Viscount Castleton's Regiment
1694: Saunderson's Foot

1699: Disbanded

1702: Reformed as Thomas Saunderson's Regiment of Marines. Designated 1st Marines until 1714

1704: Known until 1751 by the names of the colonels:-
1704: Thomas Pownall; 1705: Charles Willis; 1716: George Lord Forrester
1717: Thomas Stanwix; 1717: Andrew Bissett; 1742: Henry de Grangue
1743: Charles Frampton; 1749: George, Earl of Loudoun

1717-18, 1747, 1761-3, 1795: Served as marines
1747: Ranked as 30th Regiment

1751: Redesignated by number

1782: Redesignated as 30th (the Cambridgeshire) Regiment of Foot

1881: 30th Regiment of Foot amalgamated with the 59th
(2nd Nottinghamshire) Regiment [raised 1755]
to form The East Lancashire Regiment

1958: Amalgamated with The South Lancashire Regiment to form
The Lancashire Regiment (Prince of Wales's Volunteers)

1970: Amalgamated with The Loyal Regiment (North Lancashire) to
form the Queen's Lancashire Regiment

East Lancashire Regiment

[120] Aytoun, James. *Redcoats in the Caribbean.* Blackburn: Recreation Services Department for the East Lancashire Regiment Museum, 1984. **Locations: 3, BM**

[121] Bannatyne, Neil, Lieutenant-Colonel. *History of The Thirtieth Regiment, now the First Battalion East Lancashire Regiment, 1689-1881.* Liverpool: Littlebury Brothers, 1923. **Locations: 1, 3, 8, 12**

[122] Behrend, Arthur. *Make Me A Soldier: a Platoon Commander in Gallipoli.* London: Eyre and Spottiswoode, 1961. **Locations: ***

[123] Blackburn County Borough. *The County Borough of Blackburn presents an Address of Honour to the East Lancashire Regiment, 17th April, 1948.* Blackburn: Blackburn Corporation, 1948. **Locations: 6**

[124] Blackburn. Witton Park. *Army Display at Witton Park, 19th to 21st September, 1969.* [1969] **Locations: 6**

[125] Burden, G. W. P. N., Brigadier, (ed.). *History of The East Lancashire Regiment in the War, 1939-1945.* Manchester: H. Rawson & Co. Ltd, 1953. **Locations: 13, 33, LRO**

[126] Burnley Corporation. *Presentation by His Worship the Mayor to The East Lancashire Regiment, of the Scroll Conferring on the Regiment the Honour of Marching within the County Borough on all Ceremonial Occasions... 6th June, 1953.* Burnley: Burnley Corporation, 1953. **Locations: 9**

[127] East Lancashire Division. *Sixty-sixth East Lancashire Division Dinner Club.* Manchester: George Falkner and Sons, 1924. **Locations: 6, 13, LRO**

[128] East Lancashire Regiment. *1st Battalion The East Lancashire Regiment. Saar Plebiscite, 1935.* Aldershot: Gale & Polden Ltd, 1935. **Locations: 6, RMP**

[129] --- *An Appeal for Funds for the East Lancashire Regiment War Memorial.* 1947. **Locations: 9**

[130] --- *Commemoration Service in memory of all ranks of the Regiment who lost their lives at the Battle of the Somme 1st July 1916.* 1961. **Locations: 9**

[131] --- *Commemoration Service on the 61st anniversary of the Battle of the Somme, Sunday 3 July, 1977, in Blackburn Cathedral.* 1977. **Locations: 6**

[132] --- *Commemoration Service, on the Seventieth Anniversary of the Battle of the Somme, 1st July 1916, on July 6, 1986 [in Blackburn Cathedral].* 1986. **Locations: 6**

[133] --- *The East Lancashire Regiment. War Bulletins. Nos. 1-6 (7-17). 1st October 1944-1st March 1945 (1st April, 1945-1st February 1946).* 2 vols. Preston: The Regiment, 1946. **Locations: 3**

[134] --- *The East Lancashire Regimental Association Journal.* Preston: The Regiment, 1959

[continuation of 137]   **Locations: 9 (1959-63); 6 (1959-65); 21 (1959-65)**

[135]   --- *The East Lancashire Regimental Bulletin.*   Preston: The Regiment, 1946-.   **Locations: 1 (1948); 3 (1948-52); 12 (1950)**

[136]   --- *East Lancashire Regimental Journal.*   Vol. 1, no.1-vol.8, Feb. 1931- Sept. 1939. Aldershot, 1931-39.   [incorporating the "XXX" and "The Lilywhites Gazette"] **Locations:3 (1931-39); RMP (1931-39)**

[137]   --- *East Lancashire Regimental Journal.*   Vol. 1: Jan 1955-.   Preston: East Lancashire Regiment, 1955-58.   **Locations: 3 (1955-); 21 (1955-58)**

[138]   --- *First Battalion East Lancashire Regiment in Belgium and France 23rd August 1914-1st March 1915.*   Winchester: Warren & Son, 1915.   **Locations: RMP**

[139]   --- *Formation, Early History and Amalgamation.*   [n.d.]   **Locations: 9**

[140]   --- *Historical Records of The XXX Regiment.*   London: W. Clowes & Sons, 1887. **Locations: 1**

[141]   --- *History of The East Lancashire Regiment in the War, 1939-1945.*   Manchester: H. Rawson & Co., 1953.   **Locations: 1, 3, 7, 9, 11, 18, 21, 23, 102**

[142]   --- *The Lilywhites Gazette. A Paper for the 2nd Batt., East Lancashire Regiment.*   Vol. 16, no.1-vol.17, no.6. Aug. 1898-Feb. 1899. New Series: vol.1, no.1-10, no.5 Sept. 1921-Nov. 1930. Ranikhet, Bareilly, 1898-1930.   **Locations: 3 (1898-1930)**

[143]   --- *Order of Service at the laying-up of the Colours of the former 1st Battalion of the East Lancashire Regiment, by the 4th Battalion, Blackburn Cathedral 1959.* 1959.   **Locations: 6**

[144]   --- *Regimental Bulletin, May 1948: Special edition commemorating the granting of the Honorary Freedom of the Borough of Blackburn to the Regiment.*   1948.   **Locations: 6**

[145]   --- *Roll of Honour. 1939 World War 1945.*   Preston, 1948.   **Locations: 3, LRM**

[146]   --- *A Short History of The East Lancashire Regiment.*   Preston: T. Snape & Co. Ltd., 1952. **Locations: 3, 6**

[147]   --- *Soldiers Died in The Great War, 1914-19. Part 35: East Lancashire Regiment.* London: H.M.S.O., 1921.   **Locations: 3**

[148]   --- *Soldiers Died in The Great War, 1914-19. Part 35: East Lancashire Regiment.* Polstead: J.B. Hayward with Imperial War Museum, Dept. of Printed Books, 1989. **Locations: 3, 4, 6, 18, LRO**

[149]   --- *XXX. A Paper for the Men of the 1st Battalion East Lancashire Regiment.* 1904-1912; New Series: 1922-1930.   Dublin, Woking etc., 1904-30.   **Locations: 3 (1904-30)**

[150]   Entract, J.P.N. "The Tramore and Kinsale Tragedies, 30th January 1816 (His Majesty's 59th, 62nd and 82nd Regiments)", *Journal of the Society for Historical Research* 46 (1968) 225-34.   **Locations: 1**

[151] Garwood, John M. *Chorley Pals: "Y" Company, 11th (Service) Battalion, East Lancashire Regiment: a short history of the Company in the Great War, 1914-1919.* Manchester: Neil Richardson, 1989. **Locations: 3, CL**

[152] Hopkinson, Edward Campbell, Captain. *Spectamur Agendo: 1st Battalion, The East Lancashire Regiment, August and September 1914.* Cambridge: Heffer & Sons Ltd., privately printed, 1926. **Locations: 1, 3, 9**

[153] Huckle, Eileen, and Huckle, John. *The House of Uttley: the Story of a Pennine Family.* Aylesbury: Jade Publishing, 1991. **Locations: 3**

[154] Hyndburn Borough Council. Development Services: Leisure Section. *The Accrington Pals: 11th (Service) Battalion (Accrington) East Lancashire Regiment: A Brief History, Town Trail, Museums and Events.* Hyndburn: Borough Council [1993]. **Locations: 3, 19, 21, 26**

[155] James, Francis M., Second Lieutenant. *The Annals of the "Five and Nine": being the history of H.M. 59th Regiment (2nd Nottinghamshire), now the Second Battalion East Lancashire Regiment.* Poona: S. Shalom and Bros., 1906. **Locations: 3, 6, BM**

[156] Kirby, Henry L., and Walsh, R. Raymond *Drummer Spencer John Bent, V.C.* Blackburn: T.H.C.L. Books, 1986. **Locations: 3, 6, BM**

[157] --- *Private William Young, V.C. East Lancashire Regiment, 1914-1918: One of Preston's Heroes of the Great War.* Blackburn: T.H.C.L. Books, 1985. **Locations: 3, 6, BM**

[158] Lewis, Adrian S. *The Lilywhite 59th: 2nd Nottinghamshire and 2nd Battalion East Lancashire Regiment.* Blackburn: Blackburn Recreation Department for East Lancashire Regiment Museum, 1985. **Locations: 3, 6, BM**

[159] Liverpool Record Office. *East Lancashire Regiment: A bibliography of books held in Liverpool Record Office.* Record Office: Liverpool, 1980. **Locations: 2, 40**

[160] Marshall, William. *Accrington Pals: teachers' pack.* Preston: Lancashire County Council, 1992. **Locations: 3, 19**

[161] Mellersh, Harold Edward Leslie. *Schoolboy Into War.* London: Kimber, 1978. **Locations: ***

[162] Nicholson, C. Lothian, Major-General Sir., and McMullen, H. T. Major, (comps.). *History of The East Lancashire Regiment in The Great War, 1914-1918.* Liverpool: Littlebury Bros. Ltd, 1936. **Locations: 1, 2, 3, 9, 10, CL, LRO**

[163] Pendlebury, J. W., Brigadier. *1st Battalion, The East Lancashire Regiment; France, 1940.* Ringwood: Brown & Son (Ringwood) Ltd., printers, 1946. **Locations: 3**

[164] Royal British Legion. *Service in Blackburn Cathedral, 11 September 1977 on the laying up of the old County Standard and the dedication of the new Standard.* 1977. **Locations: 3**

[165] Turner, William. *The Accrington Pals: 11th (Service) Battalion, (Accrington), East Lancashire Regiment. A Pictorial History.* Preston: Lancashire County Books, 1992. (2nd rev. edition) **Locations: 2, 3, 4, 19, 21, 57**

[166] --- *The Accrington Pals Remembered. A Guide to their Resting Places and Memorials.* Accrington: Hyndburn Local History Society, 1993. **Locations: 3, 19**

[167] --- *"The Accrington Pals". The 11th (Service) Battalion, (Accrington), East Lancashire Regiment. A Pictorial History.* Preston: Lancashire County Council, Library and Leisure Committee, 1986. **Locations: 3, 6, 19, 20, 21, 102, CL**

[168] --- *Pals: the 11th (Service) Battalion (Accrington) East Lancashire Regiment.* Barnsley: Wharncliffe Publishing Ltd., 1988. **Locations: 3, 6, 7, 19**

[169] Whelan, Peter. *The Accrington Pals.* London: French, 1982. **Locations: ***

[170] --- *The Accrington Pals.* London: Methuen, 1984. **Locations: 4, 19, 77, 79, 115**

[171] --- *The Accrington Pals, abridged and adapted from his stage play.* 1989. **Locations: 3, 19**

[172] Wood, F. W., (ed.). *The East Lancashire Regiment XXXth and LIXth Foot: The Recruits' History of the Regiment. Compiled by Sgt. Instructor F.W. Wood, Army Educational Corps.* Preston: East Lancashire Regiment, 1927. **Locations: 9**

[173] Wood, F. W., Sergeant-Instructor. *The East Lancashire Regiment. A Short History of the Regiment. By Sgt.-Instructor F.W. Wood, with additions for the Great War by Capt. R.E.D. Green.* Preston: T. Snape & Co. Ltd., 1938. **Locations: 3**

ARCHIVES

Blackburn Library

[174] East Lancashire Regiment. *Draft amendments to the Charities for the benefit of the former 3rd Militia Battalion, East Lancashire Regiment.* 1956.

[175] --- *East Lancashire Royal Field Artillery. 'A' Battery 330 Brigade. Diary, 25th Feb. 1917 - 27th September 1918.* 1917-18.

Burnley Library

[176] East Lancashire Regiment: Memorial Cottage Homes, Burnley. *Souvenir Serviette, mounted on cardboard to commemorate the opening by H.R.H. Princess Louise on 30 Sept. 1905 of Cottage Homes, erected by public subscription to the memory of men who died in the South African War, 1899-1902.* 1905.

[177] --- *Newspaper reports of the East Lancashire Regiment in the Saar.* 1935.

Colne Library

[178] Photographic material. *Signal Section 2nd Battalion East Lancashire Regiment, Bordon April 18th 1923.*

Haslingden Library

[179] --- *East Lancashire Regiment, 2nd Volunteer Battalion. Volume of newspaper cuttings*

concerning the History of the Volunteers from their Foundation at the end of the South African War. [n.d.]

Lancashire County Library

[180]   East Lancashire Regiment. *11th Service Battalion, East Lancashire Regiment: miscellaneous items,* 1916-.

[181]   --- *Soldiers' Small Book. Issued to William Henry Hall,* 1912.

[182]   --- *Twenty-First [etc.] Annual Report, January 1946-March 1947.* 1947.

Regimental Museum, Fulwood Barracks, Preston

[183]   The principal archive relating to the East Lancashire Regiment is held at the Regimental Museum, Fulwood Barracks, Preston. At the time of preparing this guide the museum and its archive was undergoing re-organisation, and it was not possible to undertake a full survey of the archive material. Not all items in the archive have been listed but a preliminary sorting had been completed. Briefly the collection contains material relating to the two predecessor regiments (the 30th and 59th) which amalgamated to become the East Lancashire Regiment in 1881.
30th Regiment   Archive has been arranged chronologically into three boxes: (1) 1689-1693 (2) 1693-1815 (3) 1816-1881. Material deals with campaigns in which the regiment fought, some original documents relating to the establishment of the regiment, and also photographic material.
59th Regiment   Archive material has been sorted chronologically into three main boxes: (1) 1755-1793 (2) 1793-1815 (3) 1816-1881.
The archive on the East Lancashire Regiment is organised chronologically and thematically. Boxes cover the period: (1) 1881-1914 (2) 1914-1919 (3) 1919-1939 (4) 1939-1945. The archive has good coverage of the Boer War with Regimental Reports, orders, newspaper cuttings and photographs. The First World War archive is extensive, and includes a large but incomplete set of War Diaries for the battalions. It also includes a number of original diaries and accounts of the war written by soldiers and officers: E. Poe's Diary, Captain Buchanan-Brown. There is also a long run of Battalion Order Books for the 1830s onwards. Material, including pamphlets and newspaper cuttings, relating to other aspects of the Regiment's life such as Chapels and the Cottage Homes Memorials, are filed separately from the main chronological boxes. An extensive collection of photographs covers the regiment's activities from the late nineteenth century onwards in Britain, Europe, India. They range from formal photographs of officers (by Napoleon Sarony) to the regiment on manoeuvres.

National Army Museum

[184]   Preston, T. H. *41 MS letters of the period 20 July-12 November 1914 written by Captain T.H. Preston, 3rd Battalion attached to 1st Battalion, East Lancashire Regiment, to members of his family.* 1914.

[185]   Preston, Thomas. *Letters and other documents relating to 2nd Lieutenant Thomas Preston, East Lancashire Regiment.* 1898-1904.

KING'S LIVERPOOL REGIMENT: GENERAL LINEAGE

1685: Raised in London from men of Derbyshire and Hertfordshire as The Princess Anne of Denmark's Regiment of Foot

1702: Redesignated as the Queen's Regiment of Foot

1716: Redesignated as The King's Regiment of Foot (also known as the King's Hanoverian White Horse)

Known until 1751 by the names of the colonels:
1685: Robert Lord Ferrers; 1686: James, Duke of Berwick;
1688: James Beaumont; 1695: John Richmond Webb;
1715: Henry Morrison; 1720: Sir Charles Hotham;
1721: John Pocock; 1732: Charles Lenoe;
1739: Richard Onslow; 1745: Edward Wolfe.

1747: Ranked as 8th Regiment

1751: Redesignated as 8th (The King's) Regiment of Foot

1881: Redesignated as the King's (Liverpool Regiment)

1921: Redesignated as The King's Regiment (Liverpool)

1958: Amalgamated (less Territorials) with The Manchester Regiment (less Territorials) to form the King's Regiment (Manchester and Liverpool)

1968: Redesignated The King's Regiment

THE LIVERPOOL SCOTTISH, THE QUEEN'S OWN CAMERON HIGHLANDERS (TERRITORIAL ARMY): GENERAL LINEAGE

1859: Raised as the Liverpool Scottish Rifle Volunteers

1900: Raised as 8th (Scottish) Volunteer Battalion, The King's (Liverpool) Regiment

1908: Reorganized as 10th (Scottish) Battalion of of The King's (Liverpool) Regiment

1915: Renumbered as 1/10th

1920: Reconstituted as 10th (Liverpool Scottish) Battalion, King's (Liverpool) Regiment

1937: Transferred as The Liverpool Scottish, The Queen's Own Cameron Highlanders

1939: Redesignated as 1st Battalion, The Liverpool Scottish, The Queen's Own Cameron Highlanders

1967: Became the (Liverpool Scottish) Company 1st Battalion Highland Volunteers T.A.V.R.

1992: The Liverpool Scottish Company 5/8th (Volunteer) Battalion, The King's Regiment

King's Liverpool Regiment

[186] Burke-Gaffney, John Joseph, Lieutenant-Colonel. *The Story of The King's Regiment, 1914-1948.* Liverpool: Sharpe & Kellet (printer) for the King's Regiment, 1954. **Locations: 1, 2, 3, 4, 8, KRMA**

[187] Gummer, Selwyn. *The Chavasse Twins.* London: Hodder & Stoughton, 1963. **Locations: NAM**

[188] King's Liverpool Regiment. *2nd Battalion The King's Regiment (Liverpool). Trooping the Colour to commemorate the 250th Anniversary of the raising of the Regiment, 20th June, 1685; Sefton Park, Liverpool, June 25th, 1935.* Aldershot: Gale & Polden, 1935. **Locations: 2**

[189] --- "The 7th Battalion, King's (Liverpool) Regiment: a review of its origin, war services and present activities." *Liverpolitan* 5 (April 1936) 27. **Locations: 2**

[190] --- "A Brief History of a Keen Shooting Battalion: the Liverpool Rifles- 6th Rifle Battalion, "The King's Regiment"." *Liverpolitan* 5 (February 1936) 7. **Locations: 2**

[191] --- *Form and Order of Memorial Service, Liverpool Cathedral, 22nd June, 1957.* 1957. **Locations: 2**

[192] --- *Historical Record of The Eighth, or, The King's Regiment of Foot; containing an account of the formation of the Regiment in 1685, and of its subsequent Services to 1844.* London: Parker, Furnivall & Parker, 1844. Cannon's Historical Records Series. **Locations: 2**

[193] --- *Historical Record of The King's, or Liverpool Regiment of Foot, containing an account of the formation of the Regiment in 1685, and of its subsequent services to 1881; also succession lists of the Officers who served in each of the regimental ranks with biographical notices and summaries of their war services.* London: Harrison & Sons, 1883. (2nd edition) **Locations: 1, 2, 3, 17**

[194] --- *Historical Record of The King's Liverpool Regiment of Foot, containing an account of the formation of the Regiment in 1685, and of its subsequent services to 1903.* Enniskillen: William Trimble, 1904. (3rd edition) **Locations: 2, 79, KRMA, LRO**

[195] --- *King's (Liverpool Regiment). Distinguished Conduct Medal, 1914-20: Citations.* London: Stamp Exchange, 1985. **Locations: 3, 4**

[196] --- *The King's Regiment Gallery: The Story of the Regiment from 1685 to the present day.* Liverpool: City of Liverpool Museums, 1987. **Locations: 2, 3, 40**

[197] --- *King's Regiment Memorial Cross, Whitley Gardens, Shaw Street, Liverpool. History and Description.* [n.d]. **Locations: 2**

[198] --- *King's Regiment War Memorial, St. John's Gardens, Liverpool. History and Description.* [n.d.] **Locations: 2**

[199] --- *The Kingsman. The Journal of The King's [Liverpool] Regiment.* Liverpool: The

Regiment, 1946-58. **Locations: 2 (1946-58)**

[200] --- "Lancashire's Oldest Territorial Unit: the 5th (Rifle) Battalion The King's Regiment (Liverpool)." *Liverpolitan* 5 (January 1936) 19. **Locations: 2**

[201] --- "The Liverpool Corps: the 1st Volunteer Battalion The King's (Liverpool Regiment): a history." *Liverpool Athletic Times* (December 1890) 6. **Locations: 2**

[202] --- *Liverpool Scottish Regimental Gazette.* Vol. 1-, 1923-. **Locations: LSM (1923-39)**

[203] --- *Presentation of Colours to the 5th Battalion The King's Regiment and the Liverpool Scottish, the Queen's Own Cameron Highlanders, by H.M. the King....at Everton Football Ground, Liverpool, May 19th, 1938.* 1938. **Locations: 2**

[204] --- *The Record of the 11th Battalion of The King's (Liverpool) Regiment subsequently the 15th Battalion of The Loyal North Lancashire Regiment, Pioneers, 14th Light Division. August, 1914-March 1919.* London: R.E. Thomas & Co., printers, 1920. **Locations: 2**

[205] --- *Recruiting Pamphlet.* Liverpool: The Regiment, 1941. **Locations: 2**

[206] --- *Rules of the 7th (Isle of Man) Volunteer Battalion, The King's Liverpool Regiment.* Douglas: Spencer and Hannay, 1894. **Locations: MNH**

[207] --- *A Short History of The King's Regiment (Liverpool).* Aldershot: Gale & Polden, 1925. **Locations: 7, 8, KRMA**

[208] --- *Soldiers Died in The Great War, 1914-19. Part 13: The King's (Liverpool Regiment).* London: H.M.S.O., 1920. **Locations: 34**

[209] --- *Soldiers Died in the Great War, 1914-19. Part 13: The King's (Liverpool Regiment).* Suffolk: Hayward with Imperial War Museum, Dept. of Printed Books, 1989. **Locations: 2, 3, 4, 40, LRO**

[210] --- *The Swell. The Regimental Rag of The 13th Battalion The King's Liverpool Regiment.* Manchester, 1916. **Locations: 2**

[211] --- "Uniforms of the 5th Battalion The King's Regiment 1859-1967." *Military History Society Bulletin*   22 (November 1971) 50-2. **Locations: NAM**

[212] --- "The 6th King's (Liverpool) becomes the 38th (King's) Auxiliary Air Battalion, R.E." *Liverpolitan* 5 (October 1936) 19. **Locations: 2**

[213] ---- "Two famous Liverpool Battalions (the 5th Battalion The King's Regiment and the Liverpool Scottish) and how they earned their colours." *Liverpolitan* 7 (May 1938) 18. **Locations: 2**

[214] --- "What the change in status of the 5th [Battalion, King's Liverpool Regiment] means." *Liverpolitan* 6 (April 1937) 27. **Locations: 2**

[215] King's Regiment (Manchester and Liverpool). *Presentation of the Freedoms of Manchester and Liverpool to the King's Regiment (Manchester and Liverpool), May 11, 1962; and the*

marches through the two cities, May 15 and 18, 1962. 1962. **Locations: 2**

[216] Leech, J. *Extracts from the War Diary of Joseph Leech, Wigan, who served in the 11th Battalion King's (Liverpool) Regiment, December 1914-July 1919.* 1934. **Locations: 2**

[217] Liverpool Scottish Regiment. *79th News*, 1936-60. **Locations: LSM (1936-1960, incomplete)**

[218] --- *Liverpool Scottish Roll of Honour: containing the names of those men of all ranks who gave their lives for their King and Country in the Great War, 1914-1919.* Manchester: The Regiment, 1920. **Locations: 2**

[219] --- "An Outline of the 77 years' history of the Liverpool Scottish, by a military correspondent." *Liverpolitan* 5 (March 1936) 25. **Locations: 2**

[220] --- *Queen's Own Highlander Magazine.* 12 vols., 1936-46. **Locations: LSM (1936-46)**

[221] --- *Regimental Gazette*, 1910-13. **Locations: 2 (1910-1913)**

[222] MacGilchrist, A. M. *The Liverpool Scottish, 1900-1919.* Liverpool: Henry Young & Sons, Ltd., 1930. **Locations: 1, 2, 3, 7, 57, 65, KRMA, NAM**

[223] Maddocks, Graham. *List of Liverpool Pals who proceeded overseas in November 1915 and biographies of the officer casualties.* [n.d.] **Locations: 57**

[224] --- *The Liverpool Pals: History of the 17th, 18th, 19th and 20th (Service) Battalions- King's Liverpool Regiment, 1914-1919.* London: L. Cooper, 1991. **Locations: 2, 3, 7, 14, 40, 52, KRMA**

[225] Miers, R. D. M.C., Colonel. *Nominal Roll of Officers gazetted to The Liverpool Scottish, 1900-1962.* 1963 **Locations: 2, 3, KRMA**

[226] Roberts, Enos Herbert Glynne. *The Story of The "9th King's" in France.* Liverpool: Northern Publishing Co. Ltd., 1922. **Locations: 1, 2, 3, 45, 65, KRMA, NAM**

[227] Robertson, J. C. *A New Battalion of the King's.* Liverpool: Rockliff, 1902. **Locations: 2, LSM**

[228] Shepperd, Gilbert Alan. *The King's Regiment.* Reading: Osprey, 1973. **Locations: 2, 3, 40, 102, KRMA**

[229] Stanley, Ferdinand Charles, Brigadier-General. The *History of The 89th Brigade, 1914-1918.* Liverpool: "Daily Post" Printers, 1919. **Locations: 1, 2, 3, 45, 65, KRMA**

[230] Thomas, J. J., Lieutenant-Colonel. *A History of the 1st Volunteer Battalion, "The King's" (Liverpool Regiment), formerly known as the 1st Lancashire Rifle Volunteers, from its incept in 1859 to the end of June, 1908, when under Mr. Haldane's Territorial Scheme, it became the 5th Battalion "The King's" (Liverpool Regiment).* 1908. **Locations: KRMA, NAM**

[231] Threlfall, T. R. *The Story of The King's (Liverpool Regiment), formerly The Eighth Foot.*

Preface by the Earl of Derby. London: Country Life, 1916. **Locations: 1, 2, 3, 7, 16, KRMA**

[232] Williams, W. R., (ed.). *Succession Lists of the Officers of the 8th Regiment of Foot, the King's (Liverpool) Regiment, 1685-1807.* **Locations: 2**

[233] Wood, Walter. "The King's (Liverpool Regiment)." *Northern Counties Magazine* I (January 1901) 201-10. **Locations: 1, 2, 13, 28**

[234] Wurtzburg, C. E., Captain. *The History of the 2/6th (Rifle) Battalion "The King's" (Liverpool Regiment), 1914-1919.* Aldershot: Gale and Polden (printers) for the Regimental Committee, 1920. **Locations: ***

[235] Wyrall, Everard, and Synge, W. A. J. *The History of The King's Regiment (Liverpool) 1914-1919.* 3 vols. London: Edward Arnold & Co., 1928-35. **Locations: 1, 2, 7, 18, KRMA**

ARCHIVES

The principal collection of archives relating to the King's Liverpool Regiment is to be found in the regimental museum in Liverpool. The King's Regiment Collection comprises books, artifacts, manuscripts, war diaries, personal collections, photographs, order books, typescripts, newspaper cuttings, correspondence and various miscellaneous items. Archives relating to the Liverpool Scottish Regiment are held in the Liverpool Scottish Museum.

King's Regiment Archival Collection

[236] War Diaries:
1st Battalion: 12th August 1914-31st January 1918, less December 1914, May-September and December 1915; 1st February-31st October 1918, 1st November 1918-30th April 1919. Captain & Adjutant F. Hudson's Diary-12th August 1914-8th June 1918, less April 1915.
1/6th Battalion: 1st February 1915-30th April 1919.
1/8th Battalion: 1st May 1915-31st January 1918.
1/9th Battalion: 12th March 1915-31st Jan 1918.
1/10th Battalion: 1st November 1914-30th September 1919, less March, April and May 1919.
2/5th Battalion: 11th February 1917-31st January 1918, less July 1917.
2/6th Battalion: 14th February 1917-15th May 1919.
2/8th Battalion: 31st January 1917-31st May 1919.
2/9th Battalion: 1st February 1917-31st December 1918.
2/10th Battalion: 16th February 1917-4th August 1918.
4th Battalion: 4th March 1915-23rd November 1919.
5th Battalion: 1st February 1915-30th April
7th Battalion: 1st March 1915-30th April 1919, less September, October and November 1915.
11th Battalion: 17th May 1915-31st May 1918.
12th Battalion: 22nd July 1915-30th April 1919.
13th Battalion: 26th September 1915-30th September 1919.
14th Battalion: 25th October 1915-30th June 1918.
17th Battalion: 6th November 1915-30th August 1918.
18th Battalion: 3rd November 1915-15th May 1919.

19th Battalion: 6th November 1915-31st July 1918.
20th Battalion: 30th October 1915-6th February 1918.
25th Battalion: 5th May 1918-31st May 1919.
General Charles Harington: papers relating to General Charles Harington, especially those relating to the allied forces' occupation of Constantinople, c.1920, with photographs, diaries, visitors books, newspaper cuttings book, book of verses, correspondence etc. Muster Rolls of the 5th Lancashire Rifle Volunteers. Lieutenant Thomas Evans: officer's diary, 1799-1801, recording Egypt campaigns etc. Battalion Order Book, 1759. World War I Letters and Diaries. 6th Battalion: casualty books etc. Sydney Marriott, 7th Battalion, typed copies of letters. Lieutenant William Turner, 1/10th Battalion: documents and correspondence with F.H. Turner, World War I. King's Depot: Records, 1932-59. Lieutenant J. Whyte: letters and photographs. Campbell Watson, 20th Battalion: documents, correspondence, newspaper cuttings and photographs from World War I. CQMS J.A. Jack, 17th Battalion: papers and photographs-1 box. G.F. Dickinson: books and photographs, [n.d.] Miscellaneous Documents, several boxes relating to the regiment, mostly 20th Century. Photographs: 1860s onwards, mostly from World War I.

Liverpool Scottish Museum Collection

[237]   Manuscripts and documents overview: Service books, orderly books, rules and regulations, standing orders, rolls of honour, ledgers, scrapbooks, newspaper cuttings books (many with photographs), field officers' visiting books, pay books, drill muster rolls, war diaries, company rolls, attestment rolls, target registers, correspondence books, army books, field message books, letters of resignation, forms of application for enrolment, bills and accounts, warrants, commissions, minutes of meetings, discharge certificates, music books and scores, nominal rolls and other miscellaneous documents.

Manuscripts; select list:
War Diaries:
2/10th (Scottish) Battalion The King's Liverpool Regiment. Official Diary 1917-1918
No.4 Independent Company (Typescript) 1940
10th King's, 1915-1917 (3 vols)
152 (Field Service) Army Books, including "Y" Company returns of RQMS R.A.S. McFie; billeting lists, rations, returns, 1917-1919 (11 vols); Field Message Books "Y" Company-notes and returns of R.A.S. McFie, 1914-1919 (36 vols).
Personal Diaries and Documents: Orderly Book of Captain James Maxwell, No.1 (Lowland) Company, Liverpool Scottish Volunteers, 1860-1. R.A.S. McFie Volunteering, 1902-3, 1903-4, 1904-5, 1905-6 (scrapbooks). Diary of Captain Bryden McKinnell, Nov 1st 1914-June 14th 1915. Diary of Lt-Col. J.R. Davidson, 1/10th (Scottish) Battalion, King's Liverpool Regiment, Nov 1914-Aug 1916. Reminiscences of L/Cpl H.S. Taylor (No.5080) 1914-19. Diary of Pte. H.C. Dumbell No.3059 [n.d.]. Documents relating to 5771 H.M. Watson c. 1916-18. Diary of Pte. W.H. Campbell (No.4739) [n.d.]. Diary of RSM D.A.B. Marples [n.d.]. Miscellaneous documents of Pte Thomas Harold Leadbetter (12 items) c.1913-19. Diary of Captain Lionel Ferguson (Pte in King's Liverpool Regiment in 1914).
Newspaper Cuttings: Newspaper scrapbooks, 1900-6, 1914-15. 8th Volunteer Battalion, King's Liverpool Regiment, 1905-8. Pte. Hilton Spalding, 1904-6. J. Bedford with the Liverpool Scottish: Vol.1 (1914-15), Vol.2 (1915-18).
Correspondence: 152 (Field Service) Correspondence Books Jan 1915-1918, including lecture notes, "Y" Company records, Battalion orders.
Miscellaneous Manuscripts: Gaskell Papers: miscellaneous documents relating to Gaskell's connection with the British Legion.
Renison, J.D.W., Lt. Col. Regimental History of the Liverpool Scottish 1947-59 (original

manuscript copy).

Maclean, Loraine. The raising of the 79th Highlanders.

Liverpool Scottish Regimental Association, Minute Books: No.1 (1930-2), No.2 (1932-9), No.3 (1940-69).

Rosens, J.P. The Liverpool Scottish, 1914-18. (Thesis) Typescript story of a 1st Line T.F. Battalion's contribution to the war effort.

Chavasse Papers: Folder containing documents, newspaper cuttings and photographs relating to the Chavasse family of Liverpool, mostly relating to Noel Chavasse, twice awarded the VC.

Liverpool Scottish Rifle Volunteers:

Bills and accounts.

Correspondence: letters of resignation (1860-1), letters relating to: Scotch Drapers of Liverpool; St. Domingo Barracks, Everton; Corn Exchange; War Office; Lord Sefton, Lord Lieutenant; No.2 Highland Company; Uniform and dress.

Drill muster roll (1860); company notebook (No.1 Lowland); uniform notebook; Hon. Secretary's notebook (Jas. M. Dowie); Highland Company (No.2) drill book. [n.d.]

Maps include: Gorre, Lacoutre, Zillebeke (2nd Army Section), Winsles, Wielje, St. Julian area,

Ypres, Tournai, Hazebrouk, Valenciennes, Lens and maps of Belgium and France at 1:40,000.

Audio-visual material: Posters, videos, films, audio cassettes, postcards and slides relating to the history of the regiment and its members.

Artifacts: Badges, medals, helmets, uniforms, kilts, canes, cravats, kilts, sporrans, tie pins, musical instruments-bugles, drums etc., weapons-swords, pistols, rifles, bayonets etc., gas masks, goggles, plaques relating to the Liverpool Scottish Regiment.

Photographs: Some 5,000 photographs relating to the men and officers of the regiment, approximately 4,000 of these are indexed. Many photographs in bound albums.

Liverpool Libraries and Information Services, Record Office and Local History Department

[238] *2nd Volunteer Battalion, King's (Liverpool) Regiment. Minute Books; Lists of Men serving; Miscellaneous Records, 1915-22.*

Minute Books: 4 vols., 1915-1920: City of Liverpool Volunteer Guard, General Committee; Military Sub-Committee; Liverpool Area Committee of the City of Liverpool Volunteer Guard; Liverpool Corporation Employees Corps.

Lists of Men Serving: 22 vols., c.1915-1918: Enrolment Forms (18 vols.); Nominal Roll (1 vol.); Warrant officers, Non- Commissioned officers (1 vol.); Platoon Roll, by companies and platoons (1 vol.); Officers Records (1 vol.); Discharge Book etc. (1 vol.).

Miscellaneous: 4 vols., 1914-1922: Register of Documents Received (1 vol.); Correspondence and Papers (1 vol.); Receipts, invoices etc. (1 vol.); Newspaper Cuttings (1 vol.). 1915-22.

National Army Museum

[239] King's (Liverpool) Regiment. *Regimental accounts and documents relating to the 1st, 2nd and 8th Volunteer Battalions of the King's (Liverpool) Regiment for the period 1902 to 1932.*

[240] 1/6th Battalion King's Liverpool Regiment. *Certificate signed by George V, appointing 2nd Lieutenant Albert Harvey, Territorial Force, to be a Companion of the Distinguished Service Order. Dated St. James's 26 Sept 1917. Harvey was in 1/6 Bn, attached 1/5 Bn Liverpool Regt, Territorial Force. 1917.*

BORDER REGIMENT: GENERAL LINEAGE

1702: Raised at Colchester and Norwich from men of Norfolk, Essex and adjacent counties as Lord Lucas's Regiment of Foot

1740: Served as marines

Known until 1751 by the names of the colonels:
1705: Hans Hamilton;
1712: Thomas Chudleigh;
1723: Robert Hayes;
1732: Stephen Cornwallis;
1738: Lord James Cavendish;
1742: James Colmondeley;
1749: Henry Seymour Conway.

1747: Ranked as 34th regiment

1751: Designated by number

1782: Redesignated as 34th (the Cumberland) Regiment of Foot

1881: 34th Regiment of Foot amalgamated with the 55th (Westmorland) Regiment to become the Border Regiment

1959: Regiment amalgamated with The King's Own Royal Regiment (Lancaster) to become the King's Own Royal Border Regiment

King's Own Royal Border Regiment

[241] Argyle, M. A., (ed.). *Fallen on the Somme. The War Diary of 2nd Lieutenant Harold Harding Linzell M.C. 7th Border Regiment.* [n.d.]. **Locations: 5**

[242] Bardgett, Colin. *The Lonsdale Battalion 1914-1918.* Wigtown, Scotland: G.C. Book Publishers, 1993. **Locations: 5**

[243] The Border Regiment Association. Kendal Branch. *25th Anniversary of Mobilisation.* [n.d.] **Locations: 5**

[244] Green, Alan. *1st Battalion The Border Regiment, Arnheim 17th September-26th September 1944.* 1991. **Locations: 1, 5**

[245] King's Own Border Regiment. "The Border - 300 years old and singing in the rain." *Cumberland and Westmorland Herald* 19 July 1980. **Locations: 5**

[246] --- *Distinguished Conduct Medal, 1914-20: Citations: The Border Regiment.* London: Stamp Exchange, 1992. **Locations: 3**

[247] --- *King's Own Royal Border Regiment.* Morecambe: Morecambe Bay Printers, [n.d.]. **Locations: 3**

[248] --- *King's Own Royal Border Regiment: Miscellaneous leaflets.* [n.d.]. **Locations: 3**

[249] --- *The Lion and the Dragon: Regimental Gazette of the King's Own Border Regiment.* London: Combined Service Publications, 1960-. **Locations: 5 (1975-)**

[250] --- *The Lonsdale Battalion Border Regiment. September, 1914 - June 1915.* Carlisle: Thurnham, 1915. **Locations: 5**

[251] --- *Newsletter.* 1983-92. **Locations: 5 (1983-92)**

[252] --- *The Newsletter of the 110th Regiment, Royal Armoured Corps (formerly the 5th Border Regiment).* Vol. 1: parts 1-12. [n.d.]. **Locations: 3**

[253] --- "A Regiment of Fine Achievements." *Westmorland Gazette* (1968). **Locations: 5**

[254] --- *Soldiers Died in the Great War 1914-1919. Part 39: The Border Regiment.* London: Hayward with Imperial War Museum, Department of Printed Books, 1988. **Locations: 3, CURO (B)**

[255] --- *Tercentenary Parade and Presentation of Colours to The King's Own Royal Border Regiment by Her Royal Highness Princess Alexandra, Colonel-in-Chief, Weeton Camp. Preston, 11th July, 1980.* Leyland: Leyland Printing, 1980. **Locations: 3**

[256] Machell, P.W., Lieutenant-Colonel. *Records of the XI (Service) Border Batallion, Border Regiment.* J.Whitehead & Sons, 1916. **Locations: 5**

[257] May, Ralph Keogh. *Museum of the Border Regiment and the King's Own Border Regiment: an illustrated account of the Regiment's Museum housed in a building in the inner ward of*

Carlisle Castle. Derby: Pilgrim Press, 1974. **Locations: 1, 3**

[258] May, Ralph, Colonel. *The King's Own Royal Border Regiment 1680-1980: A Short Regimental History written to mark the Regimental Tercentenary on the 13th July, 1980.* 1980. **Locations: 3, 5, 28**

[259] --- "The Tercentenary of Cumbria's Regiment." *Cumbria* 30 (July 1980) 207-9. **Locations: 28**

[260] Shears, Philip J. *The Story of the Border Regiment, 1939-1945.* London: Nisbet & Co., 1948. **Locations: 3, 5**

[261] Sutherland, Douglas. *Record of the XIth (Service) Battalion Border Regiment (Lonsdale) from September, 1914 to July 1st, 1916. Commanding Officer: Lieutenant-Colonel P.W. Machell, C.M.G., D.S.O.* Appleby: J. Whitehead, 1916. **Locations: 5**

[262] --- *Tried and Valiant. The History of the Border Regiment (The 34th and 55th Regiments of Foot) 1702-1959.* London: Leo Cooper, 1972. **Locations: 3, 21**

[263] Wilkinson, Eric. "Lonsdales" The Raising of a Pals Battalion in Cumberland and Westmorland in the First World War." Liverpool University: Diploma in Local History Dissertation, [n.d.] **Locations: 5**

[264] Wylly, H. C., Colonel. *The Border Regiment in the Great War.* Aldrshot:Gale and Polden, 1924. **Locations: 5**

ARCHIVES
Researchers should note that the history of the Border Regiment, amalgamated with the King's Own Royal Regiment (Lancaster) in 1959, to form the King's Own Royal Border Regiment is covered in the Border Regiment Museum situated in Queen Mary's Tower, The Castle, Carlisle. The Museum is also the principal repository for archive material for the Border Regiment.

Cumbria Record Office. Carlisle
[265] *The Border Regiment: Records.* Contents: Lonsdale Battalion: rifle range results, rail warrants, depot files and correspondence, billeting, pay books, receipts, returns, Commanding Officer's correspondence and telegrams, training circulars and regulations, station orders, equipment ledgers, nominal rolls, medical reports, minor offences, mess books, battle orders, 1914-18.

[266] --- *World War I. The Battle Front. Medals.* 1914-18.

Kendal Library
[267] Ephemera. *King's Own Border Regiment: press cuttings and handwritten notes on Westmorland Border Regiment c.1930.* 1930-.
Military Illustrations: Departures of the Westmorland and Cumberland Yeomanry, 4 photographs and various others (1916); Westmorland and Cumberland Yeomanry Sports-various photographs [n.d.]; 4th Battalion The Border Regiment-illustrations (1910, 1930,

n.d.); 4th Battalion the Border Regiment, Aldershot, 5.11.39; 6th Battalion the Border Regiment, Kent (1940); 4th Battalion the Border Regiment, Church Parade (1937); 34th West Lancashire Royal Army Medical Corps [n.d.]; 34th West Lancashire Royal Army Medical Corps, Outside Kendal Market Hall (1914-15); 2nd Volunteer Battalion, Westmorland Home Guard, The Border Regiment [n.d.]; 11th Battalion, Westmorland Home Guard, The Border Regiment, Castle Street, Kendal [n.d.]; No.IV Troop B. Squadron, Mr. Parish and Sgt. Thompson [n.d.]; 4th Battalion The Border Regiment, India (1916); 11th Battalion Westmorland Home Guard, The Border Regiment, Westmorland and Cumberland Yeomanry, Blencow (1913); 2nd Volunteer Battalion, The Border Regiment, Kendal (1887); The Border Regiment (1969, 1972, 1982).

KING'S OWN ROYAL REGIMENT (LANCASTER): GENERAL LINEAGE

1680: Raised as 2nd Tangier, or Earl of Plymouth's Regiment of Foot

1684: Redesignated as The Duchess of York and Albany's Regiment of Foot

1685: Redesignated as The Queen's Regiment of Foot

1688: Redesignated as The Queen Consort's Regiment of Foot

1702: Redesignated as The Queen's Regiment of Foot

1703-10: Served as marines and known as The Queen's Own Regiment of Marines

1715: Redesignated as The King's Own Regiment of Foot

1747: Ranked as 4th Regiment

1751: Designated as 4th (The King's Own) Regiment of Foot

1867: Redesignated as 4th (The King's Own Royal) Regiment of Foot

1881: Redesignated as The King's Own (Royal Lancaster Regiment)

1921: Redesignated as the King's Own Royal Regiment (Lancaster)

1959: Amalgamated (less Territorials) with the Border Regiment (less Territorials) to form The King's Own Royal Border Regiment

King's Own Royal Regiment (Lancaster)

[268] Adams, W. H. Davenport. *"History of The 4th Regiment of Foot, or 'The King's Own' [Royal Lancashire Regiment]."* 1864. **Locations: 28**

[269] Barrow, Harry. "Terriers of Lancaster." *Lancashire Life* 3 (1955) 33. **Locations: 1, 28**

[270] Bigland, Editha Blanche Hinde. *The Soldier Squire: a memoir with portraits of Second-Lieutenant George Braddyll Bigland of Bigland, of the 1/4th King's Own Royal Lancaster Regiment, the immortal Fifty-first Division.* Ulverston: Kitchin, 1923. **Locations: 3, 112**

[271] Cowper, L. I., Colonel. *The Priory and Parish Church of St. Mary, Lancaster [No.4]: A History of the Monuments, Memorials and Colours in the King's Own Memorial Chapel.* Manchester: Holt Publishing Service Ltd., [n.d.] **Locations: 28**

[272] Cowper, Lionel Ilfred, Colonel, and Cowper, J. M., Colonel, (eds.). *The King's Own. The Story of a Royal Regiment. Edited from material supplied by the Members of the Regimental Historical Sub-Committee.* 3 vols. Vol I 1680-1814; Vol II 1814-1914; Oxford: O.U.P., 1939. Vol III 1914-1950; Aldershot: Gale and Polden Ltd., 1957 **Locations: 1, 3, 7, 8, 27, 28**

[273] Cross Fleury. "Roll of Officers, Non-Commissioned Officers and Men of the Line Battalion Royal Lancaster Regiment, who were killed or died in South Africa." *Cross Fleury's Journal* 90 (February 1904) 347-8. **Locations: 28**

[274] Eastwood, Stuart A. *Lions of England. A Pictorial History of the King's Own Royal Regiment (Lancaster), 1680-1980.* Kettering: Silver Link Publishing, 1991. **Locations: 1, 2, 3, 7, 112, KORM**

[275] Green, Howard. *The King's Own Royal Regiment, (Lancaster), (The 4th Regiment of Foot).* London: Leo Cooper, 1972. **Locations: ***

[276] Hall, Jasper. *Letters from the Crimea: Captain Jasper Hall of the 4th (or King's Own) Regiment of Foot, to his sister and father. Transcribed and annotated with an introduction by Edith Tyson.* Lancaster: The Museum, 1980. **Locations: 28, LRO**

[277] Harris, W. H. "English County Regiments: The King's Own." *This England* (Summer 1988). **Locations: 28**

[278] Hodgkinson, Albert, Captain, (ed.). *The King's Own T.F.; being a Record of The 1/5th Battalion The King's Own (Royal Lancaster Regiment) in the European War, 1914-1918.* Lewes: Lewes Press, 1921. **Locations: 3, 5, 28, 40, NAM**

[279] King's Own Royal Lancaster Regiment. *The Ceremony of laying up two stands of colours of the First Battalion the Royal Lancashire Militia, presented in 1806 and 1816 in the Memorial Chapel of the King's Own Royal Regiment in Lancaster Priory Church. Sunday, Sept. 18th 1932.* 1932. **Locations: 28**

[280] --- *A Gallant Regiment. A Short History of The King's Own.* Lancaster: Thomas Bell, 1914. **Locations: 28**

[281]   ---   *Historical Record of the 4th, or the King's Own, Regiment of Foot; containing an Account of the Formation of the Regiment in 1680 and of its subsequent Services to 1839.*   London: Longman, Orme & Co., 1839.   Cannon's Historical Records Series.   **Locations: 28**

[282]   ---   *The History of the 107 Regiment, Royal Armoured Corps (King's Own). June 1940-February 1946.*   Lengerich, Germany: Druck, Bischof & Klein, 1946.   **Locations: NAM**

[283]   ---   *King's Own (Royal Lancaster Regiment). Distinguished Conduct Medal, 1914-20: Citations.*   London: Stamp Exchange, 1985.   **Locations: 3, 9, 28**

[284]   ---   *The Lion and the Dragon (Regimental Gazette).*   Lancaster: 1960-.   **Locations: 28, KORM (1960-)**

[285]   ---   *The Lion and the Rose (Regimental Gazette).*   Lancaster: 1921-59.   **Locations: 28, KORM (1921-59)**

[286]   ---   *Record of the War Memorial of The King's Own Royal Lancaster Regiment, 1914-18.*   London: W.H. Smith & Son, 1924.   **Locations: 5, 28**

[287]   ---   *Soldiers Died in the Great War, 1914-1919. Part 9: The King's Own (Royal Lancaster Regiment).*   Polstead: Hayward with Imperial War Museum, Dept. of Printed Books, 1989.   **Locations: 3, 4, 28, CURO (B), LRO**

[288]   ---   *Special Supplement of The Lion and the Rose, the Regimental Magazine of The King's Own... to Commemorate the Presentation of the Freedom of the City of Lancaster to the Regiment on Aug. 29th, 1953.*   Lancaster: The Regiment, 1953.
Locations: 5, 28

[289]   Lancaster Corporation.   *Ceremony of the Honouring of the King's Own Royal Regiment (Lancaster), 29th August, 1953. Programme.*   1953.   **Locations: 28**

[290]   ---   *Presentation of the Freedom of the Cities of Carlisle and Lancaster, and the Borough of Appleby to the King's Own Royal Border Regiment, Barnard Castle, 23rd April, 1960. Programme.*   1960.   **Locations: 28**

[291]   Mason, George.   *The Journal of Captain Mason of the 4th (or King's Own) Regiment of Foot, his voyage to Australia, his service there and his return journey, 1831-1835, transcribed by Edith Tyson from the original document in the Museum of the King's Own Regiment (Lancaster).*   Lancaster: The Museum, 1981.
Locations: 3, 28

[292]   May, Ralph, Colonel.   *The King's Own Royal Border Regiment, 1680-1984: a short regimental history written to mark the 25th anniversary of the amalgamation of the King's Own Royal Regiment and the Border Regiment, 1st October 1984.*   Liverpool: North West Publications, 1984.   **Locations: 28**

[293]   Thorne, A. D., Lieutenant-Colonel.   *A Record of Articles and Monuments of Historical Interest placed in The King's Own Memorial Chapel, Lancaster, since its dedication by the Right Rev. the Lord Bishop of Manchester on 24th July, 1904.*   London: W.H. Smith, 1924.
Locations: 28

[294] Wadham, W. F. A., Lieutenant-Colonel, and Crossley, J., Captain. *The Fourth Battalion, The King's Own (Royal Lancaster Regiment) and the Great War [1914-1918].* London: Crowther & Goodman, 1935. **Locations: 5**

[295] --- *The Fourth Battalion, The King's Own (Royal Lancaster Regiment) and the Great War: Early Days.* 1920. **Locations: 3, 5, NAM**

[296] Whalley, Joseph Lawson. *The Early History of the Lancashire Regiment of Militia, now the 3rd and 4th Battalions of The King's Own (Royal Lancaster) Regiment; 1642-1799; with appendix continued to 1902.* E. Phillips & Co.: Lancaster, 1904. **Locations: 3, 29, 28, NAM**

[297] --- *Roll of Officers of the Old County Regiment of Lancashire Militia, late 1st Royal Lancashire (The Duke of Lancaster's Own); now 3rd and 4th Battalions The King's Own (Royal Lancaster) Regiment, from 1642-1889. Corrected to May 1st 1889.* London: Simpkin, Marshall and Co., 1889. **Locations: 1, 3, 7, 28, LRO, NAM**

[298] Williams, Ellis. *Ballads of the King's Own [Royal Lancaster Regiment] and other verses.* Lancaster: Beeley (printer), 1918. **Locations: 3**

[299] Williamson, Ralph John Thomas, Major. *History of the Old County Regiment of Lancashire Militia, late 1st Royal Lancashire (The Duke of Lancaster's Own); now 3rd and 4th Battalion The King's Own (Royal Lancaster) Regiment, from 1689-1856; with a continuation to 1888 by J. Lawson Whalley.* London: Simpkin, Marshall & Co., 1888. **Locations: ***

ARCHIVES

King's Own Royal Lancaster Regiment. Regimental Museum Collection

[300] The museum is the main repository for regimental archives. The collection comprises books, manuscripts, documents, artifacts, photographs, indexes and bibliographies relating to the regiment, including lists of officers from 1680 onwards and all ranks serving in the 4th Battalion. Main collections include:
Medal Rolls: from 1812 onwards.
World War I Battalion War Diaries for: 1st, 2nd, 4th, 5th, 7th, 8th, 9th, 11th Battalions.
Correspondence: relating to various members of the regiment, 18th Century onwards.
World War II Diaries for: 107th and 151st Regiments, Royal Armoured Corps. Artifacts: medals, badges, souvenirs, ephemera, invitation cards, calendars, guns, uniforms etc. relating to the regiment.
Programmes for: ceremonies, menus, re-union dinners, trooping colours, etc.
Paybooks and pension books: separate pensions and certificates in personnel files.
Newspaper Cuttings: obituaries, World War I medals awards, miscellaneous.
Maps: World War I trench maps, etc.
Postcards: regimental postcards, christmas cards.
Photographs: several thousand, from 1850 onwards, some in personal files, most split into loose photographs and albums, relating to regimental campaigns.
Oral History: personal recollections of members of the regiment.

Lancaster Library.

[301] King's Own Royal Lancaster Regiment. Regimental Museum. *Minutes of the Sub-*

Committee, 1929-1932. 1929-32.

[302] --- "Invitation from the Mayor and Corporation of Lancaster to Mr. and Mrs. Cardwell, to attend the handling of the colours of the Third Battalion of the King's Own Regiment to the Mayor for safe custody during the Battalion's service in South Africa. Feb 3rd 1900." *Lancaster Library Scrapbook* 4 (folio) (1900) 2.

[303] Lancaster Library. South African War File. *Balance sheets for the South African War Fund, 1900-3.* 1900-3.

[304] --- South African War. "Menu of supper given to the volunteer officers and men from Lancaster and district who are accepted for service in South Africa. March 21st, 1901." *Lancaster Library Scrapbook* 4 (folio) (1901) 2.

[305] --- "Plan of the proposed Memorial Chapel of the King's Own Royal Lancaster Regiment, in Lancaster Parish Church. Austin and Paley, Architects. July 1902. Scale 1.5"-50'." *Lancaster Library Scrapbook* 1 (folio) (1902) 142.

[306] Vernon, A. *Letter from A. Vernon, Royal Lancaster Regiment, 15th Division Field Forces, a serving soldier, to Mr. E. Parr.* 1900.

[307] --- *Letter from A. Vernon to "Dear Ted" [Mr. E. Parr] headed Ladysmith Camp, March 6th [1900].* 1900.

Lancashire Fusiliers

[308] Ashurst, George. *My Bit: A Lancashire Fusilier at War, 1914-1918. (Edited by Richard Holmes.)* Marlborough: Crowood Press in association with Anthony Bird, 1987. **Locations:** *

[309] Bainbrigge, Philip, Lieutenant-General. *Mis-statements in the Historical Records of the XXth Regiment in regard to the Services of the late Lieutenant-Colonel Bainbrigge in the Expedition to Holland in 1794, corrected.* London: Ford & Tilt, 1860. **Locations: LFRM**

[310] Bamford, P. G., (ed.). *Customs and Practices of XX the Lancashire Fusiliers.* Lancashire: The Regiment, 1962. **Locations: 7, 9**

[311] Barlow, Clement Anderson Montague, Sir., (ed.). *The Lancashire Fusiliers. The Roll of Honour of the Salford Brigade (15th, 16th, 19th, 20th and 21st Lancashire Fusiliers).* Manchester: Sherratt and Hughes, 1919. **Locations: 1, 13, 15**

[312] Barlow, Frederick Watkins, Lieutenant., (ed.). *Orders, Memoirs, Anecdotes, etc. connected with the XX Regiment.* Minden Press, 1868. **Locations: LFRM**

[313] Barton, John. "The XXth." *Cheshire Life* 37 (February, 1971) 36-7. **Locations: 4, 58**

[314] Bolton Museum and Art Gallery. *The Royal Regiment of Fusiliers (Lancashire Fusiliers). An exhibition of outstanding items from the Regimental Museum.* Bolton: Museum and Art Gallery, 1970. **Locations: BOM**

[315] Bury County Borough. *Honouring of The XX The Lancashire Fusiliers, 3rd August, 1946: Souvenir Brochure.* Bury: Bury County Borough, 1946. **Locations: 10**

[316] Cooper, G. "Six V.C.'s before breakfast." *Lancashire Constabulary Journal* January, 1968, 400-2. **Locations: LRO**

[317] Floyd, Thomas Hope. *At Ypres with Best Dunkley.* London: John Lane, 1920. **Locations: LFRM**

[318] Fusiliers' Association (Lancashire). *The Lancashire Fusiliers News Sheet.* Lancashire: Fusiliers' Association, 1985. **Locations: 3 (1985-)**

[319] Garratt, Stanley Reginald., (ed.). *Customs and Practices of XX The Lancashire Fusiliers.* Bury, 1960. **Locations: LFRM**

[320] Garratt, Stanley Reginald. *Customs and Practices of XX The Lancashire Fusiliers.* Sutton Coldfield, 1962. (2nd rev. edition) **Locations: 1, LFRM**

[321] Hallam, John McQ., Major. *History of the Lancashire Fusiliers 1939-1945.* Far Thrupp, Stroud, Gloucester: Alan Sutton Publishing Ltd, 1993. **Locations: LFRM**

[322] Lancashire Fusiliers, *The Ceremony of Honouring the Lancashire Fusiliers, 18th October 1947. Souvenir Brochure.* 1972. **Locations: 15**

LANCASHIRE FUSILIERS: GENERAL LINEAGE

1688: Raised as Sir Richard Peyton's Regiment of Foot

1701: Served as marines
Known until 1751 by names of the colonels:
1689: Gustavus Hamilton (afterwards Viscount Boyne);
1706: John Newton; 1714: Thomas Meredith;
1719: William Egerton; 1732: Francis, Earl of Effingham;
1737: Richard St. George; 1740: Thomas Bligh;
1746: Lord George Sackville; 1749: George, Viscount Bury.

1747: Ranked as 20th regiment

1751: Designated by number

1782: Redesignated as 20th
(The East Devonshire) Regiment of Foot

1881: Redesignated as The Lancashire Fusiliers

1968: Amalgamated with The Royal Northumberland Fusiliers, The Royal Warwickshire Fusiliers and The Royal Fusiliers to form the Royal Regiment of Fusiliers

December 1969: Disbanded as 4th Battalion The Royal Regiment of Fusiliers

[323]   Lancashire Fusiliers. *Distinguished Conduct Medal, 1914-20. Citations.* London: Stamp Exchange Ltd., 1985.   **Locations: 3, 9**

[324]   --- *The Fusilier: Magazine of the Royal Regiment of Fusiliers.* Bury: The Regiment, 1968-. **Locations: LFRM (1968-)**

[325]   --- *The Gallipoli Gazette.* 1. Egypt 2. Aldershot 3. Gibraltar: 1. Whitehead Morris (printer) 2. Gale and Polden (printer) 3. Beanland Malin (printer), 1926-68. **Locations:3 (1926-68, incomplete); LFRM (1926-68)**

[326]   --- *The Gallipolian. Journal of the Gallipoli Association*, 1992.   **Locations: LFRM**

[327]   --- *The Great War 1914-1918 and 1919. The Lancashire Fusiliers' Roll of Honour.* Bolton: 1922.   **Locations: 7, 10, 13, LFRM**

[328]   --- *Historical Record of The Twentieth, or The East Devonshire Regiment of Foot; containing an Account of the Formation of the Regiment in 1688, and of its subsequent Services to 1848. Compiled by Richard Cannon, Esq., Adjutant-General's Office, Horse Guards.*   London: Parker, Furnivall & Parker, 1848. Cannon's Historical Records Series   **Locations: LFRM**

[329]   --- *The Lancashire Fusiliers' Annual.* Manchester: Manchester Examiner, 1891 **Locations: 1 (1892-1922, incomplete); 3 (1891-1926); 7 (1902, 1903, 1905); 10 (1891-1926); LFRM (1891-1926); LRO (1919, 1921)**

[330]   --- *The Lancashire Fusiliers' Compassionate Fund. Rules.* Pendleton: P. Hampson, 1900. **Locations:LFRM**

[331]   --- *A Militia Unit in the Field: Being a Brief Account of the Doings of The Sixth Battalion Lancashire Fusiliers in the South African War, During the Years 1900 and 1901.* London: Woodfall and Kinder, 1902.   **Locations: 10**

[332]   --- *The Minden Magazine, 2nd Battalion Lancashire Fusiliers*, 1915-16.   **Locations: LFRM (1915-16)**

[333]   --- *Roll of Honour To the Glory of God and in Proud Memory of The Lancashire Fusiliers Whose Names Are Herein Recorded. These Gallant Soldiers Laid Down Their Lives for King and Country in The World War 1939-1945.* 1952.   **Locations: 13**

[334]   --- *The Royal Regiment of Fusiliers celebrates the Tercentenary: 20th Foot (The Lancashire Fusiliers), 1688-1988.* Clitheroe: Borough Printing Co., 1988.   **Locations: 3**

[335]   --- *Short History of The Lancashire Fusiliers (XX Foot).* 1931.   **Locations: 33**

[336]   --- *Soldiers Who Died in The Great War, 1914-1919. Part 25: The Lancashire Fusiliers.* London: H.M.S.O., 1921.   **Locations: 10**

[337]   --- *Soldiers Who Died in the Great War, 1914-19. Part 25: The Lancashire Fusiliers.* Polstead: J.B. Hayward & Son with Imperial War Museum, Dept. of Printed Books, 1989. **Locations: 3, 4, 13, 18, LRO**

[338]   --- *XX The Lancashire Fusiliers: A Handbook.* London, 1952.   **Locations:1, 10, 21**

[339] Lancashire Fusiliers, Sixth Battalion. *Presentation of new Queen's and Regimental Colours.* 1953. **Locations: 13**

[340] Lancashire Fusiliers Association Band. *H.M. The Queen's Silver Jubilee, 1952-1977: souvenir brochure, [prepared by Harry Johnson].* Lancashire: Lancashire Fusiliers Association Band, 1977. **Locations: 3**

[341] Lancashire Fusiliers' Compassionate and War Memorial Fund. *Report of the managers [for] year ended July 31st, 1951: list of subscriptions and donations, summary of receipts and payments and statement of balances.* 1951. **Locations: 3**

[342] Latter, John Cecil, Major-General. *The History of The Lancashire Fusiliers, 1914-1918.* 2 vols. Aldershot: Gale & Polden, 1949. **Locations: ***

[343] McCann, John. *Kohima: an Historic Village, and other short stories.* Chadderton, Oldham: The Author, 1987. **Locations: 1, 3, 7, 11, 13, 15, 18, 59, LFRM**

[344] --- *Return to Kohima.* Chadderton, Oldham: The Author, 1993. **Locations: 2, 3, 4, 18, LFRM**

[345] Potter, C. H. Captain, and Fothergill, A. S. C., Captain. *The History of the 2/6th Lancashire Fusiliers (which amalgamated successively with the 1/6th and the 12th Battalion of the same Regiment). The Story of a 2nd Line Territorial Battalion, 1914-1919.* Rochdale: Observer Printing Works, 1927. **Locations: 1, 3, 6, 7, 13, LRO, NAM**

[346] Ray, Cyril. *Regiment of the Line. The Story of XX The Lancashire Fusiliers.* London: B.T. Batsford, 1963. **Locations: ***

[347] --- *The Lancashire Fusiliers (20th Regiment of Foot).* London: Leo Cooper, 1971. **Locations: ***

[348] Royal Regiment of Fusiliers. *Short History and Description of The Royal Regiment of Fusiliers (5th, 6th, 7th, 20th).* 1975. **Locations: 15**

[349] Shaw, T. P. *HMS Euryalus and the Fusiliers.* Bury: Royal Regiment of Fusiliers, 1985. **Locations: 3, LFRM**

[350] Smyth, Benjamin. *History of The XX Regiment, 1688-1888.* London: Simpkin, Marshall & Co., 1889. **Locations: 1, 10, 13**

[351] --- *A History of The Lancashire Fusiliers (Formerly The XX Regiment), 1688-1903.* 2 vols. Dublin: Sackville Press, 1903-4. **Locations: 1, 3, 7, 10, 13, LFRM, LRO**

[352] --- "Colonel John Parr, Governor of Nova Scotia and New Brunswick." *Gallipoli Gazette* 20 (July, 1935). **Locations: 18B**

[353] Stedman, Michael. *Salford Pals: a History of the 15th, 16th, 19th, and 20th (Service) Battalions Lancashire Fusiliers, 1914-1919: a History of the Salford Brigade.* London: Leo Cooper, 1993. **Locations: 1, 2, 3, 4, 10, 18, 52, CL**

[354] Surtees, George, Major-General. *A Short History of XX The Lancashire Fusiliers.* London:

Malcolm Page, 1955.   **Locations: 1, 3, 4, 7, 13, 15, 21, LFRM, LRO**

[355] --- (ed.). *XX The Lancashire Fusiliers Handbook.* London: Malcolm Page, 1952. **Locations: 1, 13**

[356] Wheeler, Kenneth. *If I Goes West! By a Tommy*. 1918.   **Locations: 3**

[357] Wood, Walter. "The Lancashire Fusiliers." *Northern Counties Magazine,* III (April-May 1901) 91-7. **Locations: 1, 2, 13, 28**

ARCHIVES
The main collection of archives relating to the Lancashire Fusiliers is held in the Regimental Museum at the Wellington Barracks in Bury.

Bury Archives
[358] --- *Lancashire Fusiliers Memorial papers 1905.*

[359] --- *Messrs. Woodcock and Sons, solicitors, of Bury. Miscellaneous photographs etc.* 1915. **(Limited Access)**

[360] --- *Town Clerk's Papers.* Contents include correspondence referring to Lancashire Fusiliers rifle range 1939; adoption HMS Martin and HMS Zodiac 1942-1946; Local Defence Corps 1940; Red Cross etc.: correspondence with Bury PoWs 1939-1945.

[361] Packman, John B., Captain. *War diary and miscellaneous papers and photographs with reference to war service in France, 1913-1920.*

Lancashire Fusiliers Regimental Museum Archives
[362] Archive Files. The Museum's archive has a number of files which relate to various aspects of the regiment's history. A summary is given below.
Coronation Programmes: 1. George VI (12th May 1937), Peking and Tientsin Times, N. China, programme. 2. Elizabeth II (2nd June 1953), souvenir album with programme of celebrations.
Regimental Anniversaries and Celebrations, includes:
1. Royal Regiments of Fusiliers V, VI, VII, XX Presentation of Colours, Friday 23rd April, 1993.
2. Royal Regiment of Fusiliers V, VI, VII, XX Presentation of Freedom of the City of Birmingham, Saturday 5th June, 1993.
3. Royal Regiment of Fusiliers: To Celebrate the Bicentenary of the Battle of Minden (1759) Dinner at Guildhall in the City of London, Monday 27th July 1959.
4. The Parade to Mark the Closing of the Depot at Wellington Barracks, Bury, Friday 17th March 1961.
5. Programme of the Opening Ceremony of the XX Regimental Museum, Sunday 29th April 1934.
6. Collection of Dinner Menus: annual reunion, "Minden Day", Christmas, regimental,

royal, birthday dinners etc.
7. 250th Anniversary XX The Lancashire Fusiliers, 1688-1938, Souvenir Programme (1938)
Photographs of the Museum: Colour and black & white photographs of the Museum and its exhibits-esp. uniforms.
Sympathy Cards: Cards and letters of sympathy sent to relatives of members of the regiment, various dates.
Invitation and Greeting Cards: Cards and invitations to dinners, parties, official openings, VIP and royal parties etc., various dates.
Commemoration Services and Ceremonies of Honour: Souvenir brochures, Orders of Service, including those for:
1. The Parish Church of St. Mary's, Bury, April 25th 1965.
2. County Borough of Bury: Honouring of XX the Lancashire Fusiliers 3rd August, 1946.

3. City of Salford: Ceremony of Honouring XX The Lancashire Fusiliers, 18th October, 1947.
Posters: Honouring those fallen in battle; Home Guard recruitment; Regimental Institute Fund posters etc.
Postcards: A collection of postcards collected by members of the regiment, including:
1. "La Belgique Historique".
2. "Campaigne 1914-1918", Cambrai after the Bombardment.
3. Field Service Pocket Book: postcards from China, Burma and Gibraltar.
War Memorials/Graves: Memorial appeals, brochures, orders of service, posters relating to the Lancashire Fusiliers, including
1. Original "Agreement as to Erection of War Memorial at the Wellington Barracks, Bury", 21st June 1921.
2. McCann, John (ex 1/8th Battalion): Folder of photographs of fallen comrades gravestones in the Far East.
Paybooks, pensions, papers etc.: Collection of paybooks for men and officers of the regiment, with travel permits, records of service and miscellaneous lists.
Men's Service Details: Discharge certificates, Ministry of Defence records for men of the regiment.
Certificates: Collection of certificates of commemoration and commendation, enrolment to Red Cross.
Ministry of Defence Leaflets: information leaflets, etc., including:
1. "The Outbreak of War" No.1 (1939) 22nd August-3rd September 1939, Ministry o f Information, London.
2. "Your Home as an Air Raid Shelter", Ministry of Home Security (1940).
Newspaper Cuttings files: 1688-1913, 1914-19, 1920-38, 1939-45, 1946-date.
Other files include poetry by men and officers of the regiment, H.M.S. Euryalus, Lancashire Fusiliers Home Guard, Medal Rolls, Ministry of Defence letters, negatives, IWW passes (safe conduct), regimental colours, audio cassettes-memoirs, interviews etc., copies of Japanese surrender documents, 1945.
Catalogue of The Lancashire Fusiliers in the Wellington Barracks, Bury. Bury: The Regiment, [n.d.] (Typescript/mimeograph ed.) **Locations: 10**
Enlistment Books. Includes enlistment books for the Regiment, April 1881-Aug 1901.
Personal Diaries. Includes diaries by:
Sergeant L. Carr, "A Sergeant's Log of Gallipoli". 3 Volumes. "...relates accurately and faithfully the various movements, engagements...hardships and privations...on the Gallipoli Peninsula." (April 1915-January 1916).
Lieutenant V.F.S. Hawkins, 2nd Battalion Lancashire Fusiliers, World War I, Western Front (1914-18).

Brigadier V.F.S. Hawkins, 5 Brigade at Kohima, 1944.
Ensign T.F. Wade, XX Regiment including the Battle of Maida 1806 and the Peninsula War, 1808-14 (1806-14).
Lieutenant-General William Kingsley including War of the Austrian Succession and 2nd Jacobite Rebellion (1742-48). 1742-.
<u>Photograph Albums.</u>   Includes albums for the following battalions. Figures in square brackets give approximate number of photographs in each album:
Regimental collections:
Lord Ilford Collection, 1860-1914, 1st Vol. & 5th Battalions. [50];
Museum collection, 1870-1930 [121]; Ireland, 1873-1914 [79]; Sudan War, 1898 [121];
Major B. Smyth album, 1907, 1st, 3rd & 4th Battalions [112];
Yeoman of the Guard, 1910 [23];
World War I Western Front, 1918 [28];
Bury, 1946 [12];
Rochdale, 1947 [57];
<u>1st Battalion</u>: 1860-70 Officers portraits [76]; India, 1911 [21]; China, 1934-8 [65], 1936-8 [272], 1937 [65]; Chinese Army 1936-8
<u>2nd Battalion</u>: G.F. Farmar album, Sudan, 1898 [30]; V.F.S. Hawkins albums, 1914-18 [158], 1919-24 [47]; Cardiff, 1929-36 [31]; 1930-39 & 1945 [39]; India, 1934 [23]
[2/5th Battalion: Lieut-Col N.J. Stanley album, France, 1915-18 [38].
<u>4th Battalion</u>: 1914-18 [103]; 1914-17 [169]
<u>6th Battalion</u>: World War I, Egypt [181]; 1915-18 [181]; 1921-30 [244]; 1926-36 [119]; 1932-50 [797]; 633rd Light AA Regiment Royal Artillery, Rochdale, 1953 [22]
<u>7th Royal Lancashire Militia</u>: Lieut Cecil B.C. Ashton album, 1873 [33]. 1900-.
<u>Record of Items of Regimental Plate</u> presented and lent by XX The Lancashire Fusiliers, 1960.
<u>Records of Service.</u>   Bound manuscript books, many containing photographs, for:
20th Regiment: 1688-1877 (presented to 2nd Bn by Lt Col W.L.D. Meares, 1st Bn); 1759-1880 (including contemporary documents and copies thereof).
<u>1st Battalion</u>: 1869-1910; 1932-43 (including Catterick, Colchester, China 1936-38, India 1938-43); Jan-Dec 1950 (including demonstration of Battalion school of Infantry, Warminster, farewell parade at Bury, voyage to and service in Egypt); Jan 1952-Oct 1953 (including Egypt and operations in Ismailia, Cyprus and Kenya); 1953-57 (including BAOR 1953-7, Cyprus 1957).
<u>2nd Battalion</u>: 1858-1914.
<u>3rd Battalion</u>: 1891-1900 (with 4th Battalion records); 1898-1906.
<u>4th Battalion</u>: 1891-1900 (with 3rd Battalion records); 1914-17.
<u>7th Battalion</u>: 1922-34.
<u>17th Lancs RV-17th Lancers (Salford)</u>: 1880-82.
<u>56th Lancs RV</u>: 1878-80. 1688-.
<u>Regimental Letter Books.</u>   Letter Books for 1st Battalion 1899-1902, 1904-5. <u>Regimental Notebooks.</u>   Notebooks include:
1759-1880: Record of members of Lancashire Fusiliers who have been pensioners of the Royal Hospital Chelsea 1718-1952.
1864: The Murder of major Baldwin and Lieut Bird at Kamkura in 1864, by Harold S. Williams and Hiroshi Naito.
1900-1914: Compiled by a soldier of The Lancashire Fusiliers of the Volunteer Company attached to the 2nd Bn Boer War Apr-Oct 1900 and mobilisation 1914.
<u>Regimental Order Books.</u> for:
<u>2nd Battalion</u>: Jan-Dec 1938.
<u>5th Battalion</u>: 1901-2.

17th Lancers (Salford) Lancs RV: 1880-85.
56th Lancs (Salford) RV: 1878-80.
Royal Lancashire Volunteers: General Orders 1798-1800.
Regimental Scrapbooks. Scrapbooks, many containing photographs, for:
20th Regiment: 1959 (Seven Years War Minden, compiled by Col J.N.H. Christie); 1946 (Ceremony of honouring by the County Borough, August 1946)
2nd Battalion: 1952-55 (Bulford 1952 parade. Trieste 1954 liaison with US Army parade inspection by Italian General. Lichfield 1955 disbandment parade).
4th Battalion: 1968 (Vesting Day, Hong Kong)
Miscellaneous Albums: Album containing photographs relating to Cyprus 1879, Limassol 1914, 2nd Bn 1914-15, 1st Bn in Dublin 1920-25 and India 1940. 1879-1940.
Regimental War Diaries. Regimental War Diaries for:
1st Battalion: 1903-7 ("E" Company Diary of Field Practices).
1/6th Battalion: 1939-41.
2nd Battalion: 1914-19.
Roll Books of Officers, Warrant Officers and Other Ranks. Includes Roll Book for 2nd Battalion 1919-24.
Sketch Books etc. Paintings, cartoons and drawings, including:
Album of 24 water colours. Caricatures of Officers of Lancashire Fusiliers, 1893-4.
Watercolours and drawings of General Sir Frederick Horn KCB during service in the Mediterranean and India 1829-37.

LOYAL REGIMENT (NORTH LANCASHIRE): GENERAL LINEAGE

1741: Raised as John Mordaunt's Regiment of Foot

1743: Redesignated as Peregrine Lascelle's Regiment of Foot

1747: Ranked as 58th Regiment

1751: Designated as 47th Regiment of Foot

1782: Redesignated as 47th (the Lancashire) Regiment of Foot

1881: 47th (Lancashire) Regiment of Foot amalgamated with the 81st (Loyal Lincolnshire Volunteers) Regiment [raised 1793] to become the Loyal North Lancashire Regiment

1921: Regiment redesignated as The Loyal Regiment (North Lancashire)

1970: Amalgamated with The Lancashire Regiment (Prince of Wales's Volunteers) to form the Queen's Lancashire Regiment

Loyal North Lancashire Regiment

[363] Allen, Frank. *The Loyals in Malaya; the First Battalion The Loyal Regiment (N.L.) Malaya, December 1958.* Bolton: Tillotsons Newspapers Ltd, 1959. **Locations: 3, 7**

[364] Berkeley, R. H. *A Short Historical Record of The Loyal Regiment (North Lancashire).* Aldershot: Gale & Polden Ltd., [n.d.] **Locations: 7**

[365] Bulloch, J.M. "The North Lancashire Regiment", *Journal of the Society for Army Historical Research,* 12 (1933) 233-9. **Locations: 1**

[366] Dean, Charles Graham Troughton, Captain. *The Loyal Regiment (North Lancashire), 1919-1953.* Preston: Loyal Regiment (North Lancashire), 1955. [Continuation of Wylly] **Locations: 1, 3, 7, 9, 102, LRO**

[367] Elletson, S. C. B. *Memoir of Daniel Hope Elletson, Second Lieutenant, Forty-Seventh (Lancashire) Regiment.* Lancashire: T. Bell, 1878. **Locations: LRO**

[368] French, Gilbert J. *A Short History of the Volunteer Movement in Bolton, by an Officer of the 2nd Volunteer Battalion Loyal North Lancashire Regiment (Bolton Loyal Volunteers).* Bolton: 1886. **Locations: 1, 7, BOM**

[369] Gaskell, Paul. *My Experiences in Gallipoli.* Chester: Courant Press, 1917. **Locations: RMP**

[370] Houghton, A. T., Major. *The War History of The 1st/4th Battalion The Loyal North Lancashire Regiment, now The Loyal Regiment (North Lancashire), 1914-1918.* Preston:George Toulmin & Son Ltd., 1921. **Locations: 1, 3, LRO, NAM**

[371] Lancashire Lad. *[Loyal North Lancashire Regiment]. On Tramp: being a journal of the march by the 1st Battalion Loyal North Lancashire Regiment from Mhow to Kamptee, by the editor of the "Lancashire Lad".* Bombay, India: Education Society, 1890. **Locations: 3, 13**

[372] Langley, Michael. *The Loyal Regiment: (North Lancashire) (The 47th and 81st Regiments of Foot).* London: Leo Cooper, 1976. **Locations: 1, 3, 7, 10, 15, 18, 29, LRO**

[373] Leech, T. *1st/4th Loyal North Lancashire Regiment 1914-18.* Horwich: Horwich Heritage, 1988. **Locations: 26**

[374] Loyal North Lancashire Regiment. *5th Battalion The Loyal Regiment (North Lancashire).* [n.d.] (Presentation of new colours by Field Marshall Sir Gerald W.R. Templar) **Locations: 7**

[375] --- *Army Day: Fulwood Barracks, Preston, 12th June 1937: Souvenir Programme.* Preston: Snape (printer), 1937. **Locations: 3**

[376] --- *Carry-On: the Trotter's Journal.* Ashford: 1916. **Locations: 3**

[377] --- *Fearful Tragedy at Fulwood Barracks: Death of Col. Crofton; Examination of the prisoner; Adjt. Hanham also dead.* Preston: Mercury, 1861. **Locations: 3**

[378]   --- *Fifth Battalion, The Loyal North Lancashire Regiment, War Memorial Committee. Order of the Proceedings at the Unveiling Ceremony by Colonel the Rt. Hon. the Earl of Derby, K.G. Hon Colonel 5th Battalion, The Loyal Regiment. Bound with a duplicated typescript of the Battalion's Roll of Honour.* [n.d.]   **Locations: 43**

[379]   --- *Form of Service to be Used at the Dedication of the Memorial Tablet to the Soldiers of the 2nd Battalion Loyal North Lancashire Regiment who Fell in The Great War, 1914-1918 on Tuesday September 5th, 1922, in the Preston Parish Church.* Preston: Snape (printer), 1922.   **Locations: 3, 12**

[380]   --- *A Full Account of the Shooting of Col. Crofton and Capt. Hanham, the Lieutenant-Colonel and the Adjutant of The 11th Depot Battalion, at Fulwood Barracks, [Preston] by a Private Soldier of The 32nd Regiment; His Examination Before a Magistrate; Full Report of the Evidence at the Coroner's Inquest; the Funeral Processions of the Deceased; With Other Particulars of the Tragic Occurrence.* Preston: Preston Chronicle, 1861.   **Locations: 12**

[381]   --- *Horwich Territorials 1914. Scrapbook of extracts recording the exploits of the Horwich Territorials part of the 1/4th Loyal North Lancashire Regiment in the First World War 1914-1918.* 1989.   **Locations: 7**

[382]   --- *The Lancashire Lad: Journal of the Loyal North Lancashire Regiment.* Preston: Mather printers) for the Regiment, 1886-.   **Locations: 1 (1886-1887); 3 (1922-1971, incomplete); 7 (1956-date); 12 (1922-39, 1947-)**

[383]   --- *The Lancashire Lad: Journal of the Loyal Regiment (North Lancashire) Special Bicentenary Number, July, 1941.* Preston: T. Snape, 1941.   **Locations: 1, 3, 12, 29**

[384]   --- *Distinguished Conduct Medal, 1914-1920: Citations.* London: Stamp Exchange, 1985.   **Locations: 3, 7, 9**

[385]   --- *The Loyal Regiment (North Lancashire) Roll of Honour, 1939-1945.* Preston: T. Snape & Co. Ltd, 1948.   **Locations: 3**

[386]   --- *Order of Service and Procedure: the dedication of the memorial chapel and the book of honour, in remembrance of all ranks of the Loyal Regiment (North Lancashire) who gave their lives in the war, 1939-1945 and the ceremony of the laying-up of the colours of the 1st Battalion the Loyal Regiment (North Lancashire).* Preston: Loyal North Lancashire Regiment, [19--].   **Locations: 3**

[387]   --- *A Pictorial Souvenir and History of the Second Battalion, Loyal North Lancashire Regiment, Poona, India, 1910.* 1910.   **Locations: 3**

[388]   --- *The Record of the 11th Battalion of The King's (Liverpool) Regiment subsequently the 15th Battalion of The Loyal North Lancashire Regiment, Pioneers, 14th Light Division. August, 1914-March, 1919.* London: R.E. Thomas & Co, 1920.   **Locations: 2**

[389]   ---   *Regimental Association of the Loyal Regiment (North Lancashire). Handbook.* Preston, 1932.   **Locations: 3**

[390]   ---   *Roll of Honour: World War I.* [n.d.]   **Locations: 3**

[391] --- *Roll of the 8th (Service) Battalion, Loyal North Lancashire Regiment.* Lancashire: Loyal North Lancashire Regiment, [n.d.] **Locations: 3**

[392] --- *A Short History of The Loyal Regiment (North Lancashire).* Preston: T. Snape & Co. Ltd, 1943. **Locations: 3**

[393] --- *A Short History of The Loyal Regiment (North Lancashire).* London: Malcolm Page, 1954. **Locations: 7**

[394] --- *Soldiers Died in The Great War, 1914-19. Part 50: Loyal North Lancashire Regiment.* Polstead: J.R. Raymond & Son, 1988. **Locations: 3, LRO**

[395] Loyal North Lancashire Regiment. Preston. St. John's Church. *Thanksgiving service for the Preston Guild Merchant, 1952 and laying-up of colours of the Loyal (North Lancashire) Regiment, Sunday, September 7, 1952 at 10.30 a.m.* Preston: Snape (Printers), 1952. **Locations: 3**

[396] Mather, Tom. *The Story of a Battalion of the Loyal Regiment 1939-45.* 1989. **Locations: 7**

[397] Preston Corporation. *The Ceremony of Adoption of The Loyal Regiment (North Lancashire) by the Town of Preston, 6th September, 1952.* Preston: Ward (printer), for Preston Corporation, 1952. **Locations: 3, 12**

[398] *The Preston Lad, or the Third Loyal North Lancashire Gazette.* 1901, no.4 **Locations: RMP**

[399] Purdon, H. G., Major. *The Battle Honours of The Loyal North Lancashire Regiment.* Preston: G. Toulmin, 1900. **Locations: 3, 12, RMP**

[400] --- *An Historical Sketch of The 47th (Lancashire) Regiment and of the Campaigns through which they passed.* Preston: The Guardian Printing Works, 1907. **Locations: 3**

[401] Roe, Tom. *Anzio Beachhead: Diary of a Signaller.* Derby: Higham Press, 1988. **Locations: 3**

[402] Rogers, H. *Loyante M'Oblige. Historical Record of the 81st Regiment, or Loyal Lincoln Volunteers; containing an Account of the Formation of the Regiment in 1793, and of its subsequent Services to 1782.* Gibraltar: 28th Regimental Press, 1872. **Locations: 3, RMP**

[403] White, D. F. "Lancashire's Regiments: The Loyal Regiment (North Lancashire)." *Lailand Chronicle* 9 (1973) 13-14. **Locations: LRO**

[404] Wilson, J. *On the Warpath, or Our Fight to "The Sisters" (Poona Camp 1883)* Bombay: Education Society, 1883. **Locations: RMP**

[405] Wylly, Harold C., Colonel. *The Loyal North Lancashire Regiment.* Vol. 1: 1741-1914 London: Royal United Services Institution, 1933. [Continued by Dean] **Locations: 3, 5, 7, 9, 16, 18, 22, 28**

[406]   ---   *The Loyal North Lancashire Regiment*. Vol. 2: 1914-1919.   London: Royal United Services Institution, 1933. [Continued by Dean]   **Locations: 3, 5, 7, 9, 16, 18, 22, 28**

ARCHIVES

National Army Museum
[407]   ---   *Papers relating to the trial and execution of Pte P. McCaffery, 32 Foot, for shooting two of his officers at Fulwood Barracks, Preston, 14 Sept 1861.*

[408]   National Army Museum Archives. *Loyal North Lancashire Regiment. H "Ernst" Bucher: Records, 12 April 1907-Jan 1908.*

Regimental Museum, Fulwood Barracks, Preston
[409]   The principal collection of archives covering the Loyal Regiment (North Lancashire) is held in the Regimental Museum, Fulwood Barracks, Preston. The archives are arranged chronologically and thematically. Material was in the process of being sorted at the time this guide was being compiled. At the present time there is no detailed listing of the archive collection.

The archives includes material relating to the two predecessor regiments (47th Regiment and the 81st (Loyal Lincolnshire Volunteers) Regiment) though the bulk of the collection is concerned with the Loyal North Lancashire Regiment from 1881 until its amalgamation in 1970. There is a good collection of printed books and pamphlets covering the regiment's history, presentation of colours etc. The printed material also includes runs of the regimental magazine and newsletters. The archive material is organised chronologically for each battalion covering the sub-periods:

1. 1881-1914
2. 1914-1918
3. 1919-1939
4. 1939-1945
5. 1945-1970

Separate boxes of archives relate to particular aspects of the regiment's history such as Officers' and Soldiers' Records; Voluntary Battalions; Militia; Medal Rolls. The collection contains Regiment Order Books, War Diaries, Visitors' Books, Scrapbooks etc. The First World War is particularly well represented in the collection. A separate collection contains letters and other documents relating to General Sir Richard Farren, including his role in the Crimean War. A substantial collection of photograph albums and individual photographs cover the regiment's history including its operations in India and China in the interwar years.

MANCHESTER REGIMENT: GENERAL LINEAGE

1757: 2nd Battalion, 8th (The King's) Regiment of Foot

1758: Redesignated 63rd Regiment of Foot

1782: Redesignated the 63rd (West Suffolk) Regiment of Foot

1881: 63rd Regiment of Foot amalgamated with the 96th Regiment of Foot [redesignated 1824] to become the Manchester Regiment

1958: Manchester Regiment amalgamated with the King's Regiment (Liverpool) to become the King's Regiment (Manchester and Liverpool)

1968: Redesignated as the King's Regiment (Manchester and Liverpool)

Manchester Regiment

[410] Andrews, Albert Williams. *Orders are Orders: a Manchester Pal on the Somme. From the account of Albert William Andrews of the 19th Manchesters, written in 1917. Edited by Sue Richardson.* Swinton, Manchester: Neil Richardson, 1987. **Locations: 1, 102, CL**

[411] Beet, W. Ernest. "The Military Annals of The Manchester Regiment." *London Quarterly Review* 124 (July 1915) 58-68. **Locations: 1**

[412] Bell, Archibald Colquhoun, Lieutenant-Commander. *History of The Manchester Regiment: First and Second Battalions, 1922-1948.* Altrincham: John Sherratt & Son, 1954. **Locations: ***

[413] Bonner, Robert. *The Ardwick Boys went to Malta: 8th (Ardwick) Battalion The Manchester Regiment (TA) - an Illustrated Record.* Macclesfield: Fleur de Lys, 1992. **Locations: 3, 52, 59**

[414] Campbell, G. L., Captain, (ed.). *The Twenty-Four Battalions of The Manchester Regiment: a history of the Regular, Militia, Special Reserve, Territorial, Service and City Battalions since their formation; with a record of the Officers now serving, and the honours and Casualties of the War of 1914-15.* London: Picture Advertising Co., 1915. **Locations: 11, 102**

[415] --- *The Manchesters. A History of the Regular, Militia, Special Reserve, Territorial and New Army Battalions since their formation; with a record of the Officers now serving, and the honours and casualties of the War of 1914-1916.* London: Picture Advertising Co., Ltd, 1916. **Locations: 1, 18, 102**

[416] Cowell, Clement W. *Records of the Mounted Infantry Company, 2nd Volunteer Battalion Manchester Regiment, 1887-1908.* Manchester: J. H. Baxter, [n.d.]. **Locations: 1, NAM**

[417] Darlington, Henry, Colonel Sir. *Letters From Helles; With a Preface by General Sir Ian Hamilton.* London: Longmans, Green, 1936. **Locations: 1, 3, 28**

[418] Evans, Horace Carlton, (ed.). *Records of the 4th Volunteer Battalion, Manchester Regiment [1859-1900].* Manchester: Wood, Smith and Shaw (printers), 1900. **Locations: 1, 3, 14, NAM**

[419] Fraser-Tytler, Neil. *With Lancashire Lads and Field Guns in France, 1915-1918.* Manchester: Heywood, 1922. **Locations: 1, 3, 27**

[420] Hurst, Gerald Berkeley. *With the Manchesters in the East.* London: Longmans, 1918. **Locations: 1, 3, 7, 13, 102, LFRM**

[421] James, Lieutenant-Col, (ed.). *Manchester Regiment. Medal Roll (excluding V.C.'s), 1914-1920, compiled by Lieut.-Col. James. Part 1 and 2.* 1914-20. **Locations: 102**

[422] Kempster, F., and Westropp, Henry Charles Edward, (eds.). *Manchester City Battalions of The 90th and 91st Infantry Brigades: Book of Honour.* Manchester: Sherratt & Hughes,

1916. **Locations: 1, 3, 7, 13, 59, 70, 102**

[423] --- *Manchester City Battalions of the 90th and 91st Infantry Brigades: Book of Honour.* London: Sherratt & Hughes, 1917. (2nd edition) **Locations: 1, 102**

[424] King-Clark, Robert. *George Stuart-Henderson: the story of a Scottish soldier, 1893-1920.* Dumbartonshire: The Author, 1975 **Locations: 1, 3**

[425] Macardle, Kenneth C. "The Battle of Montavban." *Manchester Review* 11 (Spring/Summer 1966) 2-7. **Locations: 1, CL**

[426] Manchester City Art Galleries. "See for Your Self: Queens Park Art Gallery and Military Collections." *Cheshire Life* 46 (April 1980) 42-3, 45. **Locations: 58**

[427] Manchester Regiment. *The 12th Old Comrades...Gazette.* **Locations: 102**

[428] --- *16th, 17th, 18th, 19th Battalions: The Manchester Regiment (First City Brigade). A Record, 1914-1918* [Foreword by Brigadier General Henry Charles Edward Westropp]. Manchester: Sherratt & Hughes, 1923. **Locations: 1, 3, 7, 11, 13, 70, 102**

[429] --- *1st Cadet Battalion, The Manchester Regiment. Annual Report, 1890.* 1890. **Locations: 1**

[430] --- *The 21st Battalion of The Manchester Regiment; a History. By a Committee of Old Members of the Regiment.* Manchester: Sherratt & Hughes, 1934. **Locations: 1**

[431] --- *2nd Volunteer Battalion The Manchester Regiment... Grand Military Bazaar, St. James' Hall, April 12th-16th, 1904.* Manchester: 1904. **Locations: 1**

[432] --- *4th Volunteer Battalion Standing Orders.* Manchester: J. Heywood, 1898. **Locations: 1**

[433] --- *The Bugle Call (journal).* **Locations: 102**

[434] --- *Diary of Siege of Ladysmith. 1st Battalion, Manchester Regiment. 31st October, 1899-28th February, 1900.* 1900. **Locations: 1**

[435] --- *Distinguished Conduct Medal, 1914-20: Citations.* London: Stamp Exchange, 1985. **Locations: 3**

[436] --- "The Fifth Ardwick Volunteer Battalion, The Manchester Regiment." *Manchester Faces and Places* 7 (December 1895) 36-40. **Locations: 1, LRO**

[437] --- *First Battalion, The Manchester Regiment. Malaya, Thailand, Burma, 1939-1945.* Manchester: 1946. (Reprinted from the *Manchester Regiment Gazette*) **Locations: 1**

[438] --- *First Volunteer Battalion, Manchester Regiment. Return of the Manchesters, 1st V.B.M.R., Wigan Detachment (from S. Africa). Official Programme and Souvenir. May 1901.* Wigan: 1901. **Locations: 18**

[439] --- *The Manchester Echo (journal).* **Locations: 102**

[440] --- *The Manchester Jester (journal)*. **Locations: 102**

[441] --- *Manchester Regiment Gazette*. Vols 1-11. Manchester: 1913-58. **Locations: 1**

[442] --- *The Ninety Sixth (journal)*. **Locations: 102**

[443] --- *No. 7 Company 4th Volunteer Battalion Manchester Regiment. Regulations.* Manchester, 1891. **Locations: 1**

[444] --- *The Periscope. Being the Official Organ of The 8th (Reserve) Battalion Manchester Regiment*. Vols 1-3. Manchester: 1916-19. **Locations: 1**

[445] --- *Photographs of the Parade of the 2nd Volunteer Battalion on the Occasion of its Return from South Africa and Civic Reception at the Town Hall, 24th May, 1901.* 1901. **Locations: 1**

[446] --- *Presentation of Colour Belts to The Manchester Regiment in Albert Square, on Monday, 12th July, 1954.* 1954. **Locations: 1**

[447] --- *Presentation of Colours to the Eighth (Ardwick) Battalion The Manchester Regiment (T.A.) and the Ninth Battalion the Manchester Regiment (T.A.) by H.M. Queen Elizabeth, the Queen Mother. Audenshaw, 24 June, 1959.* 1959. **Locations: 102**

[448] --- *Presenting the Manchester Regiment, 1758-1953.* London: Malcolm Page, 1953. **Locations: 102**

[449] --- *The Pull Through.* 1915 (Journal of A Company 16th (S) Batt. while stationed at Belton Park, Grantham) **Locations: 1, 102**

[450] --- *The Quadrant (journal)*. **Locations: 102**

[451] --- *Records of the 2nd Battalion The Manchester Regiment, formerly 96th Foot. Compiled for use of Non-Commissioned Officers and Men of the Battalion.* 1899. **Locations: 1**

[452] --- *Routine of Parades, Drills, etc., etc., of The 6th Battalion, for the Year Ending October 31st, 1909.* 1909. **Locations: 1**

[453] --- *Routine of Parades, Drills, Prize Shooting, etc., etc., of The 2nd Vol Battalion for the Year Ending October 31st, 1906 and 1907.* 1907. **Locations: 1**

[454] --- *Seconds Own (journal)*. **Locations: 102**

[455] --- *The Seventh Manchester Sentry*. Khartoum:1915 (Newspaper published in Khartoum by 7th Manchester Battalion) **Locations: 1**

[456] --- *Soldiers Died in The Great War, 1914-1919. Part 59: The Manchester Regiment.* London: H.M.S.O., 1921. **Locations: 11**

[457] --- *Soldiers Died in the Great War, 1914-19. Part 59: The Manchester Regiment.* Polstead: J.B. Hayward and Sons with Imperial War Museum, Dept. of Printed Books, 1989. **Locations: 3, 4, 11, 13, 18, LRO**

[458] --- *The Sphinx, being the Official Organ of The 6th Battalion, Manchester Regt.* 2 vols. Southport: 1915-16. **Locations: 1 (1915-16)**

[459] --- *The Stand Easy. Being the Journal of The 2/7 Manchester Regiment.* Colchester: 1916. **Locations: 1(1916)**

[460] --- *Standing Orders.* Aldershot: Gale and Polden, 1907. **Locations: 7, 102**

[461] --- *The Tanglin Tribune, being the Official Organ of the Wing 1st Garrison Battalion Manchester Regiment stationed at Singapore.* Singapore: 1919. **Locations: 1**

[462] --- *The Very Light: the Journal of The 19th Battalion Manchester Regiment.* 1917. **Locations: 1**

[463] Manchester Regiment. 24th Battalion (Oldham Comrades). *Dardanelles Death Roll: Losses in the Oldham Battalion.* Oldham: Evening Chronicle, 1915. **Locations: 11**

[464] Manchester Regiment. 9th Battalion. *The Borough of Ashton-under-Lyne Presents an Address of Honour to The 9th Battalion, The Manchester Regiment, 15th July, 1950. Souvenir programme.* Ashton-under-Lyne: Ashton-under-Lyne Corporation, 1950. **Locations: 20, 102**

[465] Manchester. St. Mary's Collegiate Church. *Order of Service for the Dedication of the Restored Chapel of the Manchester Regiment, attended by Her Majesty the Queen...on Friday, 16th November, 1951 at 11-00 a.m.* Manchester: Falkner (printer), 1951. **Locations: 3**

[466] Marden, Arthur William, Major, and Newbigging, William Patrick Eric, Adjutant, (eds.). *Rough Diary of the Doings of the 1st Battalion Manchester Regiment during the South African War, 1899 to 1902.* Manchester: John Heywood, 1902. **Locations: 1, 4, 18, 102**

[467] Mitchinson, K. W., and McInnes, I. *Cotton Town Comrades: The Story of the Oldham Pals Battalion 1914-1919.* Bayonet Publications,1993. **Locations: 11**

[468] Nash, Thomas. *The Story of Private Thomas Nash (202463) 12 Platoon C Company 1/5th Battalion The Manchester Regiment, 1914-1919.* [n.d]. **Locations: 102**

[469] Oldham Corporation. *Unveiling of war memorial silver drums of 10th Battalion, Manchester Regiment...June 1st, 1924.* Oldham: Corporation, 1924. **Locations: 11**

[470] Parry, William Augustus. *Patriotic Devotion: or a People's Noble Response to Appeals for Our Soldiers. The Brave Manchesters.* Manchester: J. Heywood, 1901. **Locations: 1**

[471] Pennington, Thomas Edward. *The Signal Section of The 16th Manchesters: a Record of its Activities, 1914-18.* Bootle: 1937. **Locations: 1**

[472] Preece, Geoff. "The Museum of the Manchesters." *Manchester Region History Review* 2. i (1988) 42-5. **Locations: 1, LRO**

[473] Richardson, Sue, (ed.). *The Recollections of Three Manchesters in the Great War: Mike Lally of the Old Contemptibles [2nd Battalion]; Joe Horgan [2nd/7th Battalion] of the*

Territorials; John Hallows of Hyde [5th City Pals, later 20th Battalion]. From conversations recorded with Frank Heaton. Swinton, Manchester: Neil Richardson, 1985. **Locations: 4, 11, 15, 102**

[474] Robinson, G. "South African War Grave Inscriptions." *Manchester Genealogist* 21. i (1985) 13-14. **Locations: 1, LRO**

[475] Slack, James, Major. *[Manchester Regiment] The History of the late 63rd (West Suffolk) Regiment.* London: Army and Navy Co-operative Society Ltd, 1886.

[476] Thornycroft, C.M. *History of 3rd (Militia) Battalion The Manchester Regiment.* [n.d.] **Locations: NAM**

[477] Westropp, Henry Charles Edward. *To Manchester: a Tribute to 'the Fallen' and to 'the Spirit' of Her Great Regiment.* Manchester: 1920. **Locations: 1**

[478] Whyte, Wolmer, (ed.). *The Manchester Regiment.* London: Hutchinson & Co., 1941. **Locations: 1, 17, 102, LRO**

[479] Wigan Territorials. *Presentation of the King's Colour to the 2/5th Battalion of the Manchester Regiment (The Wigan Territorials) by His Worship the Mayor of Wigan on 17 July 1920. Instructions.* 1920. **Locations: 18B**

[480] Wigan Volunteers. "The Late Mayor Lever Robert Rowbottom V.D." *Wigan Examiner* (7/14 July 1906). **Locations: 18B**

[481] Wilde, Herbert, (ed.). *The Oldham Battalion of Comrades (24th Battalion, Manchester Regiment) Book of Honour.* London: Sherratt & Hughes, 1919. **Locations: 1, 3, 11**

[482] Wilson, S. J., Captain. *The Seventh Manchesters, July 1916 to March 1919.* Manchester: Manchester University Press, 1920. **Locations: 1, 8, 13, 102**

[483] Wood, Ernest, Sir. *Oldham Comrades in the First World War.* 1964. **Locations: 11**

[484] Wylly, Harold C., Colonel., (ed.). *History of The Manchester Regiment (late the 63rd and 96th Foot).* Vol. 1: 1758-1883 Vol.2: 1883-1922. 2 vols. London: Forster Groom & Co. Ltd, 1923-5. **Locations: 1, 3, 11, 13, 70, 102, LRO**

[485] --- *A Short History of the Manchester Regiment.* Aldershot: Gale & Polden, 1929. **Locations: 1**

[486] --- *A Short History of the Manchester Regiment (Regular Battalions).* Aldershot: Gale & Polden Ltd, 1933. (3rd edition) **Locations: 1, 18**

[487] --- *A Short History of The Manchester Regiment (Regular Battalions).* Aldershot: Gale & Polden Ltd, 1950. (4th rev. edition) **Locations: 7, 102, BOM**

ARCHIVES

The main collection of archive material relating to the Manchester Regiment is held at the Tameside Local Studies Library. The following list provides an overview of the main categories of material in this extensive archive. Tameside is also the home of the Museum of the Manchesters [472].

National Army Museum

[488]   Hopwood, Harry. *Papers relating to Harry Hopwood, CQMS, (6th Battalion Manchester Regiment) during World War I*. 1914-18.

[489]   --- *Papers relating to Sgt. Harry Hopwood (2nd Volunteer Battalion Manchester Regiment) during the Boer War, 1900-01, and his certificate of service for the years 1892-1908.*

[490]   National Army Museum Archives. *Manchester Regiment, 7th Battalion. Orders.* Copy of Lt Col Gresham's copy of the scheme marked "Secret and Confidential" giving detailed arrangements on the action to be taken on the order to mobilize. With a letter from the Adjutant, Capt. P.H. Creagh, dated 3 August 1914 discussing a minor change to the scheme. Originals in Manchester Regiment, Ashton-under-Lyne. 1913-14.

Oldham Local Studies Library Archives

[491]   *Oldham Pals- 24th Battalion, Manchester Regiment.*
Box 1: Record book listing servicemen of the regiment including list of those wounded or killed in action and decorations awarded; fragment of the bell of the church at Albert (Battle of the Somme) and explanatory details; document listing dates, localities, camps and principal events during the course of the Regiment's service in France; Trench maps-Belgium and France; Demobilization list 1919; R5 Trench log book; Registers of correspondence overseas; map of France (photocopy).
Box 2: Daily Telegraph 1936- Press cuttings of King's tribute to Canadian valour on Vimy Ridge; list of Officers who served during 1914-1918 with the Oldham Pals; correspondence 1963-1964 (1 envelope, 1 folder); war maps-Italy; envelope containing aerial photographs, trench maps, etc.; place lists, honours lists, officers lists; post-war newspaper cuttings; various photographs; Old Comrades Association Minute Book 1948-1973.
Box 3: Envelope containing photographs and newspaper cuttings; Roll Book; correspondence about Colours, the memorial etc.; company commanders' Daily Reports (duplicates); Orders and Circulars; miscellaneous items; 2 rubber stamps; souvenirs collected on re-visit April 1939.
Box 4: box file containing photographs and letters of Mayor Hautmont, France, also coloured sash; book: *Across the Piave* by Norman Gladdern (1971) with photographs enclosed; army book of wounded of the Oldham Pals; miscellaneous small documents, correspondence and press cuttings; Fifth Annual Report of the Imperial War Graves Commission and envelope of press cuttings; programme of the Somme Pilgrimage, 1966; Book:*7th Division, 1914-1918* by C.T. Atkinson (1927); envelope "War Graves, news cuttings etc.".

Tameside Local Studies Library.

[492]   *Manchester Regiment Archives Collection.*
Accounts and Pay Lists. Contents: Including 96th Regiment, 1st and 7th Battalion, five lists: 1782-1915.
Biographical and Historical Notes. Contents: Including miscellaneous notes on 96th

Regiment, 63rd Regiment, 1st Battalion and 2nd Battalion, Major-General Charles Brownlow Cumberland, Captain James Bradshaw, Captain Marmaduke Stourton, William Broadfoot, Lieutenant-Colonel H.W.E. Hitchins, 1869-1968.
Catalogues and Registers of the Regimental Museum. Contents: Registers of accessions, depositors and silver photography catalogues.
Correspondence. Contents: Foreign Service, 1854-1898; Letter to Major J.H. Abbott Anderson from 1st Battalion, South Africa, 1899-1901; Letters from abroad, 1899-1954; Miscellaneous, 1812-1958.
Ephemera. Menus, posters, leaflets, letters and poems, 1866-1965.

General Returns. Contents: 63rd Regiment: General, 1771 and 1772; On board "The Diadem", 1826; Monthly, 1836, 1844, 1845, 1847.
Histories of the Regiment. Contents: Regular Battalions, 1758-1948; Militia Battalions, 3rd, World War I; Rifle Volunteers and Volunteer Battalions, 1884-1908; Territorial Battalion, 1915-1950; Service Battalion, 1914-1918; Diaries, mainly 1st and 2nd Battalion, 1900-1953.
Illustrations and Miscellaneous Printed Material. Contents: includes postcards and cartoons, souvenirs and some orders, 1814-1960.
Miscellaneous. Contents: Sketches and drawings, 1878-1944; Sound recording, 1954. 1878-1954. *Miscellaneous Reports.* Contents: 1st and 2nd Battalions, eight reports: 1814-1950.

Newspaper Cuttings. Contents: The Regiment, 1923-1962; 1st Battalion, 1903-1957; 96th Regiment of Foot, 1824-1833; 2nd Battalion, 1911-1947; 3rd (Militia) Battalion, 1954; 1st Manchester Rifle Volunteers and 2nd Volunteer Battalion, 1875-1898; 3rd Manchester Rifle Volunteers, 1883-1884; 3rd Volunteer Battalion, 1901-1936; Territorial and Service Battalions, 1919-1959.
Crimean War, 1954 and 1962; South African War, 1899-1902; World War One, 1914-1965; World War Two, the Malaya Campaign, 1939-1950.
Rolls of honour, casualty lists, prisoners of war, 1915-1942; Rewards for gallantry, mentions in despatches, foreign decorations, 1901-1946; War memorials, memorial services, the Regimental Chapel, 1901-1958; Obituary notices (members of the Regiment killed in action), 1915; Miscellaneous cuttings relating to members and ex-members of the Regiment, 1907-1946; Obituary notices (deaths not on active service), 1919-1960; The Regimental Museum, 1935-1961.

Operational Records. Contents: Orders and reports, World War I, World War II and early 1950s. 1st and 2nd Battalions only. Also maps, plans and aerial photographs, mainly World War I period.
Papers Relating to Dress, Clothing and Equipment. Contents: Papers Relating to Dress, Clothing and Equipment: Regarding officers' dress, 1936-1956.
Papers Relating to Honours and Casualties of the Wars. Contents:
Rolls of Honour: 1854-Scutari; 1899-1900- on Ladysmith Memorial; 1900-1901- 'F' Company, 2nd Battalion; 1865-1907-Singapore; 1914-1918-All battles in World War I (listed by battalion); n/d-prisoners interned in Holland and those on Loos Memorial, France; 1928 & 1929- on Poloesgtreet Memorial, Belgium; 1920-1945- All Battalions in Mesopotamia, Ireland, Palestine and World War II; 1939-1945-at Kranji War Cemetery, Singapore.
Medal Rolls: 1845-1847 and 1917-New Zealand, Martinique and Guadaloupe; 1914-1920-Victoria Cross; 1899-1901-recommendations, South African War; 1917-1936- Re.Col. W. Elstob, V.C.

Papers Relating to Organisation and Training. Contents: Organisation, training and rules, 1860-1935; Military handbooks, manuals and War Office training pamphlets, 1798-1940;

Miscellaneous early publications, (3) 1799, 1801 and 1858.
Papers Relating to Parades and Ceremonies. Contents: papers for 1911, Delhi; 1936, Manchester; 1946, Manchester; 1948, Dunham Park; 1957, Dunkirk Memorial.
Papers Relating to the Band: 1904-1951.

Personal Documents. Contents: Relating to:- James Johnson, 1798; James W.S. Moffatt, 96th, 1846-1879; William Delaney, 96th, 1850; Private James Elliott, 63rd, 1875; Private William Thompson, 1st, 1884-1891; Private Martin Bell, 1st, 1893-1907; Private W.J. Preston, 3rd, 1894; Jonathan Broadhurst, 4th, 1896-1909; Sergeant-Major George Prosser, 2nd, 1897-1910; Corporal Thomas Smith, 6th, 1899-1909; Sergeant William Hobson, 1900; Herbert Jones, 1st Volunteer Battalion, 1900-1903; John Williams, 1907-1908; Private Robert Catling, 6th Volunteer Battalion, 1908; Private H. Valentine, 7th, 1914-1918; Brigadier-General Edward Vaughan, 1917-1933; Ensign James Fairtlough, Major James Fairtlough, 1826-1834; Lieutenant G.W.W. Knapp, 63rd, 1856-1862; J.J. Abbot Anderson, 1878-1880; Major C.H.R. Hyde, 1st Battalion.
Photographs. Contents: Album of 96th Regiment, 1st, 2nd, 3rd and 4th Battalions, at home and abroad, 1857-1958. Also separate list of photographs sub-divided into Regimental, 63rd & 1st Battalion, 3rd, 4th Special Reserve and Depot, Territorial and Service. 1857-1958.
Records of Appointments, Commissions and Promotions. Contents: Officers' Services and Army lists, 1824-1925; Commissions and warrants of appointment, 1760-1918; Attestations, 1793-1800. [n.d.]

Records of Arrests and Illegal Absences. Contents: Soldiers' illegal absences, 1923-1940; Civil arrests in Ireland, 1920-1921.
Records of Messes, Clubs and Associations Formed an Maintained by the Regiment. Contents: Mess Records: Regular Battalions, 1899-1959; other Battalions, 1900-1959; Regimental Sports Records, 1864-1939, including rifle club, shooting, cricket, game, fishing, polo and gymkhana; Records of clubs and associations, 1888-1962, including Old Comrades, married families and Regimental dinners.
Records of Service and Other Historical Records of the Regiment. Contents: includes digest of services for 1st and 2nd Battalions to World War II period and selected war diaries.
Rolls of Companies, Officers, etc. Contents: Section roll books for various companies of 63rd Regiment, 1st and 2nd Battalions, 1809, 1810, 1899, 1900, 1914, 1916 and 1935; Various lists of officers and staff, 1917, 1918, 1920 and 1939; Nominal roll of 1st Battalion, 1942-5.
Standing Orders: Battalion, Brigade and Regimental Orders; Miscellaneous Orders. Contents: Standing Orders, 1847-1950; Battalion, brigade and regimental and miscellaneous orders, 1804-1942.

QUEEN'S LANCASHIRE REGIMENT: GENERAL LINEAGE

1958: East Lancashire Regiment amalgamated with South Lancashire Regiment to form
The Lancashire Regiment (Prince of Wales's Volunteers)

1970: Loyal Regiment (North Lancashire) amalgamated with The Lancashire Regiment (Prince of Wales's Volunteers) to form
The Queen's Lancashire Regiment

See separate lineage charts for The East Lancashire Regiment, Loyal North Lancashire Regiment and The South Lancashire Regiment

Queen's Lancashire Regiment

[493] Mackenzie, B. S., Major. *"Loyally They Served". A Short History of the Queen's Lancashire Regiment, 1689-1970.* Fulwood, Preston: The Regiment, 1979. **Locations: 3, 6, 7, 9, 29, BM, LRO**

[494] Queen's Lancashire Regiment. *A Brief History of the Queen's Lancashire Regiment.* Preston: Amblers (printer), 1988. **Locations: 3**

[495] --- *The Ceremony of the Transfer of Adoption of the Loyal Regiment (North Lancashire) to The Queen's Lancashire Regiment by the County Borough of Preston, 9th September, 1972.* Preston: Mather (printer), 1972. **Locations: 3**

[496] --- *The History of Fulwood Barracks, Preston.* [n.d.]. **Locations: 3**

[497] --- *The Lancashire Lad: the Journal of The Queen's Lancashire Regiment.* Preston: Queen's Lancashire Regiment Regimental Association, 1989- **Locations: 3**

[498] --- *The Queens' Lancashire Regiment: a Ready Reference.* Fulwood: Queens' Lancashire Regiment, 1988. **Locations: 3, 40, LRO**

[499] --- *A Short History of the Queen's Lancashire Regiment.* Preston: Amblers (printers), 1974. **Locations: 3, 9**

[500] Walsh, R. Raymond, and Walsh, Jean M. (eds.). *Presentation of New Colours to the First Battalion The Queen's Lancashire Regiment 1689-1989 by Her Majesty the Queen, Colonel-in-Chief, Weeton 9 July 1990.* Blackburn: THCL Books, 1991. **Locations: 3, CL**

ARCHIVES

Archives for the Queen's Lancashire Regiment are held in the Regimental Museum, Fulwood Barracks, Preston. It is a small collection containing newspaper articles, photographs and memorabilia.

Royal Artillery

[501] *515 (Isle of Man) L.A.A. Regt., R.A. (T.A.)* Douglas: B &S Ltd.. 1949. **Locations: MNH**

[502] Ablett, H. Kellett, and Bolton, Peter (eds.). *Engravings of Joseph Bolton 1901-1988*. 1990. **Locations: 7**

[503] Bolton Artillery. *Ceremony of conferring the Freedom of the Borough on 253rd Regiment Royal Artillery (The Bolton Artillery) T.A. and on the 5th Battalion the Loyal Regiment (North Lancashire) T.A. at the Town Hall, Bolton on Saturday, 18th April, 1964 at 3.15 p.m.* 1964. **Locations: 7**

[504] Capleton, E. W. *Shabash-149: The War Story of the 149th Regiment R.A. 1939-1945.* Liverpool: C. Tinling (printers), 1963. **Locations: 65, NAM**

[505] Clague, Curwen. *Ack Ack: A History of the 15th (Isle of Man) Light Anti-Aircraft Regiment R.A., T.A.* Douglas, Isle of Man: The Old Comrades Association, 15th (I.O.M.) Regt. R.A., 1981. **Locations: MNH, RAHT**

[506] Dobson, B. Palin. *History of the Bolton Artillery, 1860-1928.* Bolton: Blackshaw, Sykes and Morris, 1929. **Locations: 3, 7, NAM**

[507] Graham, C. A. L. *The Story of the Royal Regiment of Artillery, 6th.* Woolwich: Royal Artillery Institution, 1962. **Locations: 6**

[508] Harrison, H. C. Vaughan, Captain., (ed.). *History of the 3rd Lancashire Artillery Volunteers [with Roll of Officers].* Blackburn: Aspden (printer), 1894. **Locations: 3, 22, NAM**

[509] Horsfall, Jack. *The Long March: The Story of "The Devil's Own", B/210 (Burnley) Battery, Royal Field Artillery, 1914-1919.* Preston: The Lancashire Library, 1986. **Locations: 21, CL**

[510] Hugh, James. "The Territorial Army in Cheshire - IX: 360 H.A.A. Regiment, R.A. (Cheshire)." *Cheshire Life* 17 (September 1951) 23-4. **Locations: 4, 58**

[511] --- "The Territorial Army in Cheshire - V: 420 Lancashire and Cheshire Coast Regiment, RA (TA)." *Cheshire Life* 17 (May 1951) 22-3. **Locations: 4, 58**

[512] --- "The Territorial Army in Cheshire - VIII: 493 (M) H.A.A. Regiment, Royal Artillery, T.A." *Cheshire Life* 17 (August 1951) 21-2. **Locations: 4, 58**

[513] Isle of Man Light Anti-Aircraft Regiment. *515 (Isle of Man) Light Anti-Aircraft Regiment, R.A. (T.A.) Handbook.* Douglas: B & S Ltd., 1945. **Locations: MNH**

[514] Manchester Royal Artillery. *Belle Vue Chronicle* "Newsletter of 110th Field Regiment, Royal Artillery (Manchester) T.A." (1943-45). **Locations: 1**

[515] Mather, P. R. "The Lancashire Artillery Volunteers Band (TA)." *Band International* 3.1 (March 1981) 10-2. **Locations: NAM**

[516]   Miles (pseud.). "The County's Territorials. Number 6. A Brand new unit." *Cheshire Life* 5 (March 1939) 28. **Locations: 4, 58**

[517]   Robertson, G. W. *The Rose and the Arrow: a Life Story of 136th (1st West Lancashire) Field Regiment Royal Artillery, 1939-1946.* Reigate: 136 Field Regiment, RA, Old Comrades' Association, 1988. **Locations: 3, 4, 18**

[518]   Royal Artillery Association. *Calling All Gunners. Journal of the East Lancashire and Cheshire District of the Royal Artillery Association [Formerly the E.L.C.D. News].* Vols. 1-2, 1946-9. **Locations: 9**

[519]   Royal Artillery Association. Blackburn Branch. *Ubique: the Monthly Newsletter.* 1948. **Locations: 6**

[520]   Simpson, Alexander William. *288 (2nd West Lancashire) Light Anti-Aircraft Regiment, Royal Artillery, Territorial Army: a History.* Blackpool: Gazette (printer), 1960. **Locations: 1, 3, 4, 7, 18**

[521]   Stephenson, William Henry, (comp.). *A Short History of the 1st West Lancashire Artillery Brigade. The Territorial Army.* Southport: Robert Johnson and Co., 1956. **Locations: 1, 3, 4, 8, RAHT**

[522]   Stitt, J.C., Lieutenant-Colonel. *A History of the 57th (West Lancashire) Divisional Ammunition Column, 1916 to 1919. England, France and Flanders.* Wrexham: Edwin Jones & Son, 1919. **Locations:**

[523]   Synge, Laurence Millington. *A Short History of the 59th (4th West Lancashire) Brigade R.A., T.A.* Liverpool: Daily Post Printers, 1934. **Locations: 2**

[524]   Wadsworth, W. W., Captain, (ed.). *War Diary of the 1st West Lancashire Brigade, R.F.A.* Liverpool: Daily Post Printers, 1923. **Locations: 3, LRO, RAHT**

[525]   West Lancashire Medium Regiment. *59th (4th West Lancs.) Medium Regiment Royal Artillery, 1939-1945.* 1945. **Locations: 3**

[526]   --- *History of the 359 (4th West Lancs.) Medium Regiment R.A., (T.A.), 1859-1959.* Liverpool: C. Tinling (printer), 1959. **Locations: 3, LRO, RAHT**

[527]   Wingfield, A. J. *The Bolton Artillery: a History, 1860-1975.* Bolton: B.V.A.A., 1976. **Locations: 1, 3, 7, 18, 26, BOM, LRO**

ARCHIVES

The principal archive is located in the Royal Artillery Institution, London. Established in 1778, it holds a unique collection of books and papers relating to all aspects of the history of artillery.

Lancashire Record Office.
[528]   --- *2nd West Lancashire Brigade, Royal Field Artillery: officers' services register, account book, brigade orders, history, miscellanea c.1875-c.1960.*

Liverpool Libraries and Information Services, Record Office and Local History Department.
[529]   Melly, George.   "Fourth Brigade, Lancashire Artillery Volunteers."   *George Melly's Newscuttings Album*, 121-67.   1859-61.

[530]   *War Diary of 'A' Battery, 330th Brigade, Royal Field Artillery. 1917-1918, France and Flanders.*

Oldham Local Studies Library
[531]   Hastie, Robert, Major.   *71st Searchlight Regiment, Royal Artillery (TA), Failsworth, Lancashire. Scrap book.* [n.d.]

Royal Artillery Historical Trust Archives
[532]   --- *Artifacts in the Royal Artillery Regimental Museum.*   Contents: <u>1st Lancashire Artillery Volunteers</u>: Full dress silver wire embroidered pouch 1875-1901 (reserve). <u>2nd Lancashire Artillery Volunteers</u>: Full dress silver wire embroidered pouch, 1875-1901 (on display). <u>3rd Lancashire Artillery Volunteers</u>: Helmet badge plate, 1882-1889 (on display). <u>7th Lancashire Artillery Volunteers</u>: Full dress silver wire embroidered sabretache and pouch, 1871-1901 (on display). <u>8th Lancashire Artillery Volunteers</u>: Full dress silverware embroidered pouch, 1875-1901 (reserve).

[533]   <u>Lancashire Volunteers Division</u>: Helmet badge plate, 1882-1889 (on display). <u>Lancashire Artillery Volunteers</u>: Tunic button and collar badges, c.1860 (on display). <u>The Duke of Lancaster's Own" Yeomanry</u>: Cap badge, c.1920 (on display). Lancashire Hussars Yeomanry: Cap badge, c.1930 (on display). <u>Lancashire Fusiliers</u>: Cap badge, c.1940 (on display). <u>East Lancashire Regiment</u>: Cap badge, c.1940. <u>North West Related artifacts</u>: cloth shoulder division badges 1940-45. 1860-1945.

[534]   --- *Biographical Sketch of the Career of Lt-Col Charles Butler Clay, VD (b.1856), preceded by a Memoir of his father, William Clay (b.1823).*   (Charles Butler Clay was the designer of "Clay's Breech-loading Guns" and Colonel of the 8th Lancashire Volunteer Artillery. His father raised and commanded the original volunteer corps. [n.d.])

[535]   --- *Brochure relating to the Chester Batteries of the 1st Cheshire Artillery Volunteers. The 26th Annual Carbine Prize Meeting on Monday 27th September 1886 at Sealand, near Chester.* 1886.

Royal Engineers

[536] 1st Cheshire Royal Engineers. *Regimental Orders by Col. Chas Brownbridge, V.D., Commanding. Programme of drills from May to August 1907.* 1907. **Locations: 57**

[537] Corps of Royal Engineers. *Soldiers Died in The Great War, 1914-19. Part 4: Corps of Royal Engineers.* London: H.M.S.O., 1920-21. **Locations: 34**

[538] Crook, H. T., et al. *A History of The East Lancashire Royal Engineers: compiled by members of the Corps.* London: Country Life, 1921. Country Life series of military histories. **Locations: 1, 3, 11, LRO, NAM**

[539] Davies, T. R., (ed.). *The Cheshire Royal Engineers 1860-1950, now 113 Assault Engineer Regiment, Birkenhead; a regimental history compiled (with handpainted illustrations and photographs) by Captain T.R. Davies.* 1950. **Locations: 57**

[540] East Lancashire Royal Engineers. *A History of the East Lancashire Engineers. Compiled by Members of the Corp.* London: Country Life, 1921. **Locations: 3**

[541] Hugh, James. "The Territorial Army in Cheshire-III: 113 Assault Engineeer Regiment, RE (TA)." *Cheshire Life* 17 (March 1951) 22-3. **Locations: 4, 58**

SOUTH LANCASHIRE REGIMENT (THE PRINCE OF WALES'S VOLUNTEERS): GENERAL LINEAGE

1717: Formed from independent companies in North America and the West Indies as Richard Philips's Regiment of Foot

1747: Ranked as 40th Regiment

1751: Designated by number

1782: Redesignated as 40th (the 2nd Somersetshire) Regiment of Foot

1881: 40th (the 2nd Somersetshire) Regiment amalgamated with the 82nd (Prince of Wales's Volunteers) Regiment to form The Prince of Wales's Volunteers (South Lancashire Regiment)

1938: Redesignated as The South Lancashire Regiment (Prince of Wales's Volunteers)

1958: Amalgamated with The East Lancashire Regiment to form The Lancashire Regiment (Prince of Wales's Volunteers)

1970: Amalgamated with the Loyal Regiment (North Lancashire) to form the Queen's Lancashire Regiment

South Lancashire Regiment (Prince of Wales's Volunteers)

[542] Appleton, Francis M., Capt., (comp.). *The Volunteer Service Company (1st South Lancashire Regiment) in South Africa during the Boer War, January, 1900-July, 1901, with some particulars concerning the Third Contingent.* Warrington: Mackie & Co., 1901. **Locations: 3, 14, 17**

[543] Baker, Jack. *Biting the Bullet.* Birmingham: The Word Works, 1992. **Locations: RMP**

[544] Buckton, J. D., Lieutenant-Colonel, (comp.). *9th & 49th Lancashire Rifle Volunteer Corps, afterwards entitled 1st Volunteer Battalion Prince of Wales's Volunteers (South Lancashire Regiment). A few statistics.* Warrington: Sunrise Publishing Co., 1910. **Locations: 3**

[545] Green, F.C. *The Fortieth Letters. A Record of the 40th Battalion A.I.F.* Hobart: John Vail, 1922. **Locations: RMP**

[546] Hoyle, John Baldwin. *Some Letters from a Subaltern on the Western Front, chiefly to his mother, July 1915 - June 1916.* Manchester: Faulkner for private circulation, 1917. **Locations: LRO**

[547] Jarvis, Samuel Peters. *Historical Record of The Eighty-Second Regiment of Prince of Wales's Volunteers. Dedicated to his brother officers by Brevet-Major Jarvis, 82nd Regiment.* London: W.O. Mitchell, 1866. **Locations: RMP**

[548] Jebens, F., Lieutenant-Colonel. *A Short History of The South Lancashire Regiment (The Prince of Wales's Volunteers).* Aldershot: Gale & Polden Ltd, 1951. **Locations: RMP**

[549] Longbottom, J. C. *A Short History of The South Lancashire Regiment (The Prince of Wales's Volunteers), [written by the Rev. J.C. Longbottom, M.A., for 78th County of Lancaster (Warrington) Battalion Home Guard].* Aldershot: 1943. **Locations: 17**

[550] Mullaly, Brian R., Colonel. *The South Lancashire Regiment, The Prince of Wales's Volunteers.* Bristol: White Swan Press, 1952. **Locations: 3, 7, 17, 34, 40, 102, LRO**

[551] --- *The South Lancashire Regiment, The Prince of Wales's Volunteers.* Bristol: White Swan Press, 1955. **Locations: 1, 3, 4, 7, 9, 40, 59**

[552] Neligan, T. *[Boer War, 1899-1900]. From Preston to Ladysmith with The 1st Battalion South Lancashire Regiment, (Famous Fighting Fortieth) giving a detailed account of the forced march from Estcourt to Springfield, and a graphic description of the battles of Spion Kop, Potgieter's Drift, and Pieter's Hill, and the entry of the relieving force into Ladysmith...by One of the Regiment.* Preston: Platt, 1900. **Locations: 3, 17**

[553] Oatts, Louis Balfour, Lieutenant-Colonel. *I Serve: Regimental History of the 3rd Carabiniers (Prince of Wales's Dragoon Guards).* Chester: Home Headquarters, 3rd Carabiniers (Prince of Wales's Dragoon Guards), 1966. **Locations: 4, 65**

[554] Smythies, Raymond H. R., Captain. *Historical Records of the 40th (2nd Somersetshire) Regiment now 1st Battalion The Prince of Wales's Volunteers (South Lancashire Regiment), from its formation in 1717 to 1893.* Devonport: A.H. Swiss, 1894. **Locations: 17, 58**

[555] --- *A Short Record of the 1st Battalion The Prince of Wales's Volunteers (South Lancashire Regiment) formerly the 40th (2nd Somersetshire) Regiment. Compiled by R.H. Raymond Smythies on the occasion of the Presentation of new Colours to the Battalion, 16th July, 1891.* St. Helier: Jersey Times, 1891. **Locations: 3, 17**

[556] South Lancashire Regiment. *1st Battalion The Prince of Wales's Volunteers (South Lancashire). London, Chelsea Barracks, August 15th to September 19th, 1928.* Gale & Polden Ltd: Aldershot, 1928. **Locations: 3, 17**

[557] --- *Ceremony of the Presentation of an Address of Honour to The South Lancashire Regiment (The Prince of Wales's Volunteers), 4th Oct. 1947.* Warrington, 1947. **Locations: 17**

[558] --- *Distinguished Conduct Medal, 1914-20: Citations. Prince of Wales's Volunteers (South Lancashire Regiment).* London: Stamp Exchange, 1985. **Locations: 3, 17**

[559] --- *Formation and Events in the Services of The Fortieth or 2nd Somersetshire Regiment, 1717 to 1799.* Calcutta: City Press, 1879. **Locations: 3, 17**

[560] --- *History [of The South Lancashire Regiment, Prince of Wales's Volunteers].* London: H.M.S.O., 1915. **Locations: 17**

[561] --- *The Lancashire Regiment (The Prince of Wales's Volunteers), 1689-1960.* London: Malcolm Page, 1960. **Locations: 1, 3, 4, 7, 102**

[562] --- *A Precis of the History of the Battalions of the Prince of Wales's Volunteers (South Lancashire).* Warrington: J. Walker Examiner Office, [n.d.] **Locations: 3, 17, RMP**

[563] --- *Presentation of Colours to 5th Battalion The Prince of Wales's Volunteers (South Lancashire Regiment) by the Rt. Hon. The Earl of Derby, on behalf of His Majesty The King.* St. Helens: 1929. **Locations: 14**

[564] --- *Prince of Wales's Volunteers (South Lancashire). Regimental Standing Orders and Customs.* Aldershot, 1971. **Locations: 17**

[565] --- *The Prince of Wales's Volunteers. The Royal Tournament, 1932.* Aldershot: Gale & Polden Ltd., 1932. **Locations: 3, 17**

[566] --- *The Regimental Chronicle: the Journal of The Prince of Wales's Volunteers (South Lancashire).* Vol. 1 (1925-6)- 14 (1939). Warrington: 1925-39. **Locations: 17, RMP (1925-39)**

[567] --- *The Regimental Magazine of The Lancashire Regiment (P.W.V.).* Warrington: 1963-. **Locations: RMP**

[568] --- *Regimental Standing Orders and Customs of the Prince of Wales's Volunteers.* Aldershot: Gale & Polden, 1931. **Locations: NAM**

[569] --- *A Short History of the 3rd Battalion The Prince of Wales Volunteers (South Lancashire Regiment) formerly 4th Royal Lancashire (The Duke of Lancaster's Own) Light Infantry Militia, being principally extracts from the Regimental Records.* Manchester: Taylor, Garnett and Evans, 1909. **Locations: NAM**

[570] --- *A Short History of The South Lancashire Regiment (The Prince of Wales's Volunteers)*. Aldershot: Gale & Polden Ltd, 1946.

[571] --- *Soldiers Died in The Great War, 1914-19. Part 44: The Prince of Wales's Volunteers (South Lancashire Regiment)*. London: H.M.S.O., 1921. **Locations: 14, 34, 17**

[572] --- *Soldiers Died in The Great War, 1914-19. Part 44: The Prince of Wales' Volunteers (South Lancashire Regiment)*. Polstead: J.B. Hayward & Son, 1989. **Locations: 3, 4, 18, 40, LRO**

[573] --- *The South Lancashire Regiment in the South African War, 1899-1902*. Warrington: Mackie & Co. [n.d.] **Locations: 17, RMP**

[574] --- *[South Lancashire Regiment. Prince of Wales's Volunteers 2nd Battalion] The Eighty Second*. January 1923-October 1925. 1923-25. **Locations:RMP**

[575] --- *[South Lancashire Regiment. Prince of Wales's Volunteers 6th Battalion] The Mesopoluvian*. June 1917-April 1918. Sindiyeh, 1917-18. **Locations: RMP**

[576] --- *The South Lancashire Regiment (The Prince of Wales's Volunteers) 1717-1956. Regimental Handbook*. London: Malcolm Page Ltd., 1956. **Locations: 34**

[577] --- *Presentation of Colours to the 1st Battalion the Lancashire Regiment (Prince of Wales' Volunteers) by His Excellency the Governor of Hong Kong, Sir Robert Black at the Army Polo Ground, Hong Kong, 21st November, 1958*. 1958. **Locations: 6**

[578] Whalley-Kelly, H., Captain. *"Ich Dien": The Prince of Wales's Volunteers (South Lancashire) 1914-1934*. Aldershot: Gale & Polden, 1935. **Locations: 1, 2, 3, 14, 17, 34**

[579] Whitton, Frederick Ernest, *A Short History of The Prince of Wales's Volunteers (South Lancashire) [1712-1918]*. Aldershot: Gale & Polden, 1928. **Locations: 1, 3, 4, 14, 17**

ARCHIVES

National Army Museum Archives.

[580] *South Lancashire Regiment. Scrapbook compiled by Macphail.* Contains press cuttings, letters, photographs and other items relating chiefly to Macphail's service during World War I. He served before the war in the 2nd Volunteer Battalion South Lancashire Regiment, later 5th Battalion, going to France with them in February 1915, and wounded at the Second Battle of Ypres. 1905-18.

[581] McFall, A. W. C., Lt-Col. *Volume of letters, telegrams, certificates, orders, press cuttings and other documents relating to the service of Lt. Col. A.W.C. McFall, OBE, 1881-1920.* 1881-1920.

[582] Richardson, Arthur Johnstone, Lt-Colonel. *Autobiography of Lieutenant-Colonel Arthur Johnstone Richardson, DSO, from his childhood to April 1930.*

[583] --- *Framed letter delivered by Commandant Scheepers (afterwards executed by British court-*

martial) to Lieutenant Herbert G. Clarkson 3rd Battalion South Lancashire Regiment demanding the unconditional surrender of his post on the 13th November 1900; Krugers Siding Orange River Colony. 1900.

Regimental Museum, Fulwood Barracks, Preston

[584] The principal archival collection relating to the South Lancashire Regiment is held at the Regimental Museum, Fulwood Barracks, Preston. The archive was being reorganised at the time this bibliography was being prepared. What follows is a brief outline of the main holdings to an extensive collection. Archive material covers the two original regiments that amalgamated in 1881 to form the Prince of Wales's Volunteers (South Lancashire Regiment). Boxes for:

40th Regiment 1770-1792: material relating to origins of regiments and military campaigns, particularly America. 1793-1816: correspondence, newspaper cuttings relating to Napoleonic Wars. Box 3, 1816-1881: letters, order books, cuttings, diary and journal of Henry Parkhurst.
82nd Regiment 1793-1815: manuscript material relating to Napoleonic War campaigns. 1816-1881: orders, letters, pamphlets covering the activities of the regiments.
1st Battalion Box 1, Boer War: diaries and papers relating to the Boer War from officers and private soldiers, including rough diaries by the men, manuscript accounts of the Boer War; and newspaper cuttings. World War I, booklets, some manuscript material, photographs and small printed items. 1939-1958: including printed material, pamphlets, typescript histories relating to Dunkirk and D-Day.
2nd Battalion Photographs between 1881-1914. Box 4, 2nd Battalion, World War I: War Diaries. Box 5: 2nd Battalion, 1919-1948: including printed material, photographs, particularly covering regimental service in India, typescript of Brief History of the 2nd Battalion between March 1942-July 1944. Box 6, Service Battalions, 1914-1918: War Diaries. Box 7: Territorial Army and Service Battalions, 1919-1970: including correspondence, pamphlets, scrap books and photographs. Lancashire Militia (4th Regiment): pamphlets, correspondence, photographs, play bills, battalion year books. 4th and 5th Territorial Battalions, 1914-1919: War Diaries. Volunteers: including battalion year books and order books. Separate boxes covering officers records, soldiers records, maps and charts, rolls of honour, medals and an extensive collection of photographs relating to the regiment, 1880s onwards. Other items include Digest of Services, 82nd Regiment and records of service of the 40th Regiment, plus sundry visitors books, order books, newspaper cuttings.

Separate catalogues cover the museum holdings of artifacts, paintings, silver and other materials.

III. MILITIA, VOLUNTEERS, YEOMANRY, RIFLE VOLUNTEERS AND TERRITORIALS

This section deals with the militia, those various citizens armies that have been formed, usually under the threat of foreign invasion, at different times over the last 250 years. Although not as well known as the regular army the militia form a central part of the military history of this country, and given their strong local connections they are of particular interest to the regional historian. For convenience the section is divided into five broad categories: Militia, Volunteers, Yeomanry, Rifle Volunteers and the Territorial Forces. It does not include the Local Defence Volunteers (1940-45) as these are covered in the Second World War section. In each section the printed entries are arranged alphabetically by author. These are followed by archival material.

In recent years historians have begun to acknowledge the significance of the various citizen-soldier armies that were set up essentially for the defence of the country. A number of solid book-length studies are now available to assist the local researcher in understanding the national context behind the establishment and operation of these forces. Ian Beckett has been in the van of this research, and his books, *The Amateur Military Tradition, 1558-1945* (Manchester, 1991) and *Rifleman Form: a Study of the Rifle Volunteer Movement, 1859-1908* (Aldershot, 1982) are essential starting points for any serious study. John R. Western, *The English Militia in the Eighteenth Century: The Story of a Political Issue, 1660-1802* (London, 1965) remains a most useful introduction to those political forces that re-shaped the Georgian Militia. On the Rifle Volunteers, founded as anxieties over a French invasion boiled over in the late 1850s, Hugh Cunningham's *The Volunteer Force. A Social and Political History 1859-1914* (London, 1975) should also be consulted. The Volunteers' successor was the Territorial Force, and this should be approached through P. Dennis, *The Territorial Army, 1906-1940* (Woodbridge, 1987) and Ray Westlake, *The Territorial Force, 1914* (Newport, 1988). A most welcome development in the literature is the appearance of local studies such as Glenn A. Steppler, *Britons, to Arms! The Story of the British Volunteer Soldier and the Volunteer Tradition in Leicestershire and Rutland* (Far Thrupp, Stroud, 1992). Modern research on Lancashire and Cheshire is also underway, including Stephen Bull's study of the Rifle Volunteers [755].

As the archive material indicates there is a considerable range of records awaiting examination. These range from the records of volunteer corps, such as the one founded in 1803 by Roger Barnston, a member of a prominent Cheshire family [698], to the Liverpool Independent Rifle Corps which, in true Lancastrian spirit, claimed to be the first volunteer rifle corps in the country [705].

I. Militia

[585] 4th Royal Lancashire Militia. *Standing Orders*. 1872. **Locations: NAM**

[586] Borron, J.A. *A Statement of Facts relative to the Transfer of Service of the late Warrington Volunteer Corps into the Local Militia.* Warrington: J. Haddock, 1809 **Locations: RMP**

[587] Carter, D. P. "The Lancashire Militia, 1660-1688." *Transactions of the Historic Society of Lancashire and Cheshire* 132 (1982) 155-81. **Locations:** *

[588] Chester Volunteers. "Chester Volunteers and Militia in 1782." *Cheshire Sheaf* 4 (1902) 13. **Locations: 4, 17, 58**

[589] [Lord Derby]. *A Letter From Lord Derby to Joseph Hanson Requesting that He Communicate to His Corps. (Manchester and Salford Independent Corps of Riflemen), Certain Resolutions Formed by the House of Commons. Knowsley, 3 Sept. 1803.* 1803. **Locations: 1**

[590] Illidge, Richard. *Life and Writings of Lieutenant R. Illidge of Cheer Brook, in the Township of Stapeley, Parish of Wybunbury and County of Chester.* Manchester: Reprinted by J. Gleave, 1836. **Locations: 1, 4, 57, 58**

[591] --- *A Short Account of the Life of Lieutenant Illidge, who was in the Militia of the County of Chester near Fifty Years, chiefly drawn out of his own papers.* 1710. **Locations: 58**

[592] Jarvis, Rupert Charles. "The Lieutenancy and the Militia in Lancashire and Cheshire in 1745." *Transactions of the Lancashire and Cheshire Antiquarian Society* 62 (1950-1) 111-32. **Locations: ***

[593] Lees, John, Lieutenant-Colonel. *Standing Orders for the Oldham Regiment of Local Militia commanded by Lieutenant Colonel Lees.* Manchester: Banks, 1809. **Locations: 11**

[594] Lever, Ashton, Sir. *Notice of a Recruiting Campaign at ... [portion missing] ... or at the Headquarters Bull's Head Inn: with a Martial Band of Music and Colours Flying: it is Organised by Sir Ashton Lever. Manchester 27 Sept. 1780.* 1780. **Locations: 1**

[595] Loyal Association of Manchester. *Copy of Two Letters Addressed to The Loyal Association of Manchester on the Subject of Training Twenty Thousand Men in This Town Alone, Without Serious Hindrance of Business, Loss of Time to the Parties or Expense to the Government.* [n.d.] **Locations: 1**

[596] Mallet, W. *The Tour of the Third or Prince Regent's Own Regiment of Royal Lancashire Militia, (from 1803 to 1815) during the late war.* Preston: L. Clarke, 1860. **Locations: RMP**

[597] Manchester Military Association. *Hymns, psalms and anthems, to be sung at St. Ann's Church, on Monday the 24th of February, 1783, being the day fixed for the Manchester Military Association to hear Divine Service.* Manchester: C. Wheeler, 1783. **Locations: CL**

[598] --- "Note on a Sermon Preached Before the Association by Samuel Hall, Chaplain, at St. Ann's Church, 24 Feb., 1783." *Local Gleanings* II (1887-88) 553. **Locations: 1**

[599] --- "Volunteers of The Manchester Military Association, 1783-1784. [Lists of subscribers and volunteers and other memoranda]." *Local Gleanings* I (1875-76) 159, 165, 187. **Locations: 1**

[600] Oldham Regiment of Local Militia. *Standing Orders for the Oldham Regiment of Local Militia, Commanded by Lieutenant-Colonel Lees.* Manchester: Oldham Regiment of Local Militia, 1809. **Locations: 11**

[601] Phillips, Shakespear. *The Undernamed Persons signed a declaration that they would not quit the Corps during the war, without the consent of their commanding officer, except on very urgent business. They have however thought fit to send in their resignation without the concurrence of their Commandment. Shakespear Phillips, Major Commandment.* [1804]. **Locations: 1, 15**

[602] Poole, John. *Resolutions taken at a most numerous and respectable Town's Meeting convened by the Boroughreeves and Constables of Manchester and Salford at the Bull's Head Inn, 1 May 1798 to take into consideration, the best mode of forming an additional Armed Corps of Infantry. John Poole, (Chairman).* 1798. **Locations: 1**

[603] --- *To the Inhabitants of Manchester and Salford and Their Neighbours. A Call to Arms Against the French. John Poole, (Chairman) Committee-room, Police Office. 2 May 1798.* 1798. **Locations: 1, 15**

[604] --- *To the Inhabitants of Manchester and Salford. The Committee Appointed for Forming an Additional Armed Corps of Infantry give this Public Notice - That All Loyal.Subjects are Requested to Enroll Themselves at the Police Office... John Poole, Chairman.* 1798. **Locations: 1, 15**

[605] Rawstorne, John George, Lieutenant-Colonel. *An Account of the Regiments of Royal Lancashire Militia, 1759-1870.* Lancaster: H. Longman, 1874. **Locations: ***

[606] Royal Westmorland Battalion of Militia. *Morning State of Captain Holme's Company, Royal Westmorland Battalion of Militia.* [n.d.] **Locations: 5**

[607] Royal Westmorland Militia. *Royal Warrant for holding court-martial.* 1815. **Locations: 5**

[608] Starkie, Thomas. *Sermon preached in the Parish Church of Blackburn on the presentation of the Colours, the gift of the Ladies to the Associations of Cavalry and Infantry, Tuesday 4 June, 1799.* Blackburn: Hemingway and Nuttall, 1799. **Locations: 6**

[609] Walsh, Philip J. *Township of Marton Militia List.* 1823. **Locations: 3**

MILITIA ARCHIVES

Blackburn Library
[610] Blackburn Hundred. *Militia Roll.* 1831.

Bolton Archives
[611] Contents include *Lancashire Lieutenancy Records (Bolton Sub-Division). Army Reserve, Militia, and Volunteers' Pay roll.* 1804-16; *Lancashire Lieutenancy Records (Bolton Sub-Division). Militia Enrolment Book, 1817-1825; 1826-1831*; *Lancashire Lieutenancy Records (Bolton Sub-Division). Minute Book.* 1800-60.

Cheshire County Council
[612] *Militia Lists. Bucklow Hundred includes all South Trafford.* [n.d.] **Locations: 4, 70**

Cheshire Record Office.

[613] *Militia Records*. Contents include Appointments of militia officers 1778-1814; General and sub-divisional meeting records including lists of men enrolled, principally relating to the period of the Napoleonic Wars c.1770-1815; correspondence and papers 1715 and 1745-6.

[614] *Militia Records*. 1715-1815.

Cumbria Record Office. Carlisle.

[615] *Militia Records*.
Contents include Papers concerning militia appointments and meetings (1759-71); Cumberland and Westmorland militia: orderly book, militia lists, weekly returns, account books, stock book, letter book, attendance register (1760-1805); Cumberland militia (Allerdale Below, Cumberland and Eskdale wards only): books, rolls, lists, oaths, substitutes, surgeons' certificates etc. (1762-1831); Militia accounts (1778-1802); Account for repairs to muskets and swords (1779); Nominal rolls, some recording date of birth and appearance (1779-); Warrants for militia returns to be made (1780-1); Militia Acts (1786,1797); Regulation re clothing and half mounting of militia (1801); Rate book for Army of Reserve and Supplementary Militia (1803); Militia Accounts (1804-19); Resolution re repair of militia barracks, Whitehaven (1869). 1663-1869.

Lancashire Record Office.

[616] Contents include *Quarter Sessions: Militia Records, 1837-89; Royal Lancashire Volunteer Regiment. Muster Roll 1795; Garnett Family Records, 1797-1854; Leyland and Ormskirk Militia. Orderly book, 1809-13; Lieutenancy Records. Amounderness Militia: War Office circulars 1811-1813; Loyal Kirkham Volunteers. Minutes, correspondence etc., 1798; Manchester Military Association. Minutes, accounts, etc., 1782-84.*

Lancaster Library

[617] Myers, William, Captain. "Statement signed by Capt. William Myers, of the Royal Lancashire Militia that he has received the sum of £12 from Christopher Bradshaw of Lancaster, tallow-chandler, who was balloted to serve as a militia man in the Royal Lancashire Militia, and that Capt. Myers will provide a substitute to serve in his place. 19th Nov 1761." *Lancaster Library Scrapbook* 2 (folio) (1761) 147.

[618] Bradshaw, John. "[Certificate of enrolment of John Newby as a Private in the Lonsdale Regiment of Local Militia, now assembled at Lancaster.] Signed by the Lieut. Col. commanding: John Bradshaw. 11 May 1812." *Lancaster Library Scrapbook* 2 (folio) (1812) 248.

[619] Royal Lancashire Militia Hospital. *MSS re. the premises No.1 High Street, Lancaster leased by Edmund Simpson for the use of the 10th Royal Lancashire Militia Hospital, 1871-4.*

[620] Royal Lancaster Militia. "Certificate that George Wyldman of Caton, Surveyor was balloted in the Militia for the Subdivision of the Hundred of Lonsdale, South of the Sands, and procured a substitute who was sworn in and enrolled the 15th Aug. 1803. Signed Park, Clerk to the Subdivision Meetings. Oct 25th 1803. Lancaster, Walmsley."
Lancaster Library Scrapbook 2 (folio) (1803) 227.

[621] --- "Plans of storehouse of 1st Royal Lancashire Militia, in South Road, Lancaster." *Lancaster Library Scrapbook* 2 (folio) [n.d.] 162-3.

Liverpool Libraries and Information Services, Record Office and Local History Department.

[622] *Prescot Militia Rolls.* Contents include Militia Rolls for the Prescot Sub-Division, 1808-1816, with details of name, trade, place of abode, number of children under 10 (and sometimes 14) years of ages and date of enrolment, with totals of men enrolled. St Helens Volunteer Enrolment, Rolls for 1808, 1809, 1811, 1812; Roll of supplementary volunteers "for supplying deficiencies occasioned by promotions, etc." 1813; 1814; 1815, 1816. 1808-16.

National Army Museum

[623] Brophey, John. *Documents relating to John Brophey, Col Sgt 63 Foot, Lt 3 Lancashire Militia, 1855 to 1866.* 1855-66.

[624] Cheshire Militia. *Hand coloured engraving of a Plan of Coxheath 1778 dedicated to the Hon. Willm. Keppel, Lieut. Genl. and Commander in Chief of the Forces Encamped on Coxheath by Josh. Bell and Jas. Black, soldiers in the 1st Regt. of Royals.* 1778.

[625] Royal Lancashire Militia. *Commissions to J.J. Hamilton, 1861-79.* 1861-79.

Warrington Library

[626] --- *Standing Orders of the Fourth (Duke of Lancaster's Own) Light Infantry Regiment, Royal Lancashire Militia.* Warrington, 1857.

II. Volunteers

[627] Ackers, James. *Resolutions Taken at a Meeting at the Bull's Head Inn, 28 Feb, 1797, for the Purpose of Making an Offer to Government of Raising an Armed Volunteer Corps. from Amongst the Inhabitants of Manchester and Salford: to be Called "The Manchester & Salford Volunteers".* James Ackers, Bull's Head Inn, 28 Feb. 1797. 1797. **Locations: 1, 15**

[628] Andrew, Samuel. "The Noble, Free, and Spirited Manchester Corps of Marines." *Transactions of the Lancashire and Cheshire Antiquarian Society* 23 (1905) 219-21. **Locations: 1**

[629] Ashton-under-Lyne Volunteers. "Ashton-under-Lyne Volunteers. [Resolutions of a Meeting of the Inhabitants of Ashton-under-Lyne for Raising a Volunteer Corps of Infantry, 10 Aug. 1803]." *Local Gleanings* I (1875-6) 438 . **Locations: 1, CL**

[630] Bancroft, T. *A Sermon Preached before the Officers and Privates of the Loyal Bolton Volunteer Corps of Infantry on Thursday, May 6th, 1802, being the day on which they were disembodied, and their Colours deposited in the Parish Church of Bolton, with a list of officers and privates.* Bolton: 1802. **Locations: 1, 7, CL**

[631] Barton, B.T. "Formation of a Bolton Infantry Corps in 1803." *Manchester Genealogist* 24 (April 1988) 106. **Locations: 1, 7**

[632] Borron, John Arthur. *A Statement of Facts relative to the transfer of service of the late Warrington Volunteer Corps into the Local Militia.* Warrington: J. Haddock, 1809. **Locations: 1, 17**

[633] Claye, Herbert Sandford. *Notes on the Establishment of Volunteers in Macclesfield in 1797, and other particulars of the early Volunteer Movement.* Macclesfield: Courier Office, 1894. **Locations: 3**

[634] Cumbria. Ulverston. "The Ulverston Volunteer in 1803." *North Lonsdale Magazine* 4 (1900) 35-8. **Locations: LRO**

[635] Grey de Wilton, Baron. *Standing Orders and Regulations for His Majestey's Royal Lancashire Volunteer Regiment of Foot. Issued by Colonel The Rt. Hon. Lord Grey de Wilton, at Porchester, May 1st 1798.* [Private copy of Col. Clayton of Carr Hall, with mss. notes.] London: Whitehall Military Library (T. Egerton [printers]), 1798. **Locations: 9**

[636] Grimshaw, N. *Observations on the Reply to a Statement of the Question Respecting the Comparative Rank of the two Corps of Preston Volunteer Infantry.* Preston: Croft, 1805. **Locations: 3, 12**

[637] Hall, Samuel. *A Sermon Preached Before the First Battalion of the Manchester and Salford Volunteers at St. Peter's Church in Manchester on Tuesday, June 4th, 1799.* Manchester: 1799. **Locations: 1, CL**

[638] Hanson, Joseph. *Brief Remarks on the Present Volunteer Establishment, by Joseph Hanson, Lieutenant Colonel Commandant of the Manchester, Salford &c. Independent Rifle Regiment.* Salford: 1805. **Locations: 1, 13, 15**

[639] --- *A Letter to Lieutenant Colonel Joseph Hanson containing concise observations on his brief remarks on the present Volunteer Establishment. By a Volunteer.* Manchester: 1805. **Locations: 1, 13, CL**

[640] --- An Advocate for the Truth. *Cursory strictures on the Concise Observations of a Volunteer: Being a Defence of Col. Hanson's Remarks on the Volunteer Establishment. By An Advocate for the Truth.* Salford: 1806. **Locations: 1, 13**

[641] --- *Copies of Two Letters From The Earl of Derby. They Prove the Very High Opinion His Majesty Entertains of the Loyalty of the Corps I Have the Distinguished Honour to Command. Joseph Hanson, 26 Aug. 1803.* 1803. **Locations: 1**

[642] Harland, John. *The Old [Manchester] Volunteers and Rifle Corps* in Collectanae relating to Manchester and its Neighbourhood at various periods, *Chetham Society* 72 (1867) II 92-101 **Locations: ***

[643] Higham, Don, (ed.). *Liverpool Volunteers, 1759-1803: miscellaneous muster lists of volunteers and militia men.* Liverpool: Liverpool and District Family History Society, 1988. **Locations: 3**

[644] Hulme Volunteers. *Those persons who propose to join the corps intended to be formed in Hulme will please attend the field adjoining Mr. Pooley's factory for the purpose of enrolling their names.* Manchester: J. Harrop, 1803. **Locations: CL**

[645] Jenkinson, John. *To the Inhabitants of the Town of Manchester and Salford and Their Neighbourhood. Legislative Concerning the Volunteer Corps Which a Committee Appointed*

at a Public Meeting 28 July 1803 had Decided to Raise. John Jenkinson (Secretary). 1803. **Locations: 1, 15**

[646] Kendrick, James. "Some Account of the Loyal Warrington Volunteers of 1798." *Transactions of the Historic Society of Lancashire and Cheshire* 7 (1893) 22-30. **Locations:** *

[647] King's Cheshire Volunteer Legion. *Regulations and orders observed in the Stockport Troop of the King's Cheshire Volunteer Legion.* [n.d.] **Locations: 57**

[648] Lancashire Volunteer and Yeomanry Regiments. "Names of the Officers, 1804." *Local Gleanings* II (1877-8) 711, 718, 725, 727, 734 . **Locations: 1, CL**

[649] Liverpool Volunteers. *A Complete and Comprehensive Exercise Book, containing Rules and Regulations for the Formation, Field-Exercise, and Movements of His Majesty's Forces...[and] the Manual and Platoon Exercise published for the use of the Liverpool Volunteers.* [1780] **Locations: 2**

[650] Loyal Bolton Volunteers. "The Loyal Bolton Volunteers of 1802. [List of the corps of infantry formed in 1794 and disbanded in 1802]." *Local Gleanings* I (1875-6) 445. **Locations: 1, CL**

[651] Manchester 1st Battalion. *Copies of Correspondence Concerning a Report that the Service of The 1st Battalion, 4th Class Has Not Been Accepted by the Government. Also Notice of a General Meeting of Members Enrolled in the Battalion to be Held in the Bull's Head Inn, 30 August 1803.* 1803. **Locations: 1**

[652] Manchester. Volunteers. *At a most numerous and respectable Town's Meeting on Tuesday the 1st of May, 1798...the best mode of forming an additional armed corps of infantry...it was unanimously resolved, first. That an armed Corps be formed...for the defence of the towns of Manchester, Salford.* Manchester: 1798. **Locations: CL**

[653] --- *To the inhabitants of the towns of Manchester and Salford the committee appointed at your public meeting of the 28th July last, being fully sensible how well founded the opinion is that "the most effectual way of aiding the intentions of government, will be the immediate re-establishing and raising volunteer corps".* Manchester: J. Harrop, 1803. **Locations: CL**

[654] --- *We the undersigned magistrates...request such of his Majesty's loyal subjects, as intend to offer their personal military service to enroll their names at the Police-Office.* Manchester: Harrop, 1798. **Locations: CL**

[655] --- *Whereas at a meeting of a considerable number of respectable inhabitants of this town and neighbourhood, on the 31st day of May last, it was unanimously resolved, that a corps of volunteers should be immediately raised for the defence of the town and neighbourhood of Manchester only.* Manchester: C. Wheeler, 1782. **Locations: CL**

[656] Manchester. Royal Manchester Volunteers. *Procession. To meet at St. Ann's Square at ten o'clock to march to Ardwick Green on Saturday next, to meet the Seventy-Second Regiment, or Royal Manchester Volunteers, and lead them into St. Ann's Square.* Manchester: [n.d.] **Locations: CL**

[657] Manchester and Salford Independent Volunteer Rifle Regiment. *Rules and Regulations to be Observed by the Members of the Manchester and Salford Independent Volunteer Rifle Regiment.* Manchester: 1809. **Locations: 1, 15**

[658] Manchester and Salford Light Horse Volunteers. *As the Manchester and Salford Light Horse Volunteers are to be presented with standards tomorrow, the Boroughreeves and Constables request the gentlemen of the town and neighbourhood to proceed to the parade in Dawson Street; from thence to attend the corps to High Street, where the standards to be presented.* Manchester: J. Harrop, 1798. **Locations: CL**

[659] --- *Regulating Code of Laws for the Manchester and Salford Light Horse Volunteers passed at a general meeting of the Corps September the First MDCCXCVII.* Manchester: G. Bancks, 1797. **Locations: 1, 15**

[660] --- *Regulating Code of Laws passed at a general meeting of the Corps July, 1798.* Manchester: 1798. **Locations: 1**

[661] --- "Roll of the 2nd Troop, July 1808 [from the original in the Chetham Library]." *Local Gleanings* I (1875-6) 32. **Locations: 1, CL**

[662] --- "Roll [of the whole Regiment], July, 1798." *Local Gleanings* I (1875-6) .52, 63, 73. **Locations: 1**

[663] Manchester and Salford Royal Volunteers. "Extracts from the Regimental Order Book, 1804." *Local Gleanings* I (1875-6)182, 189, 196. **Locations: 1, CL**

[664] Manchester and Salford Volunteer Corps of Infantry. *A List of Promotions in the Manchester and Salford Volunteer Infantry copied from The London Gazzette, 20 Sept. 1803.* 1803. **Locations: 1, 15**

[665] --- *Notice of the Consecration of Colours of The Manchester and Salford Volunteer Corps of Infantry. The Ceremony Will Take Place on 14 Feb 1798. The Procession will proceed from the Bull's Head Inn to the Church in St. Ann's Square. Manchester 7 Feb. 1798.* 1798. **Locations: 1, 15**

[666] Manchester and Salford Volunteers. *Attention! To all fathers of families, to all married men above the age of 30...a fellow-member of the Fourth Class, [Manchester and Salford Volunteers] presumes to address himself.* Manchester: 1803. **Locations: CL**

[667] --- *To the Inhabitants of Manchester and Salford. My Countrymen. It is not an Alarmist, nor a Ministerial Hireling who presumes to address you...Prove Your Attachment to Your King and Country by contributing to the General Fund or enrolling yourselves with the First or Second Battalion of Manchester and Salford Volunteers.* [1798]. **Locations: 1, 15**

[668] Manchester and Salford Volunteers, 1st Regiment. *Statement of the Officers of the Late 1st Regiment of Manchester and Salford Volunteers [on resigning their commission after refusing to serve under other officers].* Manchester: 1804. **Locations: 1, 15**

[669] Manchester. Scottish Volunteers. *The Scotchmen in This Town who are attached to Their King and Country are requested to attend a meeting at Mr. Smith's Boar's Head, Hyde's Cross in order to determine on raising a Corps of Volunteers to consist entirely of their own*

countrymen. Manchester 11 April 1798. 1798. **Locations: 1**

[670] Manchester Volunteers. *The Manchester Volunteers. A new song. Come all you Manchester Heroes, of Courage Stout and Bold.* Manchester: [n.d.] **Locations: CL**

[671] McGuffie, T. H. "The Royal Manchester Volunteers [1777-83]." *Manchester Review* 7 (Summer 1955) 209-12. **Locations: 1**

[672] Pendleton Volunteers. *To the inhabitants of Pendleton. By virtue of an Act of Parliament passed on 11th August 1803, all persons who shall be returned in the Muster Roll of a Volunteer Corps, now forming, will be exempted to serve in the army of reserve.* J. Harrop: Manchester, 1803. **Locations: CL**

[673] Poole, John. *An Address by John Poole to His Friends and Fellow Countrymen Calling Them to Unite in Defence of Their Country Against the French. John Poole, Committee-Room, Bull's Head Inn, Manchester. 28 Feb. 1798.* Manchester: 1798. **Locations: 1**

[674] Rochdale Bolton and Stockport Volunteers. *A List of Manoeuvres to be performed by The Rochdale, Bolton and Stockport Volunteers, on Thursday, 25 August, 1796 on Kersal Moor.* 1796. **Locations: 1, 7, 13, 59**

[675] Royal Lancashire Volunteers. *Several gentlemen of the towns and neighbourhood of Manchester and Salford, having submitted the propriety of shewing every possible mark of respect to the Royal Lancashire Volunteers on their return to their native country.* Manchester: J. Harrop, 1802. **Locations: CL**

[676] Royal Lancaster Volunteers. *Returns of the Royal Lancaster Volunteers 1798-9: Working Men 1 July 1798, and Morning Report 26 Mar 1799.* 1798-9. **Locations: 1**

[677] Royal Manchester and Salford Volunteers. *Glorious Victory. The Boroughreeves, Constables and Gentlemen of the towns of Manchester and Salford request the inhabitants to meet in St. Ann's Square where the Royal Manchester and Salford Volunteers will fire a feu de joye, on the brilliant victory obtained by Admiral Nelson over the French fleet.* Manchester: 1798. **Locations: CL**

[678] Royal Manchester Regiment. *Royal Manchester Regiment. All young men of spirit...have now an opportunity of engaging in the above regiment; commanded by Major Delhoste.* Manchester: Swindells, [n.d.] **Locations: CL**

[679] Royal Manchester Volunteers. *All Young Men of Spirit have now an opportunity of engaging in the above Regiment commanded by Major Delhoste. A large bounty will be given ... bringers of recruits will be liberally rewarded.* 1780. **Locations: 1**

[680] --- *As a Few Recruits are Wanted for The Royal Manchester Volunteers Any Young Men of Spirit may now have the opportunity of maintaining the honour and dignity of their King and Country... applying to Capt. Aytoun or Capt. Wilson. None but Lancashire men need apply.* 1777. **Locations: 1**

[681] --- *Fifty-Seven Men Are Wanted to complete The 72nd Regiment of Foot or Royal Manchester Volunteers For Which Six Guineas will be given to any man Five Feet Six, Inches, and a Guinea more Per Inch for All Above. The Regiment is to be reviewed by*

Major General Sir David Lindsay, 30 March 1778 in Castle Field, Manchester. 1778. **Locations: 1**

[682] --- *A new song composed on the Royal Manchester Volunteers. Now in Manchester they are raising, Royal volunteers so bold.* Manchester: [n.d.] **Locations: CL**

[683] --- "A Recruiting Serjeant's Handbill, 1777." *Local Gleanings* I (1877)566. **Locations: 1, CL**

[684] Royal Welsh Volunteers. *To the Warriors of Manchester. An Encouragement to the Young Men of Manchester, to become British Soldiers and join the Royal Welsh Fusiliers and campaign in Spain and Gibraltar against Buonaparte. Applications to be made to Serjeant Capon, St. Paul's Tavern, Turner Street.* 1813. **Locations: 1**

[685] Rutter, David. "The Volunteer Movement in Ulverston, Lancashire, 1803-1967." *Lion and the Dragon* 6 (Spring 1978) 251-60. **Locations: NAM**

[686] St. George's Volunteers. *Notice is Hereby Given that by Virtue of an Act of Parliament Passed on the 11 Aug. 1803, All Persons who shall be returned in the Muster-Roll of this Corps will be exempted from being balloted or enrolled to serve in the Army of Reserve.* 1803. **Locations: 1**

[687] Sale Moor. *[Programme of] a Review of Volunteers at Sale Moor on Thursday 12 April, 1804, by H.R.H. Prince William Frederick.* 1804. **Locations: 1**

[688] Salford Volunteers. *List of men who served in the Salford Volunteers.* 1813. **Locations: 15**

[689] Scotch Brigade (Third Regiment). *Third Regiment of The Scotch Brigade, Ilay Ferrier, Commander. From Five to Thirteen Guineas Bounty Besides One to Two Guineas for Bringers ... All Lancashire Heroes Bold who please to enlist in the above Corps, may depend on good treatment in all respects.* 1795. **Locations: 1, 3**

[690] Silvester, J. *A Letter to the Inhabitants of Manchester and Salford, but particularly to the Non-Commissioned Officers and Privates of the Late Second Battalion of Manchester and Salford Volunteers, informing them that the services of the Second Battalion have again been tendered to the Government. J. Silvester, Manchester, 20 Aug., 1803.* 1803. **Locations: 1, 15, CL**

[691] Stockport Independent Cavalry. *Rules for the Stockport Independent Cavalry.* [179-]. **Locations: 1**

[692] Stockport Volunteers. "Stockport Volunteers of 1794." *Cheshire Sheaf, 3rd series* 7 (1917) 24. **Locations: 4, 58, 65**

[693] Ulverston Volunteer Infantry. *Exercise of Light Infantry with some instructions for their conduct in the field intended for use of Ulverston Volunteer Infantry.* Ulverston: 1804. **Locations: 5**

[694] Walton, D. "The Salford Volunteer Movement (1794-1814)." *Military History Society Bulletin* 18 (August 1967) 18. **Locations: NAM**

[695] Widditt, John, Rev. Curate of St. John's Church. *A Sermon preached at Lancaster on Tuesday, August 8th, 1797, on the Presentation of the Colours, to the Royal Lancaster Volunteers, to which is prefixed the prayer delivered on the consecration of the colours, by the Rev. J. Widditt.* Lancaster: Jackson, 1797. **Locations: 28**

VOLUNTEER ARCHIVES

Bolton Archives
[696] *Lancashire Lieutenancy Records (Bolton Sub-Division). Muster Roll: Bolton Light Horse Volunteers at Preston. 13 Jun 1805.*

Cheshire Record Office
[697] *Stockport Loyal Volunteers papers, 1798; Stockport Rifle Corps Papers, 1803-1804*

Chester City Record Office
[698] *Roger Barnston's Volunteer Corps: Records.*
Contents include a printed notice signed by Barnston; copy agreement between H. Lewis and twenty others (named) to subscribe two guineas each to provide a substitute...to serve in the militia of Cheshire; Original enrolments [of volunteer corps raised by Roger Barnston]

[699] *William Morris Collection.* William Morris was clerk to the lieutenancy of Chester and Cheshire, 1852-71, with particular responsibility for the militia and the volunteers. The collection includes commissions; correspondence; and nominal rolls of volunteer corps.
Records of the Clerk of the general meetings of Lieutenancy: Minutes of Eddisbury sub-divisional meetings and commission entry book 1804-45. Commissions of deputy lieutenants and officers serving in: Royal Regiment of Cheshire Yeomanry Cavalry (various troops); King's Cheshire Volunteer Legion; Royal Cheshire Militia. Muster rolls of the King's Cheshire Yeomanry Cavalry, 1845-1849.
Records of the Clerk of the Lieutenancy: Letters to William Morris, clerk of the lieutenancy, St. Werbergh Street, Chester, mainly acknowledging the receipt of commissions in the Royal Cheshire Militia. 1852-1856.
Nominal Rolls of persons enrolled and now serving in the Volunteer Corps 1872: Returns from: 1st-4th Cheshire Artillery Volunteer Corps; 1st Cheshire Engineer Corps, Birkenhead; Cheshire Rifle Volunteer Corps, 1st-36th, 1804-72.

Chetham's Library
[700] Ormerod, George. *Transcripts of material relating to Royal Manchester Volunteers, 1777-78.* 1868.

Cumbria Record Office. Carlisle
[701] *Volunteer Corps.* Contents include papers relating to Maryport Loyal Volunteer Corps: vouchers, enrolments, agreement for formation, equipment subscription list (1778,1803); Loyal Edenside Rangers/Cumberland Rangers: pay-lists, regulations, establishment tables, equipment, drill instructions, financial records, muster rolls, correspondence, drill attendance registers, etc. (1801-19); Muster roll of the Loyal Wedgewood Independent Corps of Mountaineers (1803); Papers re raising regiments of volunteers (1803-7); Memo re formation, organisation, instruction of Volunteer Corps raised c.1804; Workington, Harrington and Maryport Volunteers: muster roll (1804-5); Letter book and papers re the Loyal Leath Ward Volunteer Infantry (1805-19); certificate of enrolment [n.d.]; Returns...of volunteer officers, numbers of men and recruits, and payments (1806).

Greater Manchester County Record Office

[702] *Egerton Family of Heaton Park, Earls of Wilton. Papers.*
Royal Lancashire Volunteers.
Contents include Register of recruits, 1779-82; Account book, mainly recording bounties paid to recruits, 1779; Receipted accounts for bounties, 1779; Schedule of payments (purpose unstated), c.1780.
Roll of noncommissioned officers, 1779-81; Weekly and monthly returns of numbers of officers and men, 1779-81; Weekly returns, 1779-83; Schedule of men absent on pass, January-June, 1782.
Fair copy Brigade order book, Danbury Camp, 8 June-4 November, 1781; Brigade orders notebook, Danbury Camp, 5 July-9 August, 1781; Brigade orders notebook, Danbury Camp, 31 August-4 November 1781; Brentwood 5 November 1781-28 June 1782; Cox Heath Camp, 29 June-19 August, 1782; Brigade orders notebook, Cox Heath Camp, 2 July-10 November 1782,
Correspondence and papers relating to the Regiment including monthly returns, agreement to lease a house at Danbury, accounts and abstracts of expenses, returns of arms and equipment, and officers' call rolls, 1781-82.
Muster Roll for 25 December 1780-24 June 1781.
Papers relating to court-martials, including warrant for holding a court-martial, 1779;
Accounts, some receipted, chiefly for supplies, 1779-84; Further statistical returns of personnel, 1779-82; Warrant for regulating the Non-Effective fund of the several regiments of Infantry, 1766.
Accounting instructions from War Office, c.1780, 1766-1780.
Correspondence relating to the formation of the Regiment, 1778.
Royal Lancashire Volunteers. Later papers.
Contents include Letter from Isaac Shakespeare offering his services as a recruiting sergeant for the regiment Lord Wilton was raising, 25 October 1793; Letter from Henry Blundell to Lord Wilton, seeking his support for the promotion of Lt. Col. Blundell, 12 Nov. 1794; List of grenadiers and light infantry, 24 November 1794.
Royal Manchester Volunteers (72nd Regiment).
Contents include Returns of officers, correspondence, strength returns, embarkation list and related papers, January-April, September 1778; Accounts of subscription for the relief of soldiers wounded and the widows and orphans of soldiers killed in the defence of Gibraltar. c.1782.

Kendal Library

[703] *The Volunteer Forces in Westmorland, 1803-08.* 1803-8.

Lancashire Record Office

[704] *Garnett Family Records*, 1797-1854; *Royal Lancashire Volunteer Regiment. Muster Roll 1795.*

Liverpool Libraries and Information Services

[705] *Liverpool Independent Rifle Corps Records.* Contents include Liverpool Independent Rifle Corps: Committee Minute Book, July 1803-June 1804- with lists of men.

Manchester Central Library. Local Studies Unit

[706] Manchester. St George's Regiment of Volunteers. *Copies of Official Papers, Relative to the St. George's Regiment of Volunteers at Manchester, Transmitted to the Right Hon. the Earl of Derby.* Manchester: 1804.

[707] --- *Copies of Papers [relating to disaffection towards the commanding officer].* Manchester, 1804.

Rochdale Local Studies Library
[708] *Long Roll of Captain Royd's Troop*, 1846.

Stockport Local Studies Library
[709] Stockport Corps of Riflemen. *Minute Book, 1803-1804.*

Wigan Heritage Services. Archives
[710] Military History Records include Letters relating to the Wigan Armed Association 1798-1799; Papers relating to Wigan Loyal Volunteers 1798-1804; Rules of Wigan Volunteer Light Horse 1820.

III. Yeomanry

[711] Barker, John. "The Duke of Lancaster's Own Yeomanry Takes on a New Job." *Lancashire Life* 4(November 1956)24-5. **Locations: LRO**

[712] Barlow, L. and Smith, Robert Jeffrey. *Duke of Lancaster's Own Yeomanry.* Tunbridge Wells: Robert Ogilby Trust, 1983. **Locations: 2, 3, 7, 18, 20, 40, CL**

[713] Bastick, J. Desmond. *Trumpet Call. The Story of the Duke of Lancaster's Own Yeomanry.* Worsley, Manchester: Duke of Lancaster's Own Yeomanry, 1973. **Locations: ***

[714] Colley, T. "Yeomanry Cavalry. Origin of the Corps in Cheshire and Lancashire." *Cheshire Notes and Queries* 3 (1898) 69-76. **Locations: 4, 58**

[715] Cooke, John H., (ed.). *5,000 Miles with the Cheshire Yeomanry in South Africa. A Series of Articles compiled from Letters and Diaries, written by Officers, Non-Commissioned Officers and Men of the 21st and 22nd (Cheshire) Companies of Imperial Yeomanry, relating their experiences during the South African War in the years 1900-1901.* Warrington: Mackie & Co. Ltd, 1913-14. **Locations: GM, NAM**

[716] Duke of Lancaster's Own Yeomanry. *Duke of Lancaster's Own Imperial Yeomanry, Blackpool Troop: Grand Military Bazaar, Victoria Hall, Winter Gardens, Blackpool, Sept. 28th, 29th, 30th & Oct. 1st, 1904.* Blackpool: Times, 1904. **Locations: 3**

[717] --- *A Brief History of The Duke of Lancaster's Own Yeomanry.* 1951. **Locations: 3**

[718] --- *Official opening of the Regimental Museum, the Old Sessions House, Stanley Street, Preston, 21st October 1984.* 1984. **Locations: 3**

[719] --- *Presentation of a New Guidon by Her Majesty the Queen, Colonel-in-Chief, at Belle Vue Stadium, Manchester, on Wednesday 24th May 1961.* Manchester: George Falkner & Sons Ltd., 1961. **Locations: NAM**

[720] --- *South African War: with the 23rd Imperial Yeomanry (Duke of Lancaster's Own) from*

Blackpool to Faber Putt, Cape Colony, 1900. 1904. **Locations: 3**

[721] Duke of Lancaster's Own Yeomanry Cavalry. *An abridgement of the standing orders of cavalry regiments, arranged by order of Lieut. Colonel The Earl of Ellesmere for the use of the Duke of Lancaster's Own Regiment of Yeomanry Cavalry. R. Gerard, Major. May 26, 1848.* 1848. **Locations: 28**

[722] Earl of Chester's Regiment of Yeomanry Cavalry. *The Earl of Chester's Regiment of Yeomanry Cavalry, its formation and services 1797-1897.* Edinburgh: Privately printed, 1898. **Locations: CL**

[723] Earle, T. Algernon. *List of officers who have served in the Lancashire Hussars Yeomanry; with some short Notes and annals of the Regiment since its formation in 1848 to the present time.* Liverpool: T. Brakell, 1889. **Locations: 1**

[724] Fielding, J. H. *The Story of the Oldham Horse Association and the Oldham Troop Yeomanry Cavalry, 1798-1873.* [n.d.] **Locations: 11**

[725] Hargreaves, Percy, Colonel, and Freeman, Benson, Eng.-Lieutenant. *Old Time Yeomanry. The Manchester Corps.* Chester: Chester Courant, 1910. **Locations: 1**

[726] Johnson, Louis H. *The Duke of Lancaster's Own Yeomanry Cavalry, 23rd Co., I.Y. A record of incidents connected with the services of the First Contingent of the D.L.O.Y.C. in the South African Campaign of 1899-1900-1901-1902 of interest also to the Westmorland and Cumberland Yeomanry, 24th Co.I.Y., who were our partners and comrades-in-arms.* Bolton: Tillotson & Son, Ltd, 1902. **Locations: 1, 3, 6, 7, 13, 28, 102, NAM**

[727] Jolley, Thomas. "The Yeomanry: the regiments and present constitution, etc. of the force." *Cheshire Notes and Queries* 3 (1898) 123-5. **Locations: 4, 58**

[728] King's Own Border Regiment. "The Westmorland and Cumberland Yeomanry." *The Border Magazine* (March 1954). **Locations: 5**

[729] Leary, Frederick, (ed.). *The Earl of Chester's Regiment of Yeomanry Cavalry: its formation and services, 1797-1897.* Edinburgh: Ballatyne Press, 1898. **Locations: 1, 57, 58, 70**

[730] Manchester and Salford Yeomanry Cavalry. *Regulations and Orders observed in the Manchester and Salford Yeomanry Cavalry.* Manchester: Bancks & Co., 1820. **Locations: 1, 15**

[731] Oldham Troop Yeomanry Cavalry. *Muster Roll of the Oldham Troop Yeomanry Cavalry commanded by John Taylor, Esq, May, 1826.* 1826. **Locations: 11**

[732] Philips, Francis of Longsight Hall. *An exposure of the calumnies circulated by the enemies of social order and reiterated by their abettors against the Magistrates and the Yeomanry Cavalry of Manchester and Salford.* London: Longman, 1819. (2nd edition) **Locations: 1, 13, NAM**

[733] Pomeroy, Ralph Legge, Major the Hon., (ed.). *The Story of a Regiment of Horse: Being the Regimental History of the 5th Princess Charlotte of Wales' Dragoon Guards.* 2 vols. Edinburgh and London: W. Blackwood and Sons, 1924. **Locations: 1, 3**

[734] Prince of Wales' Regiment of Dragoon Guards. *3rd Carabiniers, Prince of Wales' Dragoon Guards and Cheshire (Earl of Chester's) Yeomanry, Territorial Army. Recruiting Handbook.* London: Malcolm Page, 1964. **Locations: 3**

[735] --- *3rd Carabiniers-Prince of Wales' Dragoon Guards-and Cheshire Yeomanry, T.A.* London: Malcolm Page, 1961. **Locations: 3**

[736] --- *3rd Carabiniers, Prince of Wales' Dragoon Guards and Cheshire Yeomanry, T.A. (Recruiting Handbook).* London: Malcolm Page, 1962. **Locations: 3**

[737] --- *The Feather and Carbine, Regimental Journal of the 3rd Carabiniers.* 1936-. **Locations: 3**

[738] --- *Historical Record of the Third, or Prince of Wales' Regiment of Dragoon Guards [1685-1838].* 1838. **Locations: 3**

[739] Princess Charlotte of Wales's Regiment of Dragoon Guards. *Historical Record of the Fifth, or Princess Charlotte of Wales's Regiment of Dragoon Guards [1685-1838].* 1839. **Locations: 3**

[740] Read, Fergus. *The Duke of Lancaster's Own Yeomanry: a short history compiled from regimental and other records.* Preston: Lancashire County Books, 1992. **Locations: 3, 7, 13, 40, LRO**

[741] Scott, Daniel. *The Westmorland and Cumberland Yeomanry.* Cumbria: Penrith Observer, 1912. **Locations: 5**

[742] Stockport Yeomanry. "The History of the Original Troop of Stockport Yeomanry." *Cheshire Notes and Queries* 6 (1903) 129-36. **Locations: 4, 58**

[743] Thomas, L. J. *The 77th (DLOY) Medium Regiment- North West Europe Campaign, June 1944 - May 1945.* Lancaster: The Regiment, [1946]. **Locations: 3**

[744] Verdin, Richard, Sir. *The Cheshire (Earl of Chester's) Yeomanry, 1898-1967: the last regiment to fight on horses.* Birkenhead: Wilmer Brothers, 1971. **Locations: ***

[745] Wigan Volunteer Light Horse. *Rules and Regulations Adopted by the Members of the Troop of Wigan Volunteer Light Horse.* Wigan: 1820. **Locations: 18**

YEOMANRY ARCHIVES

Cheshire Record Office
[746] *Cheshire Yeomanry Cavalry records 1797-1820.*

Cumbria Record Office. Carlisle
[747] *Westmorland and Cumberland Yeomanry.* Records include Regimental order books, service record book, photographs, muster rolls, letter book, nominal rolls, pay list, appointment, sports programme (1838-1914); Appleby Troop: accounts, mess regulation, return of members, regimental orders, historical sketch, etc (1859-1912).

Lancashire County Regimental Museum

[748]   Duke of Lancaster's Own Yeomanry. Regimental Archive. Photographs, histories and files relating to the regiment.

National Army Museum

[749]   *Two documents of the Antrobus Family*. 1. Commission to E.C. Antrobus as Captain 50th Regiment from 3 Aug 1855, dated 7 Aug 1855. 2. Illuminated address to G.C. Antrobus, "late Captain of the Congleton Troop of the Earl of Chester's Yeomanry Cavalry" from the NCOs and men of the troop on his leaving the regiment, dated 18 May 1855-60.

[750]   Stockport. Yeomanry. *Reproduction of poster, dated Stockport 6 April 1798, announcing a meeting to consider raising a Troop of Horse for local defence in the event of a French invasion*. Stockport: Published by the Rev. Charles Prescot, JP., 1798.

[751]   --- *Two orders for the Stockport Troop of the Lancashire Yeomanry Cavalry, dated 8 June and 11 July 1821*. 1821.

Wigan Heritage Services. Archives

[752]   Minutes of Wigan Yeomanry Cavalry 1828-1841.

IV. Rifle Volunteers

[753]   Appleton, F. M. "The Warrington Volunteers in South Africa." *Warrington Literary and Philosophical Society Proceedings* 1901-2 (1902) . **Locations: 3, 17, 115**

[754]   Blackburn. Witton. *Ye Anciente Citie of Witton. Home-coming of our Volunteers from South Africa, on Monday, June 10th, 1901*. 1901. **Locations: 6**

[755]   Bull, Stephen. *"Volunteer!" The Lancashire Rifle Volunteers, 1859-1885*. Preston: Lancashire County Books, 1993. **Locations: 3, 21**

[756]   Burnley. 17th Lancashire Rifle Volunteers. *Rules of the 17th Lancashire Rifle Volunteers*. Burnley: 17th Lancashire Rifle Volunteers Headquarters, 1860. **Locations: 9**

[757]   Connellan, J. H. *Hints to Officers, N.C. Officers and Men of The 4th Lancashire Rifle Volunteers*. Manchester: 1882. **Locations: 18B**

[758]   Crompton, Walter, and Venn, George. *Warrington Volunteers, 1798-1898*. Warrington: Sunrise Publishing Co., 1898. **Locations: 1, 3, 17, 112, LRO, NAM**

[759]   Disbrowe, Ernest John Welbourn, Captain, (ed.). *History of the Volunteer Movement in Cheshire, 1914-1920. Edited and compiled from official documents*. Stockport: Swain & Co., 1920. **Locations: 1, 4, 58, 59, 63, 102, NAM**

[760]   Eccles Volunteers. "Note on the Old Flag, and List of Volunteers." *Local Gleanings* I (1875-6) 436 **Locations: 1, CL**

[761]   Engels, Friedrich. *Selected Writings.* Edited and introduced by W.O. Henderson. Harmondsworth:Penguin, 1967. **Locations: 1, 25, 49, 111**

[762]   England. Volunteers. *The Defence of England by The Volunteers, with particular reference to the defence of Liverpool.* London: W. Mitchell, 1862. **Locations: NAM**

[763]   Forshaw, C. F. "The Stockport Volunteers." *Cheshire Notes and Queries* 5. i (1900) 53-4. **Locations: 4, 58**

[764]   Harris, William A. *Our Volunteers in Belgium; giving a description of the fetes at Liege, Spa, and Brussels in September 1869.* Liverpool: Liverpool Printing and Stationery Co, 1869. **Locations: LRO**

[765]   Hayhurst, Thomas H. *A History and Some Records of the Volunteer Movement in Bury, Heywood, Rossendale and Ramsbottom.* Bury: T. Crompton, 1887. **Locations: ***

[766]   Hesketh, W. T. "1st M.R.V.- Our First Encampment (Whit Week, 1879)." *Manchester Magazine* 1 (1879) 132-7. **Locations: 1**

[767]   Lancashire Artillery Volunteer Corps. *21st Lancashire Artillery Volunteer Corps: distribution of prizes, Theatre Royal, January 20, 1873: book of words of entertainment.* Preston: Snape (printer), 1873.
Locations: 3

[768]   --- *Manual Explanatory of Artillery Terms, with illustrations. compiled for the use of the 15th Lancashire Artillery Volunteer Corps.* London; Liverpool: Whittaker & Co., 1871. **Locations: 1, 2**

[769]   24th Lancashire Artillery Volunteers. *Rules of the 24th Lancashire Artillery Volunteers, Services accepted, June 1865. Rules approved, April 7th 1869.* Lancaster: Clark, 1869. **Locations: 28**

[770]   Lancashire Military Musters. *Lancashire: Military Musters. Letter and Instructions From the Privy Council to the Lord Lieutenant of Lancashire and Others Relating to the Provision and Inspection of Arms and Armour and the Training of Men for the Defence of the Realm.* 1869. **Locations: 1**

[771]   Lancashire. Military Volunteers. *The Lancashire and Cheshire Volunteer. A monthly journal devoted to Volunteer affairs in Lancashire and Cheshire.* 895-6. **Locations: LRO**

[772]   Lancashire Rifle Volunteers. *The "Second's Own" Camp Gazette.* 1882-3. **Locations: 1**

[773]   --- *Rochdale Rifle Volunteers. Rules and Regulations of the 24th Lancashire or Rochdale Rifle Volunteers.* Rochdale: 1860. **Locations: 13**

[774]   --- *Rules of the 17th Lancashire Rifle Volunteers. May 1860. Headquarters - Burnley.* Burnley: 1860. **Locations: 9**

[775]   --- *Twenty-Eighth Lancashire Regiment of Rifle Volunteers. Rules and regulations of the [28] Lancashire or Second Manchester Regiment of Rifle Volunteers.* Manchester: 1860. **Locations: 1**

[776] --- *VII Lancashire Rifle Volunteers, Ashton-under-Lyne. Guide to the Grand Persian Fancy Fair and Bazaar, Drill Hall, Ashton-under-Lyne, 5th, 6th, 7th and 8th May, 1886.* Ashton-under-Lyne: The Volunteers, 1886. **Locations: 102**

[777] --- *Fourth Lancashire Rifle Volunteers (Companies A to E forming the Wigan Detachment) Camp Gazette.* Deganwy: 1883. **Locations: 18**

[778] --- "A List of Lancashire Volunteer Regiments." *Local Gleanings* II (1887-8) 685, 689, 696 **Locations: 1, CL**

[779] 1st Battalion The Lancastrian Volunteers. *The Lancastrian.* 1972. **Locations: 28**

[780] Lancaster. 10th Rifle Corps. *Verses sung by one of the visitors at Wennington Hall after the dinner given by Captain Saunders to the 10th Rifle Corps on Whit Tuesday, May 29, 1860.* 1860. **Locations: 28**

[781] Liverpool Volunteers. *The Proposed Changes in the Regulations of the Volunteer Force (Report thereon by the Field Officers of the Liverpool Volunteers).* Liverpool: 1870. **Locations: 1, 2**

[782] Manchester Rifle Volunteers. *First Manchester Rifle Volunteers, Annual Distribution of Prizes. On Friday Evening, Dec. 15th 1865 a Grand Dramatic Performance will be given by the Gentlemen Amateurs of Manchester consisting of Shakespeare's play of 'The Merchant of Venice' after which Major-Gen. Sir Sydney Cotton K.C.B. will present the prizes in the Free Trade Hall.* 1865. **Locations: 1**

[783] --- *First Manchester Rifle Volunteers. Bazaar Book.* Manchester: Taylor, Garnett, Evans (Printers), 1884. **Locations: 1,3**

[784] Miller, John Christie. *A Record of the Stockport Volunteers and their Armoury.* Stockport: Swain & Co., 1969. **Locations: 102**

[785] Munn, Lieutenant-Colonel. *Standing Orders of the 3rd Battalion of Lancashire Rifle Volunteers.* 1863. **Locations: 26**

[786] Mursell, Arthur. *A Letter. Men of Manchester.* Manchester: 1860. **Locations: 1**

[787] Newton-in-Makerfield Local Militia. "Muster Roll of the Second Company." *Local Gleanings* II (1877-8) 800. **Locations: 1**

[788] Nield, James. *The End of the Mursell Volunteer Controversy.* Manchester: 1860. **Locations: 1**

[789] Preston, Thomas. *Patriots in Arms: addresses and sermons by celebrated preachers of the last century in praise of the Volunteer Movement; with an introduction and interesting historical notes by Thomas Preston.* London: Whittaker, 1881. **Locations: NAM**

[790] Preston Volunteer Training Corps. *The G.R.'s, by one of them.* Preston: Guardian Press, 1915. **Locations: 3, 12**

[791] Reeves, D. "Liverpool Rifle Volunteers 1859." *Military History Society Bulletin* 22 (February 1972) 78. **Locations: NAM**

[792] --- "Liverpool Rifle Volunteers 1859 The Liverpool Rifle Volunteer Corps." *Military History Society Bulletin* 24 (1975) 139-41. **Locations: NAM**

[793] Riley, C. O. L. *Church Parade of Preston Volunteers: Address.* Preston: Guardian (printer), 1888. **Locations: 3**

[794] Rose, R. B. "Liverpool Volunteers of 1859." *Liverpool Libraries, Museums and Art Committee Bulletin* VI (1956) 47-66. **Locations: 1, 2**

[795] Simpson, Frank. The *Old Chester Volunteers and Their Colour.* Chester: G.R. Griffith Ltd., 1911. **Locations: 4, 57, NAM**

[796] Stanley of Alderley. "Letter from Maria Josepha Lady Stanley to her father Lord Sheffield." *History Today* 4 (1954) 628. **Locations: 7, 17, 112, 115, NAM**

[797] Taylor, Edward Lyon. "The Volunteer Movement in Rochdale." *Rochdale Literary and Scientific Society Transactions* 12 (1914-16) 37-41. **Locations: 1, 13**

[798] Terry, Astley, Captain. Historical Records of the 5th Administrative Battalion Cheshire Rifle Volunteers. Sandbach: 16th C.R.V.C., 1879. **Locations: 3**

[799] Usher, H. Y. "Helmets of the Lancashire Mounted Rifle Volunteers and the 1st Lancashire Light Horse Volunteers." *Journal of the Society for Army Historical Research* 36 (December 1958) 156-7. **Locations: 1**

[800] Volunteer Journal. *Volunteer Journal.* 2 vols. 1860-62. **Locations: 1**

[801] Wigan and District Volunteer Rifles. *Rules and Lists of the Original First and Second Companies as formed in 1859.* Wigan: 1859. **Locations: 18**

[802] Wigan Drill Hall. *Grand Military Bazaar and Encampment, to Pay Off the Debt Existing on the Drill Hall.* Manchester: 1886. **Locations: 18**

[803] Wilkinson, Eric R. "Rifle Volunteers in North West Lancashire." *Centre for North West Regional Studies Regional Bulletin* 7 (Summer 1993) 19-22. **Locations: LRO**

[804] Winder, Eric. *Lancashire's Part Time Soldiers, 1690-1890.* Blackburn: Borough Recreation Department (Arts Division), 1978. **Locations: ***

[805] Yarwood, Derek. "Confined to Barracks." *Cheshire Life* 55 (June 1989) 52-7. **Locations: 4, 58**

RIFLE VOLUNTEERS ARCHIVES

Bury Archives
[806] *Tottington Rifle Corps: miscellaneous correspondence re. establishment 1860, including list*

of personnel. 1860.

Cheshire County Libraries

[807] --- *Seventh (Eighth) Annual Report of...the 27th Cheshire, or Wilmslow and Alderley Edge Volunteer Corps...1878 (1879). Ninth Annual Report of H and K Companies of the 5th Cheshire Rifle Volunteers, 1880.- 5th Cheshire Rifle Volunteers: H and K Companies. Financial Report, 1880-1881. -5th Cheshire Rifle Volunteers: H and K Companies. Annual Report, 1882-1883 [-1886-7]. -5th Volunteer Battalion, The Cheshire Regiment: H and K Companies. Annual report, 1887-8.* Wilmslow, 1879-88.

Cumbria Record Office. Carlisle

[808] *Volunteer Corps.* Contents include papers relating to 7th Cumberland Rifle Volunteers, Workington: minute book, enrolments, account book, equipment ledger (1864-74); letter re subscription (1893) 1st Cumberland Voluntary Artillery: money raised towards drill hall (1899).

Lancaster Library

[809] Whalley, Joseph Lawson, Colonel., (ed.). *Scrapbook of newspaper cuttings, 1867-1875, to do with 24th Lancashire Artillery Volunteers, presented to the Lancashire Position Batteries, 5th Lancashire Volunteer Artillery, by Col. J.L. Whalley, Dec 1893.* 1867-75.

[810] --- "Rules and Regulations to be observed by the Royal Lancaster Volunteers. June 17th 1797." *Lancaster Library Scrapbook* 2 (folio) (1797) 270.

Liverpool Libraries and Information Services, Record Office and Local History Department

[811] *39th (Welsh) Lancashire Rifle Volunteers. Records*, 1859-77; *Altcar Rifle Range Committee: Letter Book, 1865-1869- with accounts for 1864.* 1 vol. 1864-9.

Merseyside Record Office

[812] *Liverpool Rifles Association, 1882-1977.* (Notes: The papers of P.S. Pennington, as Secretary of the Liverpool Rifles Association; the veterans association of the 6th (Rifle) Battalion, the King's (Liverpool) Regiment. Contents of collection include <u>Annual General Meetings</u>: Minute book, 1934-76; attendance book, 1948-77; Treasurer's expense book, 1947-75; Annual account balances and Secretary's expense accounts, 1967-74; Lists of members; A.G.M. and annual re-union agendas; Biannual newsletter; Correspondence, programmes, photographs, articles cartoons and menus relating to annual reunion dinner; menus for annual reunion dinner; photographs of the regiment; Memorabilia.

National Army Museum

[813] 8th Lancashire Artillery Volunteer Corps. *Commission issued by the Earl of Sefton, Lord Lieutenant of Lancashire to George Russell Rogerson as Captain in the 8th Lancashire Artillery Volunteer Corps, 10 Dec 1870.* 1870.

[814] Merseyside Volunteer Infantry Brigade. *Printed papers relating to the Cannock Chase manoeuvres of July and August 1894.* 1894.

Oldham Local Studies Library

[815] Oldham Chronicle. *The Volunteer Movement in Oldham 1859-1939. Cuttings from the Chronicle.* [n.d.]

V. Territorial Forces

[816] 13th Lancashire Battalion, The Parachute Regiment T. A. *Presentation of Colours by Field Marshall The Viscount Montgomery of Alamein, 25th October, 1953.* 1953. **Locations: NAM**

[817] 156 (Merseyside and Greater Manchester) Transport Regiment RCT (V). *156 (Merseyside and Greater Manchester) Transport Regiment RCT (V) Regimental History.* Liverpool: North West Publications, 1981. **Locations: 3**

[818] Barnes, Wally. *The Battle of Burtonwood: Bewsey Bridge-Gate 4 August 1942.* Wigan: Owl Books, 1991. **Locations: 2, 4, 14, 18, 40**

[819] Bigwood, George. *The Lancashire Fighting Territorials.* London: Country Life, 1916. **Locations: 3, 18, LRO**

[820] --- *The Lancashire Fighting Territorials in Gallipoli.* London: Country Life 1916. (2nd edition) **Locations: 1, 13**

[821] Bolton, George. "Battle Royal." *Lancashire Life* 3 (Winter 1954-5) 35-7. **Locations: 1, LRO**

[822] Cheshire Territorial and Auxiliary Forces Association. *Short history of the units administered by the Cheshire Territorial and Auxiliary Forces Association.* London: Reid-Hamilton, 1950.
Locations: 4, 102, NAM

[823] Cook, A. L. Michael. *Altcar: the story of a rifle range.* Liverpool: Territorial, Auxiliary and Volunteer Reserve Association for the N.W. & I.O.M., 1989. **Locations: 3, LRO, LSM**

[824] County Borough of Oldham. *Ceremony of the honouring of the 41st (Oldham) Royal Tank Regiment (T.A.). The Town Hall Oldham, Saturday 17th July, 1954.* 1954. **Locations: 11**

[825] Cumberland and Westmorland Joint Territorial Force Association. *Regulations and Instructions to Commanding Officers.* 1911. **Locations: 5**

[826] East Lancashire Division (Territorial Force). *Programme of the Royal Review of The East Lancashire Division (Territorial Force) held by His Most Gracious Majesty the King at Worsley Park, on the 6th July 1909.* Altrincham and London: 1909. **Locations: 1, 16, 25, 53**

[827] East Lancashire Territorial and Auxiliary Forces. *Review of the Territorial and Auxiliary Forces of East Lancashire.* 1951. **Locations: 1**

[828] Hugh, James. "The Territorial Army in Cheshire - VII: 102 Amphibious Transport Column RASC (TA)." *Cheshire Life* 17 (July 1951) 25-7. **Locations: 4, 58**

[829] --- "The Territorial Army in Cheshire - XI: R.E.M.E." *Cheshire Life* 17 (November 1951) 23. **Locations: 4, 58**

[830] --- "The Territorial Army in Cheshire-VI: Royal Signals." *Cheshire Life* 17.6 (June 1951) 22-3. **Locations: 4, 58**

[831] --- "The Territorial Army in Cheshire - XII: 23 (W) Field Ambulance RAMC (TA)." *Cheshire Life* 17 (December 1951) 27. **Locations: 4, 58**

[832] Lancashire: Voluntary Territorial Army Units. "An Account of Their Traditions and Work." *Defence* III (April 1938). **Locations: 7**

[833] Liverpool Rifles Association. *The Greenjacket: official publication of the Liverpool Rifles Association.* Liverpool: The Association, 1924-8. **Locations: MRO**

[834] --- *Programme for the official opening of the new drill hall, Mather Avenue, Liverpool.* Liverpool: The Association, 1938. **Locations: MRO**

[835] --- *Rifle, Lewis gun and machine gun programmes, 1934-1936.* Liverpool: The Association, 1934-6. **Locations: MRO**

[836] --- *Terms and Conditions of service in the Territorial Army.* Liverpool: The Association, 1922. **Locations: MRO**

[837] Lomas, A.D., Lieutenant-Colonel, (comp.). *West Lancashire Territorial Force.* Southport: Visitor Office, 1911. **Locations: 3**

[838] Miles (pseud.). "The Territorial Army in Cheshire. Number 2. The Cheshire Yeomanry (Earl of Chester's)." *Cheshire Life* 17 (February 1951) 22-3. **Locations: 4, 58**

[839] --- "The County's Territorials. Number 3. The 170th Cavalry Field Ambulance." *Cheshire Life* 5 (December 1938) 50. **Locations: 4, 58**

[840] Stephenson, W. H., (ed.). *West Lancashire Territorial and Auxiliary Forces' Association: Golden Jubilee, 1908-1958.* Southport: Johnson, 1958. **Locations: 3**

[841] Territorial, Auxiliary and Volunteer Reserve Association for the North West and The Isle of Man. *North West 75th Anniversary Booklet, 1908-1983.* North West Publications: Liverpool, 1983. **Locations: 3, 7, 57, 102**

[842] West Lancashire Division (Territorial Forces). *Is it my Duty to Serve my Country.* 1911. **Locations: 17**

[843] West Lancashire Territorial and Auxiliary Forces Association. *A Short History of the Units administered by the West Lancashire Territorial and Auxiliary Forces Association.* 1952. **Locations: 3, 16**

[844] --- *Twenty-sixth Lancashire Battalion Stand-down parade Sunday 3rd December 1944.* 1944. **Locations: 18B**

TERRITORIAL FORCE ARCHIVES

Cheshire Record Office
[845]   *Cheshire Territorial Association correspondence file. 1909-66.*

Clitheroe Local Studies Library
[846]   *Cheshire Territorial Force, National Reserve and Territorials, 1911-1922: Records. 1911-22.*

Cumbria Record Office. Carlisle.
[847]   *Territorial and Auxiliary Forces Association of Cumberland and Westmorland. Records, 1908-76; World War I. The Territorial Army. Minutes of the Territorial and Auxiliary Forces Association for the counties of Cumberland and Westmorland, 1914-18; World War II. The Home Front. Territorial Army Records. Minute Book of the Territorial and Auxiliary Forces Association for the counties of Cumberland and Westmorland, 1939-45.*

Lancashire County Library
[848]   East Lancashire Association. Territorial Force. *Association minutes and abstracts of committee proceedings, 1908-14.*

Wigan Heritage Services. Archives.
[849]   Military History Records include "Wigan Military Chronicle": unpublished MS history by G. Derbyshire (1949-74): Vol.1: The Yeomanry and Volunteers; Vol.2: The Territorial Force; Vol.3: The Territorial Army; Vol.4: The Territorial Army. A supplementary volume is entitled "The Colours-5th Battalion Manchester Regiment".

IV. ROYAL AIR FORCE AND ASSOCIATED UNITS

Although aspects of the history of the Royal Air Force in the North West have attracted the attention of a number of researchers, as the following section indicates there is no single general historical account. Informative general introductions to the history of the RAF include J.D.R. Rawlings, *The History of the Royal Air Force* (Temple Smith, 1984) and Peter Lewis, *Squadron Histories: RFC, RNAS and RAF 1912-1959* (Putnam, 1959). An excellent survey of sources is N.A. Webber, "A Guide to the Literature on the History of the Royal Air Force 1918-1968", London University, Ph.D., 1977. Researchers should also note that the Royal Air Force Museum at Hendon, contains a Department of Aviation Records with large collections of archives covering the RFC and RAF, as well as civil and commercial aviation.

[850] 613 Squadron. *613 (City of Manchester) Squadron: About the men and the machines of the 613 (City of Manchester) Squadron based at Ringway Airport, 1939 to 1945.* [196-]. **Locations: 1**

[851] Air Training Corps. Huyton. *Official Programme of the 40th Anniversary of 1982 (Huyton) Squadron of Air Training Corps.* 1982. **Locations: 40**

[852] Air Training Corps. Manchester Wing. *Wing Routine Orders, March 1941-July 1945.* 2 vols. 1942-5. **Locations: 1**

[853] Air Training Corps. North Lancashire Wing. *Location List, January 1971.* 1971. **Locations: 3**

[854] Air Training Corps. North West Command. *Commandant's Memorandum, June 1942-July 1945.* **Locations: 1**

[855] Air Training Corps. Prescot. *Official History of the Air Training Corps 1438 (Prescot) Squadron. (21st Anniversary).* [n.d.] **Locations: 40**

[856] Billings, G. M. "The Burtonwood Story." *Lancashire Life* 3.9 (1954-5) 20-3. **Locations: LRO**

[857] Braham, John Randle Daniel. *Scramble! by J.R.D. "Bob" Braham.* London: Frederick Muller, 1961. **Locations: 3**

[858] Brunskill, Keith R. "Per Ardua Ad Astra..." *Lancashire Constabulary Journal* 6.4 (Winter 1973) 169-72. **Locations: LRO**

[859] Burton, Fred H. *Mission to Burma: The story of 177 Squadron.* Bolton: Blackburns Ltd, 1991. **Locations: 1, 7, 18, 26**

[860] Butler, Philip Henry. *An Illustrated History of Liverpool Airport.* Liverpool: Merseyside Aviation Society, 1983. **Locations: 1, 2, 3, 4, 18, RAFM**

[861] Chartres, John. "The Army on Wings." *Cheshire Life* 19 (January 1953) 23. **Locations: 4, 58**

[862] Connon, Peter. *An Aeronautical History of the Cumbria, Dumfries and Galloway.* 2 vols. Penrith: St. Patrick's Press, 1982-84. **Locations: RAFM**

[863] Ferguson, Aldon Patrick. *Burtonwood: 8th Air Force Base Air Depot.* Reading: Airfield, 1986. **Locations: 3, CL, RAFM**

[864] --- *A History of R.A.F. Woodvale.* Liverpool: Merseyside Aviation Society, 1974. **Locations: 1, 2, 3, 8, 40**

[865] --- *A History of R.A.F. Woodvale.* Liverpool: Merseyside Aviation Society, 1980. (2nd ed.) **Locations: 1, 2, 3, 4, 115, RAFM**

[866] --- *A History of Royal Air Force Sealand.* Liverpool: Merseyside Aviation Society, 1978. **Locations: 1, 4, 14, 52, RAFM**

[867] --- *RAF Burtonwood: 50 years of photographs.* Wargrave: Airfield Publications, 1989. **Locations: 3, 14, 18, 40**

[868] --- *Royal Air Force Woodvale. The First 50 years.* Wargrave: Airfield Publications, 1991. **Locations: 14, 18, 40**

[869] Groom, Graham. *The Borough of Darwen Spitfire: a brief history of the VR7219.* 1993. **Locations: 3**

[870] Hodgson, J. E. G. *The War Service of 69779 Air Mechanic Joseph Gillett Hodgson 3rd Aircraft Park, Royal Flying Corps/Royal Air Force.* 1992. **Locations: 3**

[871] Hugh, James. "The Royal Auxiliary Air Force in Cheshire." *Cheshire Life* 18 (January 1952) 21. **Locations: 4, 58**

[872] James, Edward. "Farewell to Padgate." *Lancashire Life* 5 (February,1957) 20-1, 37. **Locations: 1**

[873] Kniveton, Gordon N. *Manx Aviation in War and Peace.* Douglas: Manx Experience, 1985. **Locations: MNH**

[874] Leigh Borough. *Exchange of the Coat of Arms of the Corporation of the Borough of Leigh and the Badge of the Royal Air Force Station, Padgate, at the Town Hall, Leigh, on Tuesday, the 14th December, 1954.* 1954. **Locations: 29**

[875] Manchester. Ringway Airport. "The Rousing Story of Ringway." *Cheshire Life* 12 (January 1946) 23. **Locations: 4, 58**

[876] Margerison, Russell. *Boys at War.* Bolton: Ross Anderson, 1986. **Locations: ***

[877] Mason, Ernest Mitchelson. *Imshi: a fighter pilot's letters to his mother.* London: W.H. Allen, 1943. **Locations: 1, 3, 14**

[878] Miles (pseud.). "The County's Territorials. Number 8. No. 610 (County of Chester) Squadron, Royal Auxiliary Air Force." *Cheshire Life* 5 (May 1939) 32. **Locations: 4, 58**

[879] Newnham, Maurice. *Prelude to Glory: The Creation of Britain's Parachute Army.* 1947. **Location:1**

[880] Northern Air Division. "Good-Bye to All That." *Cheshire Life* 23 (March 1957) 35-6. **Locations: 4, 58**

[881] Polish Air Force Association, Blackpool. *25th Anniversary Souvenir Brochure.* Blackpool: Polish Air Force Association, 1976. **Locations: 3**

[882] --- *Eagle Club Journal. Summer 1973.* Eagle Club: Blackpool, 1973. **Locations: 3**

[883] Radcliffe, Leslie N. "Per Ardua ad Astra." *Cheshire Life* 15 (May 1949) 14-15. **Locations: 4, 58**

[884] --- "The Steep Ascent of Heaven." *Cheshire Life* 19 (October 1953) 39-40. **Locations: 4, 58**

[885] R.A.F. Padgate. *Gateway: The Official R.A.F. Padgate Magazine.* 2 vols. Shrewsbury: Wilding and Son Ltd., 1948-9. **Locations: 17**

[886] Rainford, R. W. B. "The "Blip" Squad." *Cheshire Life* 28 (May 1962) 50-1. **Locations: 4, 58**

[887] Robinson, Brian R. *Aviation in Manchester: a short history.* Manchester: Royal Aeronautical Society (Manchester Branch), 1977. **Locations: ***

[888] Royal Air Forces Association: Preston Branch. *East Views.* Vol. 1-. Preston: R.A.F. Association, 1952-88. **Locations: 3**

[889] --- *Monthly News Letter.* December 1950-August 1952. Preston: Snape (printers), 1950-2. **Locations: 12**

[890] --- *Report and Accounts, 1953-70.* Preston: Snape (printers), 1953-70. **Locations: 3, 12**

[891] Sharp, John R. *Over the Wall: a personal history of wartime RAF Station Heaton Park, Manchester.* Manchester: J.R. Sharp, 1992. **Locations: 1**

[892] Smith, David J. *Action Stations 3: Military Airfields of Wales and the North-West.* Cambridge: Patrick Stephens, 1981. **Locations: ***

[893] --- *Action Stations 3: Military Airfields of Wales and the North-West.* Cambridge: Patrick Stephens, 1990. (2nd ed.) **Locations: ***

[894] Smith, David. "The Day Sub-Lt. Reggie Shaw got lost en route for Stretton." *Cheshire Life* 47 (December 1981) 38-9. **Locations: 4, 58**

[895] Thomson, J. *One of Many: West Africa bound airman's true war story: Adabo: written in Africa in 1943.* 1989. **Locations: 2**

[896] Walsh, George. *Personal Effects.* Lowesmoor: Square One, 1989. **Locations: 3, 13**

[897] Webb, Raymond John. *Early Ringway. An account of the aircraft visiting Ringway, as seen through the airport registers and the camera lens, June 1938-May 1940 and January 1946-December 1951*. Bramhall: Webstar Graphics, 1978. **Locations: 3, 4, 15, 52, 59, 115, RAFM**

[898] Willis, Steve, and Hollis, B. *Military Airfields in the British Isles 1939-1945*. Kettering: The Authors, 1987. **Locations: RAFM**

ARCHIVES

Bolton Archives
[899] *World War II. Royal Air Force. Aeroplane Log Book, 1943*.

Cheshire Record Office
[900] *Royal Auxiliary Air Force 610 Squadron scrapbook 1931-1946*.

Lancashire County Library
[901] Royal Air Force. Bomber Command. *Aircraft log book: type Lancaster, No.FE 186, Squadron No.61, September-December 1943*.

Lancashire Record Office
[902] *Blackpool: Women's Junior Air Corps No.41 (3rd Blackpool) Unit, management committee minutes, log books, financial records 1940-47*.

Manchester Central Library. Local Studies Unit
[903] Parachute Training School No. 1, Ringway. *Group Captain John Kilkenny; transcript of tape recorded interview*.

Trafford Local Studies Library
[904] Women's Junior Air Corps, Sale. *Miscellaneous Items*. 1940-.

Wirral Libraries
[905] Birkenhead. World War II. *Aircraft Log Book*. This log book, which will record the operational activities of an aircraft is a tribute to the success achieved by Birkenhead Savings Committee in the Wings for Victory National Savings Campaign, 1943.

V. ROYAL AND MERCHANT NAVIES

The Royal and Merchant Navies in the North West have not attracted the attention shown to the other armed forces. Nationally the history of the Royal Navy is served by an extensive bibliography of analytical studies, popular illustrated accounts and reference works. George Manwaring's bibliography should be consulted at an early stage by any serious researcher [40].

[906] Ashton, W. *1939/45 War. A Saddleworth Sailor*. 2 vols. 1989. **Locations: 102**

[907] Association of Naval Ex-Servicemen, Burnley and District. *Trafalgar Remembrance Parade and Service, 22 Oct 1950*. 1950. **Locations: 9**

[908] Branigan, D. P. "H.M.S. Chester." *Cheshire Life* 40 (October 1974) 82-3. **Locations: 4, 58**

[909] Chalmers, W. S. *Max Horton and the Western Approaches*. London: Hodder & Stoughton, 1954. **Locations: ***

[910] H.M.S. Penelope. *Our Penelope (H.M.S. Penelope), by her company*. 1943. **Locations: 3**

[911] Kemp, Paul. *Liverpool and the Battle of the Atlantic, 1939-45*. Liverpool: Maritime Books, 1993. **Locations: 2, 3, 4, 18, 57**

[912] Kennish, William. *A method for concentrating the fire of a broadside of a ship of war*. London: John Bradley, 1837. **Locations: MNH**

[913] Lane, Tony. *The Merchant Seaman's War*. Manchester: Manchester University Press, 1990. **Locations: ***

[914] Manchester. Navy. *King George and the Wooden Walls of Old England Forever! Wanted for the Townships of Pool and Helperby, eight active young men for His Majesty's Navy. [Manchester] [1795] By applying to Robert Walker at Edw. Roden's Weaver's Arms, Cockpit Hill, or Wm. Club, the Seven Stars, Heaton Lane, Manchester*. 1795. **Locations: 1**

[915] Pertwee, Jon. *Moon Boots and Dinner Suits*. London: Elm Tree, 1984. **Locations: 3, 4, 8, 10, 14, 20, 52, MNH**

[916] Pugh, N. R. "Coastal convoy memories." *Sea Breezes* 46 (1972) 116-19. **Locations: 2, MMM**

[917] --- "H.M.Y. Eradne: another yacht at war." *Sea Breezes* 44 (1970) 342-6. **Locations: 2, MMM**

[918] Robertson, Terence. *Walker, R.N. The story of Captain Frederic John Walker, C.B., D.S.O. and three bars, R.N.* London: White Lion Publishers Ltd., 1975. **Locations: ***

[919] Robinson, H. A. "The Five Ships of Rock Ferry." *Cheshire Life* 22 (April 1956) 71. **Locations: 4, 58**

[920] Roeder, Charles. "Francois Thurot (1727-1760) and his Naval Engagement off the Isle of Man." *Manx Notes and Queries* (1904) 1-16. **Locations: MNH**

[921] Roskill, Stephen Wentworth. *A Merchant Fleet in War: Alfred Holt and Co., 1939-1945.* London: Collins, 1962. **Locations: 1, 2, 3, 4, 8, 10, 13, 57, MMM**

[922] Scarth, Alan J. *Liverpool as HQ and Base. Academic paper for The Battle of the Atlantic- a conference organised jointly by the Society for Nautical Research, the Merseyside Maritime Museum and the Naval Historical Branch (M.o.D.). at the Merseyside Maritime Museum, Albert Dock, Liverpool, 25-28 May, 1993.* 1993. **Locations: MMM**

[923] Sotheby's. *Catalogue of Military and Naval Campaign Medals, Gallantry Awards and other English and Foreign Orders, Medals and Decorations. The property of the late Albert Broadley Esq. and other owners. Date of Sale Thursday 8th July 1982.* 1982. **Locations: 94**

[924] Southport Royal Naval Artillery. *Rules of the Southport Royal Navy Artillery Volunteers.* [1876]. **Locations: 16**

[925] Spring, Howard. "Seaman Arnold Baker, Merchant Navy." in Derek Tangye (ed.), *Went The Day Well*. 1942. pp.131-8. **Locations: 7**

[926] Stewart-Brown, Ronald. *Liverpool Ships in the Eighteenth Century.* Liverpool: University Press, 1932. **Locations: 1, 8, 14, 45, 85, 202**

[927] Tallon, J. *Warrants from the Mayor and Mr. J. Tallon, Justices, to the Constables and Serjeants at Mace of Lancaster to search for idle unemployed persons and rogues, for service in the Navy. 8 Sep. 1795, 6 Oct. 1795.* 1795. **Locations: 28**

[928] Tatham, William. *Return of persons enrolled as volunteers in H.M. Navy at Lancaster, by William Tatham, Churchwarden, at the Petty Sessions, Lancaster. 10 April 1795.* 1795. **Locations: 28**

[929] Travis, Arthur. *From War to Westhoughton.* Warrington: P. & D. Riley, 1992. **Locations: CL**

[930] Wardle, Arthur C. "The King's Ships Named Liverpool, 1741-1941." *Transactions of the Historic Society of Lancashire and Cheshire* 93 (1941) 131-3. **Locations: ***

[931] Warren, C. E. T., and J. Benson. *The Admiralty Regrets. The Story of H.M. Submarines "Thetis" and "Thunderbolt".* 1958. **Locations: ***

[932] Wemyss, David Edward Gillespie. *Walker's Groups in the Western Approaches; illustrated with many official photographs, with a foreword by Admiral Sir Max Horton.* Liverpool: Liverpool Daily Post and Echo Ltd., 1948. **Locations: 1, 2, 4, 9, MMM**

[933] Williams, Jack. *H.M.S. Penelope: the history of those ships of the Royal Navy which have borne the name "Penelope".* Blackpool: The Author, 1983. **Locations: 3**

[934] Williams, Mark. *Captain Gilbert Roberts, R.N. and the Anti-U-Boat School.* London: Casell Ltd., 1979. **Locations: ***

[935] Winton, John. *Hands to Action Stations: Naval Poetry and Verse from World War II.* Denbigh: Bryn Clwyd, 1980. **Locations: 1, 2, 57, 59**

[936] Wood, Richard. *Abandon Ship.* 1985. **Locations: 3**

ARCHIVES

Colne Library
[937] Colne Library. Photographic material. *H.M.S. Colne adopted by Colne, Trawden and Foulridge during Warship Week March 1942.*

Cumbria Record Office. Barrow
[938] *Vickers Ltd., Barrow: Rolls of technical drawings, particularly from the Naval Armaments Office.* 1900-.

Lancashire Record Office
[939] *Hulton of Hulton Miscellaneous Papers.* c.1645-82.

Lancaster Library
[940] Atkinson, Robert. *Letter from Robert Atkinson at Liverpool to his parents in Lancaster.* 1760.

[941] Brockbank, John. "Certificate that William Mackreth, employed by John Brockbank, as a journeyman shipwright is to pass free and unmolested. Signed by John Brockbank, and William Haygarth, Commander of the Impress. Lancaster, 8th Feb. 1780." *Lancaster Library Scrapbook* 2 (folio) (1780) 222.

[942] H.M.S. Lancaster. *Message of greeting and signatures of the crew of H.M.S. Lancaster. Also poem by one of the ship's company. Warship Week, Feb. 28th-March 7th, 1942.* 1942.

[943] Lancaster Library. Naval Records. *Certificate of the service of Robert Hanlon of Lancaster, in the Royal Navy 1901-1902.*

[944] --- *Warrant for the pardon and release of John Wheeler and others, imprisoned in Lancaster Castle for a year for assisting in rescuing John Coopley from being impressed into the Royal Navy. 16 Apr. 1810.*

Manchester Central Library. Local Studies Unit
[945] Cochrane, D. B. *Collection of Nautical Press Cuttings, including 3 vols. on the Port of Manchester, 1920-73.*

Merseyside Maritime Museum.
[946] *World War I and World War II Archives.* The museum has selective holdings of World War I and World War II records only. See main entry in World War I section.

Wigan Heritage Services. Archives.
[947] Freeman, Raymond. *Letter about sinking of Wigan's adopted ship H.M.S. Janus by a survivor.* [n.d.]

VI. 1750-1914

This section identifies publications and archives from the mid-eighteenth century up to the outbreak of the First World War. It includes accounts covering the Napoleonic Wars, Crimean War and the Boer War. It includes entries which did not fit easily into the sections devoted to individual regiments, and the reader should be aware that relevant material for this period will also be found in those sections covering the region's regiments.

[948] Anon. "Soldiers' life in Hulme Barracks." *Sphinx Magazine* (1868). **Locations: 15**

[949] Axon, William. "The Thin Red Line." *Cheshire Gleanings*. Manchester: Tubbs, Brook & Chrystal, 1884. pp.95-100. **Locations: 4, 17, 69, 76**

[950] Bancroft, James W. *The Way to Glory: Men of the North West who rode in the Charge of the Light Brigade*. Swinton, Manchester: Neil Richardson, 1988. **Locations: 3, 7, 21, 102, BOM**

[951] Bowers, Maunsell, Lieutenant-Colonel. *A Short History of the 5th Princess Charlotte of Wales's Dragoon Guards*. Meerut: "Official" Machine Printing Press, 1896. **Locations: 1**

[952] Bury Loyal Association. *A Sermon Preached in the Parish Church of Bury on. 18th of October, 1798... on the Occasion of the Colours Being Presented to The Bury Loyal Association; Together with the Form of Presentation*. Bury: Bury Loyal Association, 1798. **Locations: 10**

[953] Coward, B. "The Lieutenancy of Lancashire and Cheshire in the Sixteenth and early Seventeenth Centuries." *Transactions of the Historic Society of Lancashire and Cheshire* 119 (1968) 39-64. **Locations: ***

[954] Cox, Bernard William. *The Dress Distinctions of the 3rd Carabiniers-P.O.W.D.G.* Cambridge: Langridge's Military Publications, 1962. **Locations:**

[955] De Curzon, Alfred. *Dr. James Currie and the French Prisoners of War in Liverpool, 1800-1801*. Liverpool: Howell, 1926. **Locations: NAM**

[956] An Englishman, (pseud). *A Letter to Lieut. Colonel Hanson. By an Englishman*. Manchester: 1806. **Locations: 1**

[957] Farrow, John. *Oldham at War 1793: Extracts from the annals of William Rowbottom*. 1793. **Locations: 11**

[958] Fell, Alfred. *A Furness Military Chronicle*. Ulverston: Kitchin & Co., 1937. **Locations: 1, 3, 5, 6, 112, LRO**

[959] Holcroft, Fred. *The Devil's Hill; Local Men at the Battle of Spion Kop*. Wigan: Heritage Service Publications, 1992. **Locations: 18B**

[960] Kersal Moor. *An Account of a sham fight which was fought on Kersal Moor, 15 January 1804*. 1804. **Locations: 1**

[961] Kirby, Henry L. *The Russian Guns: the Story of Preston's Crimean War Memorial*. Preston: The Author, 1982. **Locations: 3**

[962] Knowles, Robert. *The War in the Peninsula: some letters of Lieut. Robert Knowles, a Bolton Officer. Arranged by Sir Lees Knowles.* Bolton: 1909. [Reprinted from Bolton Journal and Guardian for private circulation]. **Locations: 1, 7, CL, LRO**

[963] Lancashire and Cheshire Regiments. *The Story of the Lancashire and Cheshire Regiments: the History of the Heroic Deeds of the Soldiers of Lancashire and Cheshire, in All Parts of the World Since 1685, including the Part Taken by these Regiments in the Present War; Together With Accounts of the Organization and Lists of the Officers of the Regiments as now Constituted.* 1914. **Locations: 2, 8, 16, 57**

[964] Lancaster. Commissioners. *Impress warrant from the Commissioners to the constables, serjeants at mace, churchwarden and overseers of the poor of Lancaster, to search for idlers etc. for the army and navy. 1 March 1779.* 1779. **Locations: 28**

[965] Liverpool Fusiliers. *Proceedings of the General Court Martial in the Trial of Alexander Grant Carmichael, Captain and Adjutant of the Liverpool Fusiliers, on a charge exhibited against him by William Earle, Esq., Lieutenant-Colonel Commandant. Published from the notes of a short-hand writer.* Liverpool: W. James, 1804. **Locations: LRO**

[966] McKenzie-Annand, A. "An Officer of the 1st Lancashire Light Horse Volunteers and a Lady c.1865." *Journal of the Society for Army Historical Research* 48 (1970) 195-204. **Locations: 1**

[967] Manchester. Grand Review of Troops, 1870. *Official Programme of the Grand Review of Troops Under the Command of Major General Sir J. Garvock, K.C.B. Commanding Northern District, This Day Saturday June 18th, 1870 on the Manchester Racecourse.* 1870. **Locations: 1**

[968] Manchester. Royal Marines. *Two Guineas Bounty, and a Crown to Drink His Majesty's Health. For all aspiring, active, well made young fellows able and willing to serve in marines. Applying to Sergt. Aylward at the Sign of the Weavers Arms, Sugar Lane.* 1796. **Locations: 1**

[969] Mayer, Joseph. *On the arming of levies in the Hundred of Wirral, in the County of Chester, and the introduction of small fire arms as weapons of war in place of bows and arrows.* 1859. **Locations: 1, 57**

[970] Parker, Rev Canon, and Rev R. Jackson Cuppage. *In Memoriam. Records of the death and funeral, with brief notices of the life and military career, of the late lamented Sir Jas. Yorke Scarlett, G.C.B. and the funeral sermons.* Burnley: W. Waddington (printer), 1872. **Locations: CL**

[971] Partridge, M. S. "Cannon or Commerce? The Case of the Liverpool Battery 1824-1885." *Transactions of the Historic Society of Lancashire and Cheshire* 135 (1986) 83-98. **Locations: ***

[972] Perrett, Bryan, (ed.). *A Hawk at War: the Peninsular War. Reminiscences of General Sir Thomas Brotherton, CB.* Chippenham: Picton, 1986. **Locations: 3**

[973] Peters, H. "Fleetwood and the Military Connexion." 1976. **Locations: 3**

[974] Preston, Henry, Ens. *Journal of Ens. Henry Preston 90th Foot, 12 April 1849-17 October 1851 kept during service in Ashton-under-Lyne, Manchester and Cork.* 2 vols., 1849-51. **Locations: NAM**

[975] Regiment of Body Guards. *Wanted a Few Good Recruits to Complete His Majesty's First Regiment of Body Guards...12 Guineas Bounty by Applying to Sgt. Huff, at the Black Bull, Deansgate, Manchester.* 1795. **Locations: 1**

[976] Sargeaunt, B.E. *A Military History of the Isle of Man.* Arbroath: T. Buncle & Co., 1949. **Locations: 1, MNH**

[977] --- *The Royal Manx Fencibles.* Aldershot: Gale & Polden, 1947. **Locations: 1, MNH**

[978] Smith, Sam D., (ed.). *James Yorke Scarlett: A Burnley Balaclava Hero: Lecture to the Burnley Historical Society, March 1955.* Burnley: Historical Society, 1971. **Locations: 3**

[979] Towneley Hall Art Gallery and Museum. *The Regiments of Lancashire: Programme of a Military Exhibition, (held at) Towneley Hall Art Gallery and Museum, Burnley, 14th April-30th September, 1973.* Burnley: County Borough of Burnley, Art Gallery and Museums sub-committee, 1973. **Locations: 3, 9, 23, 33, 111, BOM**

[980] Whalley, J. Lawson. *Catalogue of British War medals, crosses, badges, decorations, medals for saving life, and miscellaneous medals, in the collection of J. Lawson Whalley.* Lancaster: Printed for private circulation, 1877. **Locations: 28**

[981] Wright, John. "Balaclava to Burnley." *Lancashire Life* 3 (July,1986) 31. **Locations: LRO**

ARCHIVES

Bolton Archives

[982] *Lancashire Lieutenancy Records (Bolton Sub-Division). Bolton Sub-Division Minute Book, 1800-1809, 1809-1860.*

[983] Bolton Museum and Art Gallery. Collection of Medals. From the Peninsular War to World War I and World War II and after with, in a number of cases, accompanying documents, photographs, diaries and information. Many recipients were local men serving in various regiments, local and non-local, in the Navy and RAF.

Bolton Libraries

[984] Bolton Regiments. *Miscellaneous notes.* [n.d.]

Burnley Library

[985] Burnley Barracks. *Documents relating to the sale of Burnley Barracks, 1906.*

[986] Burnley. General Scarlett. *Miscellaneous papers connected with preparations to commemorate the centenary of the death of General Sir James Yorke Scarlett.* [n.d.]

Bury Archives

[987] *Geoffrey Hutchinson, Lord Ilford of Bury: Family Papers.* Contents include correspondence of John Richard Hutchinson, papers with reference to scheme for army reform, 1904-5.

Cheshire Record Office

[988] *Crimean War. Letters and papers of General Sir Richard Wilbraham and of Colonel Robert Hibberts.* [n.d.]; *Napoleonic War. Diary of Lieutenant Colonel William Tomkinson.* [n.d.]; *Officers' commissions 1855-1889.*

Chester City Record Office

[989] *Welsh and Midland Command and Western Command: Specialist Sanitary Officer: Records.* These include correspondence, orders, reports and returns, 1902-14.

Chetham's Library

[990] Greenhalgh, Joseph Dodson. *Diary of Roger, otherwise Captain Dewhurst, of Halliwell Hall, Parish of Deane.* Bolton, 1881.

Colne Library

[991] Colne. Red Lion Inn. *Minutes of a meeting at the Red Lion Inn, Colne to take into consideration the proposal of forming an armed association for defence of the country against foreign and domestic enemies 8th May, 1798.* 1798. **Locations: 1, 23**

[992] Photographic material. *Colne Ambulance men in South Africa War,* 1899-1902.

Cumbria Record Office. Carlisle

[993] *Boer War. Records.* Contents: Diary of Private J. McLoughlin of M. Company 1st Border Regiment (copy) (1899-1900); Transvaal War Relief Fund: reports, accounts, subscription lists, correspondence (1899-1932); Esme Howard's experiences including military service with the Duke of Cambridge's Corps, 13th Regiment Imperial Yeomanry (1900); Correspondence re the war and its consequences (1900-2); Cumberland Transvaal Relief Fund: minute books, accounts, applications for relief, service verification (1903-32).

[994] *Crimean War. Records.* Contents: 18 letters from a Captain serving in the 21st Fusiliers; written from Sebastopol and Malta; includes campaign maps (1854-6); 54 letters re experiences in the Crimean War (1854-6). 1854-56.

Lancashire Record Office

[995] *Dawson-Greene of Whittington: letter of Captain D.C. Greene from Crimea 1856, commissions of D.C. Greene 1856, and H. Dawson-Greene 1880; James Brown: photocopy transcripts of correspondence of James Brown of Manchester, with diary of service overseas in East Essex (44th) Regiment of Foot 1798-1801; Peters, H. William Robinson, Waterloo Veteran.* [n.d.]; *Private W. Cooper: Letter from Private W. Cooper at Lucknow (India) to sister Annie at Blackburn,* [n.d.]; *Quarter Sessions. Defence of the Realm. Lieutenancy Records, 1796-1866; Quarter Sessions. Defence Records, 1795-6; Stanley, Earls of Derby. Correspondence and Miscellaneous Records, 1692-1814.*

Lancaster Library

[996] Fleming, Michael. *Letter from Michael Fleming at Kendal to his father Sir Daniel Fleming re. the desertion of his men at Preston. 18 Dec 1695.* 1695.

[997] Lancaster. Army and Navy. "The names of the persons who have subscribed as under for raising a sum of money to be applied in purchasing cloaths, or other necessary articles for the seamen and soldiers now employed in His Majesty's Service. Lancaster, 17th December 1793." *Lancaster Library Scrapbook* 2 (folio) (1793) 257.

[998] Thomas Pownall's Troop of Dragoons. *Receipt signed by four inhabitants and innholders of Lancaster for payment for quartering Capt. Thomas Pownall's Troop of Dragoons. 8 Aug 1689.* 1689.

Liverpool Libraries and Information Services, Record Office and Local History Department

[999] *60th Regiment.* Records include Alphabetical Roll of No.6 (Captain R. Tempest's) Company, 1st Rifle Corps 60th Regiment- with details of number, rank, age size, etc., followed by a progress report on each soldier, 1828.

National Army Museum

[1000] Clay, J. G., Maj-Gen. *Copies of the correspondence (157 letters) of Maj-Gen J.G. Clay, March 1804 to August 1835.* Clay served in Manchester between 1804-13, as Inspecting Field Officer, later commander of the Garrison during the disturbances of 1808 and 1812. 1804-35.

[1001] Warre, William, Lt-Gen Sir. *Papers of Lt Gen Sir William Warre (1784-1853).* The collection relates to Warre's military career 1807-49, including many letters received during the Peninsular War, documents relating to service at the Cape of Good Hope 1813-21, and diaries 1843-48 as GOC NW District at Chester containing notes on inspections and the use of troops in aid of the civil power. 1807-49.

[1002] Seager, Edward, Captain. *Copies of letters written to members of his family by Capt. Edward Seager, 8th Hussars, 5 Jun 1854-15 Aug 1855, describing his service in the Crimean War.* 2 vols. Contains descriptions of Seager's voyage from Malta to Varna; landing in the Crimea; his command of the Cavalry Depot at Scutari (Feb 1855); a description of the Charge of the Light Brigade; and letters referring to the people of Bootle, who presented gifts to the 8th Hussars. 1854-5.

[1003] Hopwood, Harry. *Papers relating to Sgt. Harry Hopwood (2nd Volunteer Battalion Manchester Regiment) during the Boer War, 1900-01, and his certificate of service for the years 1892-1908.* The papers comprise manuscript and typescript versions of 44 letters from Hopwood to his parents and family in England, and one letter from a soldier-friend in South Africa named James Hurst. 1900-1.

Salford Archives Centre

[1004] *Records of Military Service includes* Private James Bell: "Account Book" or pay book (printed in 1859) of James Bell of Pendleton, near Manchester, groom, son of William Bell of Salford, enrolled in the 12th Regiment of Foot...in 1861; Certificate of Discharge...(1 parchment doc.).

[1005] Militiaman's Small Book issued to Thomas Deakin, born in Salford parish...enlisted in the 4th Battalion of the Manchester Regiment...(1 item, also containing printed militia regulations); Certificate to Sergeant Arthur Henry Cauldwell (born 1879, enlisted in 1897), Loyal North Lancashire Regiment, of discharge from the Army (1 doc.).

Wigan Heritage Services. Archives

[1006] *Military History Records includes* Military papers of Col. Nathaniel Eckersley (1779-1837); Discharge certificate, accounts etc. of James Higson, Queen's Regiment 1842-63, and lodge-keeper at Haigh Hall; Papers relating to militiamen may be found amongst records of some of the townships and parishes. Miscellaneous items are scattered amongst family, estate and artificial collections. 1642-1974.

VII. WORLD WAR I

As a pivotal event in the history of the modern world the First World Ward has attracted the attention of all types of historian. Military historians have studied the conflict from innumerable angles and the researcher should be aware of the bibliographies to the secondary literature [15, 18]. Guides are also available to the manuscript material [41]. This section does not repeat those studies which have been already listed already under regiments but it does includes divisional histories such as those by Coop [1050] and Gibbon [1066]. A section on manuscript material follows the listing of published and printed items. Once again, the user should be aware that the archive section in other parts of this guide will contain relevant material.

Much of the published literature identified here appeared during or shortly after the end of the war. It includes remembrance and victory souvenir pamphlets and books published by regiments, firms and societies, many with their rows of closely-printed names of the dead. Whilst not all of the written histories of those units that fought in the war were published there is a reasonably solid coverage of the military activities of the region's regiments. Although, in recent years there has been a welcome upsurge of interest in the First World War in the region there is still comparatively little work of serious intention. Enormous opportunities exist for the study of the impact of the war on individual communities, and as Geoffrey Moorhouse's study of Bury has shown it is possible to use military history to develop a social history of communities [1097]. The interest in the Pals battalions initiated by William Turner and others continues to grow [165, 353, 467]. Individual incidents such as the munitions explosion in Ashton-under-Lyne can also be a revealing point of entry into the war and the local community [1015]. More local studies on specific aspects of the war such as Keith Grieves's work on manpower tribunals is required [1068]. Necessary and important as this work on individual communities is, there is a need for studies comparing and contrasting the experiences of communities; neither should we forget the perspectives that can be opened up by contrasting the First World War with the impact of earlier and later great wars. Much remains to be done on the war's impact in the region on themes such as civilian health, education and the changing role of women, as well as examining the economic and social history of the immediate post-war years as lives were readjusted in communities fit for heroes. Once again an awareness of the questions being addressed in the general secondary literature should be kept in mind. Arthur Marwick, *The Deluge* (Oxford, 1965) is still one of the most readable and question-provoking of such accounts. As can be seen from the following list there is much archival straw to help make these historical bricks. Long-distance researchers will also need to familiarise themselves with the holdings of the great national collections, in particular those of the Imperial War Museum. Researchers living in the north-west should also note that Hyndburn Library at Accrington holds a substantial collection of books on the First World War, a legacy of the collecting policy of the old Lancashire County Library.

[1007] Accrington. New Jerusalem Church. *Record of the services rendered by the young men of the New Jerusalem Church and Sunday School, Accrington in the Great War, 1914-1918.* [n.d.] **Locations: 3**

[1008] Adelphi Lads Club. *In Remembrance of the 1080 members who served their country in the Great War 1914-19.* Manchester: Hardman & Co., [n.d.] **Locations: 15**

[1009] Allen, Madeline. "Chester's Great Film Epic." *Cheshire Life* 35(December,1969)138-9. **Locations: 4, 58**

[1010]　Allinson, Sidney. *The Bantams: the Untold Story of World War I.* London: Howard Baker, 1981. **Locations:** *

[1011]　Armitage, John Basil. *Captain John Basil Armitage killed in action in France, May 17th, 1917: Extracts from Letters.* Manchester: Palmer, Howe (printers), [n.d.] **Locations:** 3

[1012]　Athletes' Volunteer Force (Blackburn Unit). *First Annual Report. 1914-1915.* Blackburn: Athletes' Volunteer Force, 1915. **Locations: 6**

[1013]　Behrend, Arthur. *As From Kemmel Hill: an adjutant in France and Flanders, 1917 & 1918.* London: Eyre & Spottiswoode, 1963. **Locations:** *

[1014]　Bell, Ernest W. *Soldiers killed on the first day of the Somme.* Bolton, Lancashire: Ernest W. Bell, 1977. **Locations: 21**

[1015]　Billings, John, and Copland, D. *The Ashton Munitions Explosion 1917.* Tameside:Tameside Leisure Services 1992. **Locations: 102**

[1016]　Birkenhead, County Borough of. *Unveiling the Town's War Memorial, 5th July 1925.* 1925. **Locations: 57**

[1017]　Birkenhead News. *Victory Souvenir of the Great War 1914-1919.* 1919. **Locations: 57**

[1018]　Blackburn, C. J. *How the Manx Fleet helped in the Great War: the story of the Isle of Man Steam Packet Boats on service.* Isle of Man: Louis G. Meyer, 1923. **Locations: MNH**

[1019]　Blackburn and District Discharged Sailors and Soldiers Association. *A Brief Description of the Formation and Work of the Association.* 1918. **Locations: 3**

[1020]　Blackpool. Arnold School for Boys. *Roll of Honour, 1918.* 1918. **Locations: 3**

[1021]　Blackpool Herald. *Blackpool Herald Victory Souvenir Supplement: Blackpool's share in the Great War reviewed: tributes from various sources.* Blackpool: Herald, 1919. **Locations: 3**

[1022]　Blackpool. World War I. *Heroes of the Great War: a record of gallantry and sacrifice from Blackpool and the Fylde.* Blackpool: Herald (printer), [n.d.] **Locations: 3**

[1023]　Boderke, David, (ed.). *Words from the Wounded: injured soldier's view of the trenches of the First World War.* 1988. **Locations: 3**

[1024]　Bolton County Borough. War Memorial Committee. *Roll of Honour of Bolton Men and Women who gave their lives in the Great War 1914-1918.* 1919. **Locations: 7**

[1025]　Bolton Evening News. Prisoners of War Fund. *Tea and entertainment to the returned prisoners of war by the Editor and Committee of the Bolton Evening News' Prisoners of War Fund at the Drill Hall, Silverwell Street, Bolton, on Saturday June 21st 1919.* Bolton: Evening News, 1919. **Locations: 7**

[1026] Bolton Journal. *Roll of Honour Supplement, December 7th 1917, December 28th 1917.* 1917. **Locations: 7**

[1027] Bolton Journal and Guardian. *When the "Zepp" came to Bolton.* 1918. **Locations: 7**

[1028] Bolton Museum and Art Gallery. *Roll of Honour of Bolton Men and Women who gave their lives in the Great War, 1914-1918.* Bolton: Museum and Art Gallery, [n.d.] **Locations: BOM**

[1029] Bolton. World War I. *Bolton peace souvenir and programme of festivities 1919.* 1919. **Locations: 7**

[1030] --- *Farnworth Journal. Roll of Honour Supplement, December 28th 1917.* 1917. **Locations: 7**

[1031] Bowdin, Tom. *Blacko, Lancashire, War Memorial, 1914-1918, 1939-1945.* Birkenhead: Cull Reprographics for Rossendale Society for Genealogy, [n.d.] **Locations: 3**

[1032] Brack, Alan. "Floscenka." *Cheshire Life* 40 (October 1974) 78-9. **Locations: 4, 58**

[1033] Bradshaw, Brian. *Bolton Bred.* Swinton: Neil Richardson, 1984. **Locations: 1, 3, 18, 59, 115**

[1034] British Limbless Ex-Servicemen's Association. *The BLESMA home for limbless ex-servicemen: official opening by H.R.H. the Duchess of Gloucester, Saturday 25th June 1949; souvenir.* Manchester: Ferndale Marshall (printer), 1949. **Locations: 3**

[1035] British Red Cross Society. East Lancashire Branch. *An Illustrated Account of the Work of the Branch during the First Year of the War.* Manchester: Sherratt and Hughes, 1916. **Locations: 1, 3, 19, 24, 50**

[1036] Bruckshaw, Horace. *The Diaries of Private Horace Bruckshaw, 1915-1916.* Edited and introduced by Martin Middlebrook. London: Scholar Press, 1979. **Locations: ***

[1037] Bryant, G. J. "Bolton and the outbreak of the First World War." *Transactions of the Historic Society of Lancashire and Cheshire* 138 (1988) 181-200. **Locations: ***

[1038] Burne, Richard Vernon Higgins. *Knutsford: the story of the Ordination Test School 1918-41.* 1960. **Locations: 1, 4, 57**

[1039] Burnley Express. *Greater Burnley and the Great War: Roll of Honour, 1914-1919.* Burnley: Express [n.d.] **Locations: 3, 23**

[1040] Cartmell, Harry. *For Remembrance: an account of some fateful years.* Preston: Toulmin, 1919. **Locations: 1, 3, 12, 25, 28, 30**

[1041] Chavasse, F. J. *The War and the Diocese: a charge delivered to the clergy of the Diocese of Liverpool, Nov 25th, 1914, in the Church of St. Peter, Liverpool.* 1914. **Locations: 2**

[1042] Cheshire. Victoria Cross. "Cheshire Victoria Cross holders." *Cheshire Life* 18 (September 1952) 31. **Locations: 4, 58**

[1043] Civic Service League. *Report of work done at the War Depot, 110 and 112 Bold Street, Liverpool, Aug 1917-Aug 1918.* 1918. **Locations: 2**

[1044] Clarke, David A. *Great War Memories: Soldiers' Experiences, 1914-1918.* Blackburn: T.H.C.L. Books, 1987. **Locations: 1, 3, 6, 14, 15, 20, 52, 102**

[1045] Clemesha, Henry Wordsworth. *Food Control in the North-West Division [Lancashire, Cheshire, Cumberland and Westmorland].* Manchester: University Press, 1922. **Locations: 1, 3**

[1046] Colne and Nelson Times. *The Colne and District Roll of Honour and War Record, 1914-1919.* Colne: Colne and Nelson Times, 1920. **Locations: 3, 23**

[1047] --- *War Album, 1914-1915: 500 portraits and biographical sketches of heroes from North-East Lancashire...heroes from the West Riding...who have been killed or wounded in action, or who have died on active service for their King or country; and also of men who have won distinction during the war.* Colne: Hyde, 1915. **Locations: 3, 23**

[1048] Connell, A. *Commemoration Day, 1919: Sermon preached in Sefton Park Presbyterian Church, Liverpool, on Sunday, 27th July, 1919, and the roll of names of "The sons of our own homes and church" who have fallen during the Great War, 1914-1919.* 1919. **Locations: 2**

[1049] Coop, J. O. "Liverpool and the Great War." *Cox's Liverpool Annual and Year Book.* Liverpool: Cox, 1923. (pp.104-7) **Locations: 2**

[1050] Coop, James Ogden. *The Story of The 55th (West Lancashire) Division.* Liverpool: Daily Post, 1919. **Locations: ***

[1051] Dawson, Thomas H. *Preston Port to Flanders Field: An Autobiography, (1896-1919).* Lancashire: Lancashire Polytechnic, Community History Project, 1987. **Locations: 3**

[1052] Disbrowe, E.J.W., (ed.) *History of the Volunteer Movement in Cheshire, 1914-1920.* Stockport: Swain & Co., 1920. **Locations:**

[1053] Ellis, A. E. *As it was and Twenty-one Today: reminiscences of Edwardian Bolton and World War I.* Bridge Press: Church, [n.d.] **Locations: 7**

[1054] Ellison, Norman Frederick. *Three Musketeers and a Gunner.* 1924. **Locations: 2**

[1055] Fallows, James. "For Valour: Wirral family's double distinction." *Cheshire Life* 22(January 1956) 20. **Locations: 4, 58**

[1056] Farnworth Journal. *Journal War Supplement and Roll of Honour 1916. Farnworth Journal January 5th 1917.* 1917. **Locations: 43**

[1057] --- *Roll of Honour Supplement. December 28th 1917.* 1917. **Locations: 7**

[1058] Farnworth Urban District Council. *Peace Celebrations. August 2nd 1919: United Sunday and Day Schools Festival. Programme.* 1919. **Locations: 7**

[1059] --- *Peace Celebrations: concert and public presentation. Moor Hall, Farnworth, July 31st 1919.* **Locations: 7**

[1060] Fisher, C. A. *How Peace came to Blackpool: Scenes of 1918 Recalled.* Blackpool: Times, 1931.

[1061] Fisher, P. J. *Figures and Phases of the War 1916-1919.* London: Odhams Ltd, 1919. **Locations: MRO**

[1062] Flixton, Parish of. *Peace Celebrations 1919. Official programme.* 1919. **Locations: 52**

[1063] Floyd, Thomas Hope. *At Ypres with Best-Dunkley.* London: J. Lane, 1920. **Locations: 1, LRO**

[1064] Foulger, L. E. "A Cheshire Village at War: a commentary on the Appleton Thorn War Memorial." *Cheshire History* 27 (Spring,1991)15-19. **Locations: 4**

[1065] Francis, Alfred E.F., Sergeant. *History of the 2/3 East Lancashire Field Ambulance. The Story of a 2nd Line Territorial Unit, 1914-1919.* Salford: W.F. Jackson & Sons, 1930. **Locations: 1**

[1066] Gibbon, Frederick P. *The 42nd (East Lancashire) Division, 1914-1918.* London: Country Life, 1920. **Locations: ***

[1067] Grieves, K. R. "The Liverpool Dock Battalion: military intervention in the Mersey Docks, 1915-1918." *Transactions of the Historic Society of Lancashire and Cheshire* 131 (1981) 131-58. **Locations: ***

[1068] Grieves, Keith. "Mobilising Manpower: Audenshaw Tribunal in the First World War." *Manchester Region History Review* 3.2 (Autumn/Winter 1989-90) 21-9. **Locations: 1, LRO**

[1069] Haslingden, Borough of. *Programme of arrangements: unveiling of the Haslingden War Memorial, in the Greenfield Memorial Gardens, on October 25th 1924, by the Rt. Hon. the Earl of Derby.* 1924. **Locations: 26**

[1070] Haythornthwaite, Philip J. "The Blackpool Volunteers, 1916." *Dispatch: the Journal of the Scottish Military Collectors Society* 98 (Spring 1982) 11. **Locations: NAM**

[1071] Hope, Maurice. "The Fort That Never Fought." *Cheshire Life* 44 (1978) 42-4. **Locations: 4, 58**

[1072] Hyde Tipperary League. *Hymns.* 1914-18. **Locations: 102**

[1073] Hyde. World War I. *United Memorial Service, Hyde Town Hall, Sunday August 4th, 1918.* Hyde: Corporation, 1918. **Locations: 102**

[1074] Borough of Hyde. *Souvenir programme of the Peace Celebrations: 19th July, 2nd and 4th August 1919.* Hyde: Herald, 1919. **Locations: 102**

[1075] Imperial War Graves Commission. *The War Graves of the British Empire: the register of the names of those who fell in the Great War and are buried in cemeteries and churchyards in the South-Eastern part of the Administrative County of Lancaster (exclusive of Manchester and Stockport).* London: Imperial War Graves Commission, 1930. **Locations: 11,12, 13, 59, CURO (B)**

[1076] Irwin, Francis, and Cecil Chichester-Constable. *Stonyhurst War Record. A memorial of the part taken by Stonyhurst men in the Great War.* Derby: Bemrose (printer), 1927. **Locations: 1, 6, 9**

[1077] Isle of Man. Great War 1914-1918. *Roll of Honour.* Douglas: Isle of Man Local War Pensions Committee, 1934. **Locations: MNH**

[1078] Jackson, T., Sgt. Major. "Four Days from a Field Message Book, July 29-Aug 4, 1918." *Manchester Genealogist* 25 (July 1989) 34-5. **Locations: 7**

[1079] James, A. H., Lieutenant-Colonel. *A Short Memoir of Lt. Col. A.H. James, D.S.O.*, 1918. **Locations: CURO (C)**

[1080] Kennedy, W. B. Bill. *Bill Kennedy M.M.: Egypt, Gallipoli, France and Flanders with the 42nd (East Lancashire) Division in the Great War, 1914-1919.* Edited by Sue Richardson. Swinton, Manchester: Neil Richardson, 1990. **Locations: 1, 3, CL**

[1081] King's Lancashire Convalescent Hospital. *The Return: Journal of the King's Lancashire Convalescent Hospital.* 1916-17. **Locations: 3**

[1082] Kirby, Henry L., and Walsh, R. Raymond. *The Four Blackburn V.C.'s. James Pitts, Manchester Regiment. William H. Grimbaldeston, KOSB. John Schofield, Lancashire Fusiliers. Percy T. Dean, RNVR.* Blackburn: T.H.C.L. Books, 1986. **Locations: 3, 6, 18, BM**

[1083] Lancashire Family History Society. Lancaster and Morecambe Branch. *Record of names listed on war memorials in the area of Lancaster, Morecambe and district.* Lancashire: L.F.H.S., 1992. **Locations: 3**

[1084] Lancashire Museum Service. County and Regimental Museum. *The Trench Army, 1914-18.* Preston: County and Regimental Museum, 1991. **Locations: 3**

[1085] Lancashire Volunteer Regiments. *Annual Report 10th Battalion Lancashire Volunteer Force (Late Athletes' Volunteer Force), 1915/16.* 1915-16. **Locations: 6**

[1086] Lancashire Volunteer Regiments. *3rd Manchester City Battalion. C. Company (Crumpsall Platoon). To Every Man Between 17 and 70 Years of Age not in Military Training.* 1916. **Locations: 1**

[1087] Lancaster War Memorial. *Lancaster War Memorial and Garden of Remembrance: Unveiling and dedication of the Memorial in the Town Hall Garden, Wednesday December 3 1924.* Lancaster: J.J. Wigley (printer), 1924. **Locations: 3**

[1088] Lattimer, Amy. "Touching the Sile." *Cheshire Life* 40(October 1974)105. **Locations: 4, 58**

111

[1089]   Lee, John A. *Todmorden and the Great War, 1914-1918: a local record.* Todmorden: Waddington, 1922. **Locations: 3, 112**

[1090]   Lever Brothers Ltd. *Port Sunlight War Memorial Golden Book, 1914-1919.* [n.d.] **Locations: 4**

[1091]   Liverpool University. *The University of Liverpool Roll of Service August, 1914 to November, 1918.* Liverpool: University Press, 1921. **Locations: 2, 79A**

[1092]   Liverpool. World War I. *Gwasanaethmawl dathlu heddwch, y Sun Hall, Kensington, nos Sadwrn, Hydref 18 fed, 1919: trefn y gwasanaeth ac enwau rhai a syrthiasant yn y Rhyfel (1919).* 1919. [Service of Praise for Peace... the names of those who fell] **Locations: 2**

[1093]   Longbottom, F. W. *Chester in the Great War.* Chester: Phillipson & Golder, 1920. **Locations: 4**

[1094]   Long Preston. St Mary the Virgin. *Great War, 1914-1918 Muster Roll and the War of 1939-1945 Roll of Honour.* 1989. **Locations: 3**

[1095]   McCauley, John. *A Manx Soldier's War Diary.* 1932. **Locations: MNH**

[1096]   Mather and Platt Ltd. (Park Works, Salford Iron Works, Boiler Yard). *A Record of the part taken by all Employees during the Great War 1914-1919.* **Locations: 15**

[1097]   Moorhouse, Geoffrey. *Hell's Foundations: a Town, its Myths and Gallipoli.* London: Hodder and Stoughton, 1992. **Locations: ***

[1098]   Morecambe Corporation. *Roll of Honour, the Great War, 1914-1918.* Morecambe: Corporation, [n.d.] **Locations: 3, 28**

[1099]   Morten, J. C. *I remain, your son Jack: letters from the First World War; edited by Sheila Morten.* 1993. **Locations: 3, 102**

[1100]   Musgrove, W., (ed.). *Borough of Haslingden. Haslingden's Roll of Honour in the Great War 1914-1918. Compiled by W. Musgrave, Town Clerk.* 1918. **Locations: 26**

[1101]   National Association of Discharged Sailors and Soldiers. Blackburn Branch. *A Brief Description of the Formation and Work of the Association.* 1919. **Locations: 6**

[1102]   National Publishing Company. *The National Roll of the Great War 1914-18. Section XIV- Salford.* London: N.P.C., 1922. **Locations: 1, 15**

[1103]   --- *The National Roll of the Great War. 1914-1918. Section XI- Manchester.* London: N.P.C., [n.d.] **Locations: 1, 15**

[1104]   Nayler, J., (ed.). *Lancashire: Biographies, Rolls of Honour. Introduction by Ralph Hall Caine.* 1917. Counties' Whos' Who Series. **Locations: 2**

[1105]   Nelson. Borough Council. *Thanksgiving Service for the Declaration of Peace, Sunday 3rd August, 1919, Nelson Cricket Field at 3 p.m.* Nelson: Coulson (printer), 1919. **Locations: 3**

[1106] Nelson Leader. *The "Leader" Local War Record, 1914-1915: with letters from the front, list of fallen heroes, and local roll of honour.* Nelson: Coulton, [n.d.] **Locations: 3**

[1107] North West Sound Archive. *The War to End All Wars: Memories of the Great War, 1914-1918.* 1992. **Locations: 3**

[1108] Northwich War Memorial. *Unveiling and Dedication of the War Memorial, June 13th 1922.* Northwich: Albert Wood, Castle Press (printer), 1920. **Locations: 69**

[1109] Ogle, Henry. *The Fateful Battle Line: the Great War journals and sketches of Captain Henry Ogle, MC.* London: Leo Cooper, 1993. **Locations: 2, 3, 4, 8, 18**

[1110] Oldham Chronicle. *Our Local Heroes: Portraits of soldiers and sailors of the Oldham district who have been killed, and of those who have gained distinction on the battlefield. Jan 9, 1915-Dec 23, 1916.* 1915-16. **Locations: 11**

[1111] Oldham Corporation Tramways Department. *Welcome Home to our Returned Ex-Servicemen. In the Greenacres Co-operative Hall, Christmas Day, 1919.* Oldham: Corporation, 1919. **Locations: 11**

[1112] Oldham Metropolitan Borough. *Order of proceedings on presentation to the Mayor of Oldham of the Victoria Cross awarded to Sergeant John Rogan 20th February 1915.* Oldham: Metropolitan Borough, 1984. **Locations: 11**

[1113] Preston Guardian. *Preston During the Great World War, 1914-1918: a record of some interesting facts and events, extracted from the "Preston Guardian".* 1986. **Locations: 3**

[1114] Preston War Memorial. *The Unveiling of the Preston War Memorial, by Admiral of the Fleet, Earl Jellicoe of Scapa: Sunday, June 13, 1926.* Preston: Corporation, 1926. **Locations: 3**

[1115] Preston. World War I. *An Open Air Service of Thanksgiving and Memorial for those who were killed in action or died of wounds or sickness during the Great War, 1927-38.* Preston: Seed (printer), [n.d.]. **Locations: 3**

[1116] --- *Preston's Roll of Honour.* Vols. 1-3., 1918. **Locations: 3**

[1117] Radcliffe, Leslie N. "Private Todger Jones, VC." *Cheshire Life* 14 (September 1948) 21. **Locations: 4, 58**

[1118] Richardson, Neil, and Richardson, Sue. *Fallen in the Fight: Farnworth and Kearsley men who died in the Great War, 1914-1918.* Manchester: Neil Richardson, 1990. **Locations: 3, 7, 13, CL**

[1119] Rossendale Society for Genealogy and Heraldry, and Mrs Higginson, (eds.). *Colne, Lancashire, war memorial, 1914-1918, 1939-1945.* Birkenhead: Cull Reprographics [for] Rossendale Society for Genealogy and Heraldry, Lancashire, [n.d.]. **Locations: 3**

[1120] Rossendale Society for Genealogy and Heraldry, Pendle Branch. *Christchurch, Colne, Roll of Honour and War Memorial 1914-1919 and 1939-1945.* [n.d.] **Locations: 23**

[1121] St. Annes-on-Sea. *The Order of the solemn ceremonial and service appointed for use on the occasion of the unveiling of the memorial to the men of Saint Anne's who fell in the Great War, 1914-1918, on Sunday 12th October, 1924.* St. Annes-on-Sea: Fylde Press, 1924. **Locations: 3**

[1122] Sargeaunt, Bertram Edward. *The Isle of Man and the Great War.* Douglas: Brown and Sons, 1920. **Locations: 1, MNH**

[1123] Short, Walter. *Pictures from France.* Manchester: Sherratt & Hughes, 1919. **Locations: 1, 8, 102**

[1124] Sidebotham, Randal. *Hyde in Wartime: soldiers, sailors, and civilians' deeds.* Hyde: Herald, 1916. **Locations: 1, 102**

[1125] Smith, Leslie. *The German Prisoner of War Camp at Leigh, 1914-1919.* Manchester: Neil Richardson, 1986. **Locations: 3, 18B**

[1126] Smith, Peter J. C. *Zeppelins Over Lancashire. The Story of the Air Raids on the County of Lancashire in 1916 and 1918.* Manchester: Neil Richardson, 1991. **Locations: ***

[1127] Stubbs, S., and Ward, Ron. "P.O.W. Camps in Lancashire and I.O.M. during World Wars I and II." *Lancashire Mail* 2 (1964) 39-41. **Locations: LRO**

[1128] Tapley. *A Tockholes Child in the First World War.* Blackburn: [n.d.]. **Locations: 7**

[1129] Taunton. The Book of Taunton. *From City of Taunton, Mass. U.S.A. to Township of Chadderton, Lancashire, England, in recognition of courtesies extended to Taunton soldiers in the World War. 1918.* Taunton, Massachusetts: C.A. Hack & Son Inc., 1918. **Locations: 11**

[1130] Taylor, F. A. J. *Tanky's War or a Private Eye View: a collection of verses on the Great War.* Taunton: Taymark, 1984. **Locations: 7**

[1131] Taylor, James. *My Experience as a Prisoner of War with the Germans, 1919.* 1919. **Locations: 7**

[1132] Thompson, George, (ed.). *Liverpool's Scroll of Fame: a memorial of Liverpool soldiers and sailors who gave their lives for their country in the Great War, 1914-1919. Part 1: Commissioned officers.* Liverpool: Quills, 1920. **Locations: 3**

[1133] Wadsworth, W.W., Captain, (comp.). *War Diary of the 1st West Lancashire Brigade, R.F.A.* Liverpool: "Daily Post" Printers, 1923. **Locations: 3**

[1134] Ward, C. H. Dudley, Major. *History of the 53rd (Welsh) Division (T.F.) 1914-1918.* Cardiff: Western Mail Limited, 1927. **Locations: 63, RAHT**

[1135] Ward, H., Staff-Sergeant. *A Citizen Soldier's Service. The War Diary of Staff-Sergt. H. Ward 1914-1919.* 1924. **Locations: 1**

[1136] Webb, Harold. *A Salford Gunner in the First World War. The 1917 diary of Gunner Harold Webb.* 1991. **Locations: 15**

[1137]   Weir and District War Memorial. *Programme for unveiling the War Memorial on Saturday 14th September 1935.* 1935. **Locations: 21**

[1138]   West Lancashire Division. *"Sub-Rosa", being the Magazine of The West Lancashire Division British Expeditionary Force, June, 1917.* Boulogne: The Division, 1917-18. **Locations: 5,17, 28, LRO**

[1139]   West, Margery. *Island at War: the remarkable role played by the small Manx nation in the Great War, 1914-18.* Laxey: Western Books, 1986. **Locations: 3, MNH**

[1140]   Westhoughton. Roll of Honour. *List of Westhoughton men killed or taken prisoner in World War I and those missing, together with those decorated.* [n.d.] **Locations: 7**

[1141]   Westmore, A.W., Thompson, M., and Allison, J.E. *The Story of the 63rd Field Ambulance (2/2 West Lancashire Field Ambulance, T.F.) 1914-1919.* Liverpool: Wood & Sloane Ltd. Printers, 1928. **Locations:**

[1142]   Whalley. Lancashire. *Queen Mary's Military Hospital, Whalley.* Bolton: Tillotson, 1916. **Locations: 3**

[1143]   Whiston, Harold W. *Welcome Home after the Great War of the Langley and Lane-Ends Village Soldiers employed by Messrs. W.M. Whiston & Sons Ltd.* Macclesfield: 1919. (Reprint from the "Macclesfield Times" of May 30th 1919 and November 14th 1919). **Locations: 63**

[1144]   Henry Young & Sons Ltd. *Memorials of Old Birkonians who Fell in the Great War 1914-1918.* Liverpool: Henry Young & Sons Ltd., 1920. **Locations: 4**

ARCHIVES

Bacup Library
[1145]   Toc. H. Rossendale Group. *Minute Book, December 1st 1931-October 10th 1943.* 1931-43.

Blackburn Library
[1146]   Blackburn Athletes' Volunteer Force. *Minute books, 1914-1916*

[1147]   --- *Miscellaneous papers and cuttings, 1914-1916.* 1914-16.

[1148]   --- *Report for 1914-1915.* 1914-15.

[1149]   --- *Second Annual Report, presented at the Annual Meeting, November, 1916.* 1916.

[1150]   --- *Special inaugural service at Blackburn Parish Church, Sunday, November 22, 1914.* 1914.

Bolton Archives

[1151] *Bolton Air Raids. Correspondence, 1916-1918; Bolton Casualties. Newspaper supplement, 1916; Bolton. National Service Authority: Photograph, 1918; Farnworth: Ministry of Reconstruction Correspondence, 1917-1920; Farnworth. Naval and Military Distinctions: Correspondence, 1917-19; Farnworth. Victory Celebrations: Correspondence, 1919; Field Ambulance Service. Albert Batty: Diaries and scrapbooks, etc, 1914-1970; France. Correspondence, postcards, etc., 1915-16; France. Description of experience, c.1914-18; Friends Ambulance Unit: Photograph Album, 1914-1917; Horwich. Military Service Tribunal: Minutes, 1916-1917; Kearsley. War Pensions Committee: Correspondence and claims, 1916-1917; Photocopy of diary, c.1916; Postcards, 1914-1918; Royal Engineers. Photographs, c.1914-1918; World War I. Royal Welsh Fusiliers. Photographs, c.1914-1918; Turton. Draft Roll of Honour, 192; Westhoughton. Military Service Tribunal Minute Book, 1916-1918; Westhoughton. Peace Celebrations Cuttings Book, 1918-1919; Westhoughton. War Charities Act: Applications, etc 1916-1922; Bolton. County Borough. Naval and Military War Pensions Act 1915: scheme framed by the Bolton Borough Council for the constitution of a Local Committee for the Borough, 1916; Bolton County Borough. War Memorial Committee. Roll of Honour of Bolton men and women who gave their lives in the Great War 1914-1918.*

Bolton Libraries

[1152] Sanderson, Thomas. *Diary 1916-18: extract 25-26 September 1916. Relating to Zeppelin Raid, together with Bolton Journal account, 27 September 1916.* 1916.

[1153] Taylor, H. *Zeppelin LZ61 (Marine L21): (an account of the raids on Bolton during the 1st World War).* 1987.

Bury Archives

[1154] *Geoffrey Hutchinson, Lord Ilford of Bury: Family Papers; Prince of Wales National Relief Fund (for families of servicemen): Bury fund records 1914-1920; Radcliffe Borough. Conscription Tribunal letterbook 1918; Tottington Urban District. Prince of Wales National Relief Fund: Tottington and Ainsworth District Committee minutes 1914-1919.*

[1155] *--- correspondence of Mrs H.O. Hutchinson with reference to search for son John of the South Lancashire Regiment missing during retreat from Mons 1914-1915 [also includes postcards collected by G.H. c.1900-1910, many of warships and cavalry.* [n.d.]

Cheshire Record Office

[1156] *First World War. Drawings and sketches on the Western Front of W.H. Hutchings, RAMC 1916-1918; First World War. Military patients register, Macclesfield Workhouse Infirmary 1914-1925.*

Chester City Record Office

[1157] *Cheshire Volunteer Regiment: Chester Company. Records.* Contents: the records of this company, which took part in the First World War, comprise a minute book (1914-1916) and a handbill of weekly orders, 27 September 1915. 1914-16.

Clitheroe Local Studies Library

[1158] *Private William Blundell: Records.*
Contents: Certificates and other documents relating to Private William Blundell of Clitheroe on his demobilisation and transfer to the reserve in 1919. Includes a Great War

Medal and *A Pocket Atlas and Gazetteer of the World* by G. Bacon, 1895. c.1919.

Colne Library

[1159] *National Day of Remembrance for the wars 1914-18 and 1934-45. Remembrance Service at the War Memorial order of proceedings 1935-1973*; Photographic material. *Colne and Brierfield Sick Berth Reservists October 8th 1914 Royal Naval Hospital, Chatham*, 1914; *Volunteers on Colne Edge, 1914*; Colne. War memorabilia. *Coupons*, [n.d.]; Colne War Memorial. *Unveiling Ceremony, 11th November, 1930.*; Colne War Memorial Committee. *Plans for war memorial*, [n.d.]; Colne War Savings Committee. *Minute Book*, 1918-29; *Foulridge War Memorial unveiling a dedication ceremony 1914-1918*; *Police air raid warning notice*, 1918.

[1160] Rossendale Society for Genealogy and Heraldry, Pendle Branch. *Christchurch, Colne, Roll of Honour and War Memorial 1914-1919 and 1939-1945.* [n.d.]

Cumbria Record Office. Barrow

[1161] *Barrow Borough Council Records. Town Clerk's department.* Contents: Roll of Honour volume, listing personnel from the County Borough who served during the Great War, 1914-1919
Minute Books from various local servicemen's welfare committees, 1914-1919

Cumbria Record Office. Carlisle

[1162] *World War I. Military Service Records*, 1914-21; *Peace Celebrations. Records*, 1918-19; *Peace Conference Records*, 1918-19; *Profiteering. Records*, 1919-21; *Rolls of Honour*, 1914-26; *War Memorials*, 1917-73; *The Battle Front. Letters Home*, 1914-21; *The Battle Front. Miscellaneous*, 1915-36; *Records of Sir Esme Howard (later Lord Howard of Penrith), Chief of the British Legation at Stockholm, Sweden, 1913-1919.*

[1163] *Conscientious Objection and Pacifism Records*, 1914-21; *Food Control Records*, 1914-20; *Liquor Control Records*, 1914-25; *Miscellaneous Records*, 1913-21; *Prisoners-of-War Records*, 1917-19; *Refugees. Records*, 1914-19; *War Charities Records*, 1914-20; Dowell, William. *Notebook re William Dowell's experiences with the Camera Repair and Photographic Section of the British Expeditionary Force in France, 1918-19.*

Haslingden Library

[1164] Haslingden Auxiliary Military Hospital. *Letters, reports, etc. appertaining to Miss B. Harrison and the Haslingden Auxiliary Military Hospital.* 1914.

Lancashire County Library

[1165] Lancashire Library. *Blackpool in the First World War: miscellaneous items, 1919-*

[1166] Preston Sailors and Soldiers Free Buffet. *Duty roster and visitors' book.* [n.d.]

[1167] Rossendale Society for Genealogy and Heraldry, and Mrs Higginson, (eds.). *Colne, Lancashire, war memorial, 1914-1918, 1939-1945.* Birkenhead: Cull Reprographics [for] Rossendale Society for Genealogy and Heraldry, Lancashire, 198-.

Lancashire Record Office.

[1168] *Book of reminiscences of life at the Auxiliary Military Hospital, Moor Park, Preston, by Nurse E.F. de Trafford, 1914-19;* George Ashworth: personal papers, 1915-35; *Royal Field Artillery, "A" Battery, 330th Brigade, official diary, 1917-18.*

Liverpool Libraries and Information Services, Record Office and Local History Department

[1169]   Liverpool. Munitions of War Committee. *Record of Work, 1915-1918.* 1919.

[1170]   *Records of the 55th (West Lancashire) Division, 1914-19. Memoranda and Papers; Daily Intelligence Summaries; Recommendations for honours and rewards; Personal Papers, Correspondence and Lectures of Major-General Jeudwine; General Maps; Local Maps.*
Note: The 55th Division was formed out of the West Lancashire Territorial Division following the Territorial and Reserve Forces Act, 1907 (7 Edw. VII, c.9) In the early part of the war, units of the division were used to reinforce other divisions, but in January 1916, the units were brought together again to form the 55th (West Lancashire) Division, under the command of Major General Jeudwine. The history of the division during the war years is described by Rev. J.O. Coop in *The Story of the 55th (West Lancashire) Division.* Jeudwine relinquished command of the division in March 1919.
Contents summary:
Memoranda and Other Papers: 6 files, 1915-1919: Memoranda on training, training instructions, tactical exercises; Summaries and lists of casualties; Summaries and lists of honours and rewards; Various Memoranda; List of code names of units, buildings, trenches etc.
Daily Intelligence Summaries: 10 files, 1916-1918.
Recommendations for honours and awards: 19 files, 3 bundles, 1916-1919. These contain narratives of acts of gallantry, and include original recommendations and copies of recommendations forwarded by Major-General Jeudwine: King's Birthday List 1916 (1 file); New Year's List 1917 (5 files); King's Birthday List 1917 (10 files, including cuttings from the *Morning Post*); New Year's List 1918 (2 files); New Year's List 1919 (1 file); Immediate Rewards (3 bundles).
Personal Papers, Correspondence and Lectures of Major-General Jeudwine: 4 vols., 18 files, 1915-1938: includes personal notebooks (4 vols.); correspondence with C.F.N. Macready; Lord Derby; Sir Arthur Conan Doyle; men of the division; Sir Douglas Haig; A Brief History of the Division; notes and lectures given at army schools; Papers relating to the German Counter-attack at Cambrai, 1917; Account written by Lt. Gen. Thomas D'O. Snow; Contemporary records and copies; Further correspondence on the records and evidence, (1925-7); Contemporary maps (8 items); Correspondence on extracts from Lord Haig's Diaries, (1936); Lecture on operations at Givenchy-Festubert, 9 Apr. 1918, (1936); Remarks on draft chapter of the Official History dealing with the Somme operations, Sep.1916, (1933-5); Note on origin of the Divisional Badge; Correspondence on the deposit of the records by Lt. Gen. Sir Hugh Jeudwine (1938).
General Maps: 6 maps, 1918, for: Enemy Order of Battle; Western Front; British Battles, showing areas gained; Map of the main prison camps in Germany and Austria.
Local Maps: 37 maps, 1915-1918, for: Amiens; Ath; Bauvin; Bethune; Beuvry; Brussels; Gorre; Hazebrouck; La Bassee; Lacouture-Estraires; Laventie to Festubert; Lens; Leuze; Lille. 1915-19. Records relating to operations.
Contents summary:
12 files, 1916-1919: Assembly of the Division; South of Arras and the Somme.
Third Battle of Ypres: Orders, lists of casualties, reports, letters and 3 maps; Narratives and reports of divisional units (including also 5th Army narrative dated 1 Sep 1917); Divisional report on operations (3 copies); Orders, summary of awards, list of casualties, strength return, trench map; Narratives and reports of divisional units; Strength returns, 4 lists; Cambrai: operations against Gillemont Farm and the Knoll; Givenchy Crater operations and the succeeding advance; Routine orders; Orders and other papers. 1914-19.

Liverpool University Archives

[1171] *Military Records.*
Contents: Minutes of the Military Education Committee, 1914-67 (3 vols).
Copies of minutes, correspondence, reports, and publications of or relating to the Military Education Committee, 1945-82.
Records and publications deposited by members of staff:
Deposited by Mr. A.N. Ricketts: R. Pizer, *Target Shooting at Manchester University* (typescript, July 1978, 1 vol.); contains a number of references to the University of Liverpool; Xerox of Mr.Pizer's manuscript notes listing the sources used in writing his account; Letters from Mr. Pizer to Mr. Ricketts about his work, 17 April and 9 October 1978.
History of the University of Liverpool Officers Training Corps up to 1984, proof, begun by the late Major F.J. Routledge, M.B.E., T.D., and expanded and completed by A.N. Ricketts (University of Liverpool, 1989) together with photographs and draft chapters updating the account (not yet published).
Students at Sea by Lieutenant-Commander Philip L. Kemp, B.A., R.N.R. (ret'd) (1992), proof, an account of the University's Royal Naval Unit's origins and development and the part played by the author in the same (not yet published).

Manx National Heritage

[1172] McCauley, John. *A Manx Soldier's War Diary*, 1932.

[1173] *Military Scrapbook: The Great War.* [n.d.]

Merseyside Maritime Museum

[1174] *World War I and World War II Archives.* The museum has selective holdings of World War I and World War II records only.
Contents summary: DX Collection: J. Thompson's experience in RAF Coastal Command, West Africa, 1943-46. Merchant Navy: Weekly Ration Book 1953-54, Clothing Book 1949; Particulars of sea service in Merchant Navy of Albert Price 1916-1959; Career papers of Captain Webster, Merchant Navy and war service during World War II; Book of War instructions for Merchant Ships, leadweighted, 1917. Royal Navy: Copies of certificates of service in Royal Navy as gunlayer on Q-ship SS Baralong, c.1915; Certificate of service in Royal Navy and Discharge Certificates of A. Glasspool, 1872. Accessions include items relating to the Battle of the Atlantic: souvenirs, newscuttings, plans of Western Approaches HQ, sailing plans for convoy HX300- the largest to cross the Atlantic- and information on Captain Walker.
Non-DX Archives: Career Papers of Lieutenant-Commander Ronald W. Keymer (1910-1957) Relating to Atlantic Convoy Duties During World War II. The Papers and Documents Provide a Valuable First-Hand Insight into the Events of the Battle of the Atlantic, Especially Concerning *HMS Gorleston* Which Keymer Commanded from August 1941.
Stubbs Family Archive Career Papers of Herbert Molyneux Stubbs (1879-1915) and His Family, 1879-1970. Stubbs Was an Engineer On *Royal Edward* Which Was Sunk During World War I (Partly Listed). The Archive Also Includes the Personal Papers and Maritime Memorabilia of His Daughter, Lillian from 1912-1970.
Special Collection of Items Re the *Lusitania* Torpedoed During World War I; McRoberts Photographic Collection Includes an Album of Royal Naval Vessels. 1914-.

National Army Museum

[1175] Hopwood, Harry. *Papers relating to Harry Hopwood, CQMS, (6th Battalion Manchester Regiment) during World War I.* The collection consists of 81 manuscript and typescript versions of letters to his family and four newspaper cuttings of the Manchester Regiment 1914-18.

[1176] National Army Museum. *James Wilkinson (1881-1951) Three certificates issued to a Bolton grocer during World War I.* 1915-18.

[1177] Roberts, W., Brigadier. *File of correspondence of July 1981-March 1982 between Brigadier W. Roberts and Dr R. Yorke on the use of army horses to launch the Formby Lifeboat during 1916.* 1981-2.

Oldham Local Studies Library

[1178] Duchess of Connaught's Own Irish Rangers. *Visit to Oldham, 1916-17. Extracts from Oldham Evening Chronicle.* 1916-17.

[1179] *Oldham recruits and local heroes. Cuttings from the Oldham Chronicle, 1914-1915.* 1914-15. *Roll of Honour. Cuttings from the Oldham Chronicle, 1914-15; Newscuttings relating to recruitment in Oldham, 1914-18.*

Rochdale Local Studies Library

[1180] Rochdale Observer. *Obituaries.* Rochdale: Observer, 1914-18.

[1181] Rochdale Times. *Obituaries.* Rochdale: Times, 1914-18.

Salford Archives Centre

[1182] *Records of Military Service.* Contents: <u>Printed diary</u> for the year 1919 of soldier serving in India and demobilized at the end of the year, containing brief entries chiefly of events in his life and of a few other individuals, 1919, incl. some entries for events occurring 1916-18 (1 small vol.).
<u>Other Records</u>: records of an army officer on the Western Front, 1916, 1918-19, [n.d.] and of an R.A.F. officer during the Second World War, 1940-45; letters on loss in action of R.A.F. Sergeant in action in 1941; Commission as Adjutant in the Third Dragoon Guards. 1859-1919.

Tameside Local Studies Library

[1183] Great Britain. Ministry of Munitions. *File of documents concerned with the Ashton Explosion, 1917.*

[1184] Morison, J. P. *Recollections of the Ashton Explosion, 3rd June 1917.* 1989.

Trafford Local Studies Library

[1185] Kidney, Ralph. *Biographical notes, letters and documents.* [n.d.]

[1186] --- *Notes on World War 1.* [n.d.]

[1187] National Registration Act 1915. *Registration cards. J. Riley and E. Riley. Flixton Road, Urmston.* 1915.

[1188] Urmston Library. *Photographs.* 1914-.

[1189] Vane, Francis, Sir. *The War and My Other Crimes. Press cuttings etc. of Sir Francis Vane*. 1914-18.

Wigan Heritage Service. Archives
[1190] *Military History Records*.
Contents summary:
Wigan Military Chronicle": unpublished MS history by G. Derbyshire (1949-74): Vol.1: The Yeomanry and Volunteers; Vol.2: The Territorial Force; Vol.3: The Territorial Army; Vol.4: The Territorial Army. A supplementary volume is entitled "The Colours-5th Battalion Manchester Regiment".
Diaries of Rifleman William Walls of Abram 1915-1919.
Papers relating to Wigan men killed in World War I.
Rolls of Honour, Lowton 1914-1916.

Wigan Heritage Service. History Shop
[1191] --- *Conduct Medal 1914-1920 Citations-Wigan men*, 1914-20.

[1192] Wigan County Borough. *Minutes of the War Memorial and Peace Celebration Committees, 1917-1922*. 1917-22.

[1193] --- *Wigan Roll of Honour 1914-1919*. 1914-19.

VIII. SECOND WORLD WAR

This section contains material relating to the Second World War. The first part lists published and printed items; manuscript and other archive materials are identified in the second section. Publications relating to the military operations of individual regiments can be found in the sections on the regiments. References to the Second World War can also be found in the sections on the Royal Air Force and Royal Navy.

The Second World War has generated an immense secondary literature. Fortunately the bibliographical control of this area is increasing and researchers should be aware of the various bibliographical aids that will help steer them through this ocean of literature. The work of Enser is an especially useful starting point for those exploring the secondary literature [16, 17]. Gwyn M. Bayliss offers a clear introduction to reference works and materials [3]. The part played by the region's regiments in the various military campaigns have been covered by a number of studies. A number of accounts of units of the Local Defence Volunteers - the Home Guard - written shortly after they were stood down can be consulted though there is clearly a need for a fuller examination of the role played by these citizen-soldiers in both counties [1235, 1250, 1271]. The literature on other aspects of the Home Front continues to develop. This includes accounts of evacuation [1207, 1251] and the blitz [1291, 1330], and the impact of the war on women [1196, 1276]. More attention needs to be given to the preparations made for the war, especially the building up of the ARP service [1264]. The publication of reminiscences about the war from all sections of society is also to be encouraged [1209, 1335]. Nonetheless numerous opportunities for research exist both into the more specific military history of the region and, as with the First World War, into the broader question of the war's impact on the civilian population. A familiarity with some of the key accounts of the social and economic history of the war - Angus Calder, *The People's War. Britain 1939-1945* (London,1969) remains an essential piece of early reading - will help develop the agenda of issues and questions that would benefit from being explored in local studies. Surprisingly little has been written about military-civilian relationships. In a region where key elements of the war machine were built much remains to be re-discovered and analyzed. Metro-Vickers is an obvious starting point. In a conflict in which the scientist became a central figure research needs to be carried out into the contribution made by the region's educational institutions into military research as well as the training of military personnel. Themes such has how the war impacted on art and literature have received little attention at the regional level. Specific themes await examination but what would be most valuable would be a study of how this *total* war impacted on the *total* community of one of the region's major towns. In short there would appear much to be done. There is hardly a shortage of archival material, to which oral historians can add another valuable dimension.

[1194]   Andrews, Charles Ferdinand. *Vickers Aircraft since 1908.*   London: Putnam, 1969. **Locations:** *

[1195]   Atherton, James Grenville. *Home to Stay: Stretford in the Second World War: from the diaries of J.G. Atherton.*   Manchester: Neil Richardson, 1992.   **Locations:** 1, 3

[1196]   Ayers, Pat. *Women at War: Liverpool Women, 1939-45.*   Birkenhead: Liver Press, 1988. **Locations:** 2, 3, 4, 14, 40

[1197]   Bancroft, James W. *Devotion to Duty: Tributes to a region's VCs.*   Eccles, Manchester: Aim High Productions, 1990.   **Locations:** *

[1198] Bannerman, Alastair. "Lest We Forget." *Cheshire Life* 18 (July 1952) 24-5. **Locations: 4, 58**

[1199] Barber, Eric S. *My War*. Stalybridge: Boyes (printer), 1985. **Locations: 3, 11**

[1200] Beckett, Norman. *The War Around Us*. Staffordshire: Sentinel Newspapers Ltd., [n.d.] **Locations: 4**

[1201] Birtill, George. *The War and After*. Chorley: Guardian Press, 1976. **Locations: 3, 18, 59, 75, 79, 115**

[1202] Blackpool. Borough Council. *Remembrance Day service: [order of service], 1969.* Borough Council: Blackpool, 1969. **Locations: 3**

[1203] Blackpool. Civil Defence Department. *Do not read this unless you are interested in preventing suffering*. Blackpool: Borough Council, [n.d.]. **Locations: 3**

[1204] Blackpool County Borough. *The Aftermath: a memorandum on welfare work after a heavy air raid*. Blackpool: County Borough, 1941. **Locations: 3**

[1205] Blackpool. Town Clerk's Department. *Record of the names of Blackpool men and women who lost their lives in the 1939-45 War for inclusion on War Memorial*. Blackpool: Borough Council, 1952. **Locations: 3**

[1206] Bolton Evening News. *Bolton at War: a special supplement to mark the 50th anniversary of the start of the Second World War on September 3rd 1939*. Bolton: 1989. **Locations: 7**

[1207] Boyce, Joan. *Pillowslips and Gasmasks: Liverpool's Wartime Evacuation*. Birkenhead: Liver Press, 1989. **Locations: 2, 3, 4, 18, 40**

[1208] Brack, Alan. "A Dormitory Wide Awake." *Cheshire Life* 44 (January 1978) 24-7, 29. **Locations: 4, 58**

[1209] Brereton, Wallace. *Salford Boy Goes To War*. Manchester: Neil Richardson, 1990. **Locations:1, 15**

[1210] Broad, Richard, and Suzie Fleming, (eds.). *Nella Last's War: a mother's diary, 1939-45*. Bristol: Falling Wall, 1981. **Locations: ***

[1211] Buchan, G. H. *Making the Magic Bullet: a History of Northwich Works 1939-1986*. 1986. **Locations: 4**

[1212] Burnley and District Association of Ex-Servicemen. *Service for Remembrance Sunday*. [n.d.] **Locations: 9**

[1213] Carver, R. M. P. *A Short History of the Seventh Armoured Division, October 1938 - May 1943*. 1943. **Locations: MNH**

[1214] Chadwick, Vince. "The Woodford Wonder." *Cheshire Life* (November 1991) 100. **Locations: 4, 58**

[1215] Cheshire County Council. *Discovering Wartime Cheshire.* Cheshire: County Council Countryside & Recreation Department, 1985. **Locations:** *

[1216] --- *Wartime Tatton 1939-45. Full Story and Trail Guide.* Cheshire: County Council, Countryside County Council, [n.d.] **Locations: 203**

[1217] Cheshire Herb Committee. "Herb Gathering: drying foxglove leaves-urgent need for drying centres." *Cheshire Life* 9 (June 1942) 15. **Locations: 4, 58**

[1218] --- "Rose Hip Collection 1944." *Cheshire Life* 11(October 1944) 11. **Locations: 4, 58**

[1219] Cheshire. Home Guard. *History of the Cheshire Home Guard. From L.D.V. Formation to Stand-Down, 1940-1944.* Aldershot: Gale & Polden, 1950. **Locations: 1, 4, 17, 52, 57, 102, 200, 201, 202**

[1220] Cholmondeley, George Hugh, Earl of Rocksavage. *A Day's March Nearer Home: experiences with the Royals, 1939-1945.* 1947. **Locations: 4**

[1221] Commonwealth War Graves Commission. *The War Dead of the Commonwealth: the register of the names of those who fell in the 1939-1945 war and are buried in Cemeteries and Churchyards in the County of Lancashire.* Vol. 1-6. Commonwealth War Graves Commission: London, 1961. **Locations: 2, 15, 102, BOM**

[1222] Cooper, Julia, Colonel. "The Proud Memory of Dunkirk [1940]." *Lancashire Life* 5 (1957) **Locations: 1, 3, 27, 53.**

[1223] Cowden, James E. *Elder Dempster 1939-1945: the Price of Peace.* Liverpool: Cotton Exchange, 1981. **Locations: 2**

[1224] Crossland, A. *Davyhulme Anti-Aircraft Gun Site and Prisoner of War Camp.* 1990. **Locations: 52**

[1225] Davies, T.R., Captain. The Cheshire Royal Engineers, formerly 113 Assault Engineer Regiment [now 113 (Cheshire) Army Engineer Regiment]. 1950 with additions to 1960. **Locations: 4**

[1226] Farnworth Borough Council. *Farnworth and Kearsley Salute the Soldier Week: 29th April-6th May 1944. Souvenir Programme.* 1944. **Locations: 7**

[1227] Farnworth Borough Council, and Kearsley Urban District Council. *Wings for Victory: Farnworth and Kearsley May 22nd-29th 1943. Target £200,000. Official Programme.* 1943. **Locations: 7**

[1228] Ferguson, Ion. *Doctor at War.* London: Christopher Johnson, 1955. **Locations: 3**

[1229] Flixton. World War II. *Particulars of gas masks required for residents of Flixton*, 1938. **Locations: 52**

[1230] Forde, Frank. "The Liverpool Irish Volunteers in World War Two." *The Irish Sword* 15 (Winter 1983) 258-66. **Locations: NAM**

[1231]   German Air Force. A map issued to the German Air Force bearing coloured symbols indicating targets in the Bolton area. 6" to 1 mile.[1939-44]. **Locations: 7**

[1232]   Goulding, Frank. *A North West Village at War: a memoir of Winwick and its environs from 1939 to 1945*. Chester: Cheshire Libraries and Museums, 1987. **Locations: 4, 14, 18, 40, 58, 63, 115, 202**

[1233]   Greenwood, Jack. *Blackpool Entertains the Troops*. Blackpool: The Author, 1986. **Locations: 3**

[1234]   Grime, Harold Riley. *The Silver Trumpet: extracts from war articles in the "West Lancashire Evening Gazette", May 1940-May 1942*. Blackpool: Gazette and Herald, 1942. **Locations: 3**

[1235]   Hampson, C. G. *The History of the Tottington Home Guard, "C" Company 21st County of Lancaster (Bury) Battalion Home Guard*. Bury: Bury Times, 1945. **Locations: 10, 115**

[1236]   Hardy, Clive, Cooper, Ian and Hochland, Henry. *Manchester at War. A Pictorial Account*. Bowdon: Archive Publications Ltd. 1986. **Locations: 1, 2, 3, 102**

[1237]   Harrer, H. "Liverpool's 5 ARP services." *Liverpolitan* 7 (September 1938) 24-5. **Locations: 2**

[1238]   Harris, G. H. *Prisoner of War and Fugitive*. Aldershot: Gale & Polden Ltd, 1947. **Locations: 65**

[1239]   Hawkes, Arthur J. *Air Raid Distress information manual*. Civil Defence Committee: Wigan, 1942. **Locations: 18B**

[1240]   Hazel Grove and Bramhall. World War II. "Salute the Soldier: Hazel Grove and Bramhall Week." *Cheshire Life* 10 (June 1944) 20-1. **Locations: 4, 58**

[1241]   Hides, Margaret. "Evacuee: destination unknown." *Cheshire Life* (1992) 104. **Locations: 4, 58**

[1242]   Hodge, Sir R. J. "Protection of the port against enemy air raids." *Liverpolitan* 6(May 1937) 23. **Locations: 2**

[1243]   Hovis Ltd., Macclesfield. *War Record of Hovis Ltd 1939-1945*. Macclesfield: Hovis Ltd., 1947. **Locations: 1, 63**

[1244]   Hughes, John. *Port in a Storm: the air attacks on Liverpool and its shipping in the Second World War*. Liverpool: National Museums and Galleries on Merseyside, 1993. **Locations: 2**

[1245]   Imperial War Graves Commission. County Borough of Birkenhead. *Civilian War Dead, World War II, 1939-1945*. **Locations: 57**

[1246]   Irby WEA Local History Class. *Wirral at War*. Birkenhead: Countyvise, 1991. **Locations: 2, 4**

[1247] Isle of Man. *Military Service Local Tribunal.* Douglas: Norris Modern Press, 1961. **Locations: MNH**

[1248] Jackson, Aubrey J. *Avro Aircraft since 1908.* London: Putnam, 1965. **Locations: 4**

[1249] --- *De Havilland Aircraft since 1915.* London: Putnam, 1962. **Locations: * 2nd ed., 1978: 2, 3, 7, 8, 10, 13, 15, 40, 59**

[1250] Jager, Harold. *The Rise and Ascent of the "Number Two Platoon" (Home Guard) "A" Company, 17th Battalion, Cheshire Regiment (Wirral Div.).* 1945. **Locations: 57**

[1251] Jones, Audrey. *Farewell, Manchester: the Story of the 1939 Evacuation.* Manchester: Didsbury Press, 1989. **Locations: 3, 21**

[1252] Jones, Bill. *The Forgotten Front: the North-West at War, 1939-1945.* Manchester: Granada TV, 1989. **Locations: 21**

[1253] Jones, Helga. *Evacuation-preparation and implementation in Birkenhead 1938-1940.* [n.d.] **Locations: 57**

[1254] Jones, Louise. "Roger." *Cheshire Life* 39 (May 1973) 70-1. **Locations: 4, 58**

[1255] Kinnear, Sandy. *Sandy Kinnear's wartime memories 1939-1945 spent in seven overseas countries.* [n.d.] **Locations: 2**

[1256] Kissack, P. D. *Home Guard Southern Company History.* [n.d.] **Locations: MNH**

[1257] Lancashire: Voluntary Territorial Army Units. "An Account of Their Traditions and Work." *Defence* III (April 1938). **Locations: 7**

[1258] Lancaster Corporation. *Unveiling and dedication of the extension to the War Memorial in the Garden of Remembrance, Thursday the 17th May 1951.* Lancaster: Beeley Bros., 1951. **Locations: 28**

[1259] Lancaster Home Guard. *Home Guard, 46th County of Lancaster Battalion. From Brassard to Battledress: the History of The 46th Battalion, County of Lancaster Home Guard; by the Company of Officers.* 1946. **Locations: 1, 28**

[1260] Lancaster Royal Grammar School. *Memorial to Old Boys who have fallen in the War. Oct. 1944.* 1944. **Locations: 3, 28**

[1261] Lappin, J. P. *If we see morning boys! An account of the explosion of the SS Makaland in Huskisson Dock, Liverpool, during the Great May Blitz on Merseyside in 1941; based on the records of John Lappin, G.M., Deputy Divisional Officer, North Docks, Liverpool Auxilliary Fire Service.* Liverpool: Merseyside Maritime Museum, [n.d.] **Locations: MMM**

[1262] Laskier, Frank. *My name is Frank: a merchant seaman talks.* London: George Allen & Unwin, 1941. **Locations: 1, 2, 3**

[1263] Linney, Peter. "Lakeland Manhunt." *Lancashire Constabulary Journal* 4 (1966) 10-11. **Locations: LRO**

[1264] Little, Eddie. "Manchester City Council and the development of air raid precautions, 1935-1939." *Manchester Region History Review* 2.1 (1988) 3-12. **Locations: 1, LRO**

[1265] Littlewoods Mail Order Stores Ltd. *From peace to war: a record of Littlewoods war-time achievements.* Liverpool: Littlewoods Ltd., 1946. **Locations: 1, 2**

[1266] --- *From this Pool a Sword: an illustrated record of the change-over from Littlewoods peacetime organisations to war industries and of the types of munitions and equipment produced.* Liverpool: Littlewoods Ltd., 1946. **Locations: 1, 2**

[1267] Liverpool Daily Post. *"Bomb Damage in the City" Pictures from the Post.* Liverpool: Daily Post, 1945. **Locations: 2**

[1268] Liverpool Daily Post and Echo. *Bombers over Merseyside: this was Merseyside's "finest hour": the authoritative record of the blitz, 1940-1941.* Liverpool: Scouse Press, 1943. **Locations: 2, 3, 4, 34, 45, 57, 65, MMM**

[1269] Liverpool Echo. *BA93 souvenir: a special pictorial tribute recording the Battle of the Atlantic commemoration.* Liverpool: Liverpool Echo, 1993. **Locations: 2**

[1270] --- *Our War: Merseyside's role in World War Two. Supplement in 3 parts: 5.* Echo: Liverpool Echo, 1989. **Locations: 2**

[1271] Liverpool. Home Guard Units. *89th County of Lancaster (Liverpool) Battalion Home Guard.* 1947. **Locations: 2**

[1272] --- *90th Battalion (Lancs) Home Guard.* [n.d.] **Locations: 2**

[1273] --- "Home Guard: a brief account of the Liverpool Group." *Liverpolitan* 9 (November 1940) 14-15. **Locations: 2**

[1274] Liverpool. World War II. "The Civil Defence of Liverpool." *Liverpolitan* 9 (January 1940) 10-11. **Locations: 2**

[1275] --- "How crisis needs were dealt with in Liverpool." *Liverpolitan* 9 (October 1938) 4-5. **Locations: 2**

[1276] --- *Liverpool Women at War: an anthology of personal memories.* Picton Press: Liverpool, 1991. **Locations: 2, 3**

[1277] --- "Precautions against air raids. Liverpool's efforts to provide protection for its citizens." *Liverpolitan* 5 (September 1936) 14-16. **Locations: 2**

[1278] Lloyd, Ian. *Rolls-Royce: the Merlin at War.* London: Macmillan, 1978. **Locations: 4**

[1279] --- *Rolls-Royce: the Years of Endeavour.* London: Macmillan, 1978. **Locations: 1, 2, 3, 4, 11, 49, 52, 57**

[1280] McCann, John. *Echoes of Kohima*. Chadderton: The Author, 1989. **Locations: 11**

[1281] Makepeace, Chris. *Manchester As It Was*. Vol. 6: War and its Aftermath. Nelson: Hendon, 1977. **Locations: 1,3**

[1282] Manchester Evening News. *Two cities go to war*. Manchester: Evening News, 1989. **Locations: 1, 102**

[1283] Marsh, B. J., and Almond, S. *The Home Port: Bootle, the Blitz and the Battle of the Atlantic*. Sefton: Metropolitan Borough Education Department, 1993. **Locations: 2, 3**

[1284] Massey, Victoria. *One Child's War*. London: British Broadcasting Corporation, 1978. **Locations: ***

[1285] Mersey Docks and Harbour Board. *Port at War: the Story of the Port of Liverpool, its ordeals and achievements during the World War (1939-45)*. Liverpool: Mersey Docks and Harbour Board, 1946. **Locations: 1, 2, 3, 8, 45, 202, MMM**

[1286] Mount, Kevin. *War Time Pendle: an account of a few of the military fighters and bombers that came to grief, in and around Pendle and District, in World War II*. Burnley: Peter Scott (Printer), 1983. **Locations: 3, 21, 23**

[1287] Nabarro, Derrick. *Wait for the Dawn: an account of an escape from a prisoner of war camp*. London: Cassell & Co., 1952. **Locations: 3**

[1288] Naylor, Bill. *Lancashire Leatherneck*. Manchester: Neil Richardson, 1985. **Locations: ***

[1289] O'Dell, Audrey. *Burgeoning Amid the Alien Corn: new life in a strange country, 1939-1989*. Bedford: The Author, 1989. **Locations: 3, 18**

[1290] Parkin, Betty C. *Desert Nurse: war memoir*. London: Hale, 1990. **Locations: ***

[1291] Perrett, Bryan. *Liverpool: a City at War*. London: Robert Hale Ltd., 1990. **Locations: 2, 3, MM**

[1292] Phoenix, J. P. "War and Merseyside" *Liverpool Daily Post* Supplement (1955) 99-103. **Locations: 2**

[1293] Polish Artillery (Manchester). *Komunikat: Artyleryjski (Irregular). The Journal of a Social Club for those who served in the Polish Artillery Regiments during World War 1 and 2, and for members of their families living in the Manchester Area*. Vol. no.1-., 1973-. **Locations: 1**

[1294] Preston Catholic College. *Roll of Honour, 1939-45*. Preston: Mather (printers), 1946. **Locations: 3**

[1295] Prisoners of War Packing Centre. "Prisoners of War Parcels Packing Centre: Somewhere in Cheshire." *Cheshire Life* 7 (January 1941) 9. **Locations: 4, 58**

[1296] Quincey, Sylvia. "It Was a Lovely War." *Cheshire Life* 37 (September 1971) 69. **Locations: 4, 58**

[1297] Ridgway, E. "Camp Guard." *Lancashire Life* 31 (1983) 54. **Locations: LRO**

[1298] Robinson, Jack. *Jack and Jamie go to war.* London: G.M.P., 1988. **Locations: 2, 4, 10, 79**

[1299] Rocke, Joan. "Fun-and-Fear in Wartime Chester." *Cheshire Life* 51 (June 1985) 62-3. **Locations: 4, 58**

[1300] Rossendale Society for Genealogy and Heraldry, Pendle Branch. *Colne War Memorial, Roll of Honour, 1914-1918, 1939-1945. Rossendale Society for Genealogy and Heraldry, Pendle Branch 1980, list of persons serving in the A.R.P. and various leaflets relating to A.R.P. work.* 1980. **Locations: 23**

[1301] Rowland, Stan. *Wartime Blackpool, 1939-46.* [n.d.] **Locations: 3**

[1302] Royal Army Medical Corps War Memorial Fund. *Exhibition, Blackpool, August 20th to September 6th, 1947.* Shrewsbury: Wilding (printer), 1947. **Locations: 3**

[1303] Search Packs on Liverpool History Topics. *The May 1941 Blitz in Liverpool.* 1979. **Locations: 2**

[1304] Sharp, C. Martin. *D H: an Outline of De Havilland History.* Shrewsbury: Airlife, 1982 (revised edition) **Locations: 1, 3, 4, 13, 20, 52, 58, 59, 68**

[1305] Shaw, Frank, and Shaw, Joan. *We Remember Dunkirk.* F. and J. Shaw, 1994. **Locations: 7**

[1306] Smith, Peter J. C. *Flying Bombs Over the Pennines: the story of the V1 attack aimed at Manchester on December 24th, 1944.* Swinton, Manchester: Neil Richardson, 1988. **Locations: 3, 102, CL**

[1307] --- "The Night the Doodlebugs Came to Cheshire." *Cheshire Life* 50(December 1984) 44-5. **Locations: 4, 58**

[1308] Spence, J. C. *"They Also Serve". The 39th Cheshire Battalion Home Guard.* Manchester: C. Nicholls & Co. Ltd. , 1945. **Locations: 4, 57, 58, 63, 102, 115**

[1309] Spooner, Tony. *In Full Flight.* Canterbury: Wingham Press, 1991. **Locations: 2, 3, 4, 8, 52**

[1310] Sprenger, Cyril H. "Lancashire: 1940. I did like to be beside the seaside." *Lancashire Life* 33 (1985) 22-3. **Locations: LRO**

[1311] Starkey, Pat. *Companions in Caring.* Ilfracombe: Stockwell, 1989. **Locations: 2, 3, 40**

[1312] --- *I Will Not Fight: conscientious objectors and pacifists in the North West during the Second World War.* Liverpool: Liverpool University Press, 1992. 7 of <u>Liverpool Historical Essays</u>. **Locations: 1, 3, 112**

[1313] Stockport Museums and Art Gallery Service. *Hidden Army: Women in the Second World War. Evaluation of a one-day event held at the Pop-In-Centre, Stockport on 4th November*

1982. Stockport: Museums & Art Gallery Service, 1982. **Locations: 102**

[1314] Summerfield, Anne. *The Artist at War: Second World War paintings and drawings from the Walker Art Gallery's Collection, 10th February to 1st April 1990.* Liverpool: National Museums and Art Galleries on Merseyside, 1990. **Locations: 2, 85**

[1315] Tameside Local Studies Library. *War and the Civilian. Collection of pamphlets issued before and during the Second World War.* 1939-45. **Locations: 102**

[1316] Tameside. World Wars I & II. *Reporter at War. A collection of Reporter Articles to commemorate the 50th Anniversary of the outbreak of the Second World War and the 75th Anniversary of the outbreak of the Great War.* 1989. **Locations: 102**

[1317] Thompson, George, (ed.). *Merseyside Militant. Section I. The Port's war effort: A pictorial presentation of facts and figures concerning the war effort organised by the Mersey Docks and Harbour Board.* Liverpool: Mersey Docks and Harbour Board, 1964. **Locations: 1, 2, 57, MMM**

[1318] Tildsley, Dorothy. *Remembrance: recollections of a wartime childhood in Swinton: incorporating a Roll of Honour for the Borough.* Manchester: Neil Richardson, 1985. **Locations: 1, 3, 7, 15, 115**

[1319] Titherington, Arthur. *One Day at a Time: a British Prisoner of War's account of 1,300 days in a Japanese slave labour camp.* Hanley Swan: Self Publishing Association, 1993. **Locations: 3, 4, 7, 8, 10, 52, 57, 59**

[1320] Townend, Michael S. *Wartime in Burnley and Pendle.* Burnley: East Lancashire Newspapers, 1989. **Locations: 3, 23**

[1321] Trescatheric, Bryn. *Barrow's Home Front, 1939-1945.* Barrow: The Author, 1989. **Locations: 3**

[1322] Trescatheric, Bryn, and D. J. Hughes, (eds.). *Barrow at War.* Chorley: Countryside Publications, 1979. **Locations: 3, 112**

[1323] Urmston Urban District Council. *Urmston "Salute the Soldier" Week, 6th to 13th May, 1944. Official programme.* 1944. **Locations: 52**

[1324] Veysey, Arthur Geoffrey. *Clwyd a'r Rhfel: Clwyd at War, 1939-45.* Hawarden: Clwyd Record Office, 1989. **Locations: 2**

[1325] Wade, Beryl. *Storm over the Mersey.* Birkenhead: Countyvise, 1990. **Locations: 2, 3, 4, 14, 40**

[1326] Walsh, R. Raymond. *Stonyhurst College War Record, 1939-45.* Blackburn: T.H.C.L., 1989. **Locations: 3, 4**

[1327] Waterhead Primitive Methodist School. *Roll of Honour.* [n.d.] **Locations: 11**

[1328] Werrell, Len. "The Mutiny at Bamber Bridge." *After the Battle* 22 (1978) 1-11. **Locations: 3, LRO**

[1329]   Westall, Robert. "The War on Merseyside." in *Children of the Blitz*. London: Viking 1985. 137-48. **Locations:** *

[1330]   Whittington-Egan, Richard. *The Great Liverpool Blitz*. Neston, South Wirral: Gallery Press, 1987. **Locations: 2, 3, 4, 8, 14, 18**

[1331]   Whitworth, R. A. *Liverpool Under Fire*. 1946. **Locations: 2**

[1332]   Whitworth, Rodney. *Merseyside at War: a day-to-day diary of the 1940-1941 bombing*. Liverpool: Scouse Press, 1988. **Locations: 2**

[1333]   Williams, W. D. "Port of Liverpool: a mighty war weapon." *Merseyside and North West District Retail Trader* (June 1946) 3. **Locations: 2**

[1334]   Wood, Brian. "The Lost Generation." *Cheshire Life* 55 (September 1989) 136-9. **Locations: 4, 58**

[1335]   Wright, Simon. *Memories of the Salford Blitz: Christmas 1940*. Swinton, Manchester: Neil Richardson, 1987 **Locations: 1, 3, 15, 102**

ARCHIVES

Altrincham Library

[1336]   Cheshire Wardens. *Minute Book of Cheshire Wardens Old Members Association, Altrincham Branch 1944-1957*. 1944-57.

[1337]   --- *Minute Book of the meetings of the Head Wardens 1938-1944*. 1938-44.

Bacup Library

[1338]   Bacup Home Guard "B" Company. Picture of the Company.

Blackburn Library

[1339]   Blackburn Emergency Committee. *Blackburn Invasion exercise and you*. Blackburn: "Times", 1940.

[1340]   Home Guard. *Minutes and Accounts, 10th Battalion Home Guard Officers' Association, November 1945 to October, 1980*. 1945-80.

[1341]   --- *Nominal Rolls, 10th Battalion; War Office Regulations; newsletter; training instructions, 1942-1980 List of Members, 1960*. 1942-80.

Bolton Libraries

[1342]   Bolton. Air Raids. "Raider Kills 11 in North-West Town." *Bolton Journal and Guardian* (Friday 17th October 1941) .

[1343]   Bolton Evening News. *Bolton at War: a special supplement to mark the 50th anniversary of the start of the Second World War on September 3rd 1939*. 1989.

[1344] --- *Bolton Evening News, Sunday September 3rd 1939. Bolton at War 50th anniversary special reprint.* 1989.

[1345] --- *Wednesday 8th May 1985. V.E. Day 40 year anniversary supplement.* 1985.

[1346] Bolton Public Libraries. *Booklists, bookmarks, notices of lectures and miscellaneous publicity material, c.1940-1950.* [n.d.]

[1347] Bolton. World War II. "1939-1945. Bolton helps and is thankful." *Bolton Journal and Guardian* (11 May 1945).

[1348] --- "Bolton in the Hours of Victory." *Bolton Journal and Guardian* (Friday 16th August 1945).

[1349] --- "Victory Celebrations: reminiscent articles on V.E. Day celebrations in Bolton May 8th 1945." *Bolton Journal* (Thursday 9 May 1985).

[1350] --- "Victory greeted quietly, but gladly." *Bolton Journal and Guardian* (11 May 1945)

[1351] Lancashire County Constabulary. Air Raid Precautions Department. *Table indicating the authority responsible for organising the several parts of the air raid precautions scheme for the Administrative County of Lancaster*, 1938.

Burnley Library
[1352] Burnley and District Association of Ex-Servicemen. *Service for Remembrance Sunday.* [n.d.]

Bury Archives
[1353] Bury Archives. *Bury War Memorial Council papers, 1947-1954.* 1947-54.

[1354] --- *Prestwich Borough. Town Clerk's Papers: WWII roll of honour 1952-61; road blocks 1940-1947; machine gun posts 1940.* 1940-.

[1355] --- *Radcliffe Borough. War Memorial fund papers 1946-1949.* 1946-49.

[1356] --- *Ramsbottom Urban District. Town Clerk's Papers.* 1909.

[1357] --- *Tottington Urban District. War Memorial Committee Papers.* 1930-51

[1358] --- *Town Clerk's Papers.* 1939-45.

Cheshire Record Office
[1359] --- *Audlem Home Guard log books*, 1940-44.

Clitheroe Local Studies Library
[1360] Clitheroe Local Studies Library *Air Raid Precautions in Clitheroe, 1938-1940: Records.* 1938-40.

[1361] --- *Articles relating to Local Defence Volunteers and Home Guard, May 1940-November 1941.* 1940-41.

[1362] --- *Clitheroe Home Guard: box file containing miscellaneous letters, instructions, minute book, etc. May 1940-November 1941*. 1940-41.

Colne Library

[1363] --- *Home Guard: Various photographs*. [n.d.]

[1364] --- Photographic material. *Unveiling of war memorials, Colne, Trawden and Foulridge*. [n.d.]

Cumbria Record Office. Barrow

[1365] --- *Wartime log book compiled by C. Wardropper of Barrow, a prisoner in Marlag and Milognord Camp, Germany, 1942-1945*. 1942-45.

Cumbria Record Office. Carlisle

[1366] Cumbria Record Office. Carlisle. *World War II. The Battle Front. Records*.
Contents: Bank Notes; War map of the Western Front; "Sudeten Freiheit"; Maps of the Middle East; Papers re Col G.M. Kinmont; Photographs of Scots Guards; Badges, buttons and awards; Diaries of Lieutenant G.W. Iredell (restricted access); Scroll commemorating the death of Sapper J. Mumberson; War map of the Mediterranean and North Africa; Safe conduct pass to Lyons; Photographs of Royal Canadian Air Force crew and places in Germany bombed; Letter from men in German P.O.W. camps; Letters re service with the 7th Battalion, Border Regiment; Letters of John Hudleston on active service; Papers re imprisonment by Japanese in Java, subsequent; "A Guide to the Preservation of Life at Sea after Shipwreck; R.A.F. service papers; Experiences of a Belgian nurse, 1939-1944; Ration books and vouchers (French); Survey of public opinion in Sicily; Message from General Montgomery to his troops in Western Europe; Indian Service records; Dutch newspaper welcoming the 53rd Welsh Division; "Escape and Liberation 1940-1945", A.J. Evans; "Pathfinders", the story of the men who found and illuminated the targets for our bombers, Wing Commander W. Anderson; demobilisation letter of Miss B. Mehls (restricted access); Photographs including German propaganda poster, injured British soldier, march of ex-servicemen. 1938-47.

[1367] Cumbria Record Office. Carlisle. *World War II. The Home Front. Air Raid Precautions. Records*. Contents: Files, papers, minute books, booklets, cigarette cards etc. and other records relating to Air Raid Precautions in World War II for the following areas: Border area, Carlisle, Cockermouth, Cumberland, Ennerdale, Penrith. 1936-48.

[1368] Cumbria Record Office. Carlisle. *World War II. The Home Front. Casualties. Records*.
Contents: File re civilian deaths due to war operations, Carlisle (1939-45); 2 Files re civilian casualties, Cumberland (1940-3). 1938-45.

[1369] Cumbria Record Office. Carlisle. *World War II. The Home Front. Civil Defence Records*.
Contents: Letters, files, circulars, wages books, postcards, minute books, certificates and other records relating to World War II Civil Defence for the following areas: Braithwaite, Carlisle, Cockermouth, Cumberland, Keswick, Millom, Penrith. 1938-45.

[1370] Cumbria Record Office. Carlisle. *World War II. The Home Front. Conscientious Objection and Pacifism Records*.
Contents: Papers re conscientious objectors; Papers re the Union of Democratic Control; Records re Women's International League for Peace and Freedom; Pacifist posters; File re conscientious objectors on corporation staffs. 1939-41.

[1371] Cumbria Record Office. Carlisle. *World War II. The Home Front. Emergency Planning Records.*
Contents: Admission registers, files, plans, booklets and other records relating to World War II emergency planning for the following areas: Carlisle, Cumberland, Keswick, Millom, Netherby, Silloth. 1939-45.

[1372] Cumbria Record Office. Carlisle. *World War II. The Home Front. Evacuation Records.*
Contents: Reports, files, registers, minute books, papers, magazines, agreements and other records of evacuation for the following areas: Border area, Carlisle, Cockermouth, Cumberland, Keswick, Lanercost, Maughanby, Penrith, Workington. 1939-46.

[1373] Cumbria Record Office. Carlisle. *World War II. The Home Front. Miscellaneous Records.*
Contents:Contents: Papers re A.R.P., petrol rationing, etc.; A.R.P. warden's hand-book, pamphlet on fire precautions, Dig for Victory pamphlets; Pamphlets re war, pacifism, refugees, etc; Papers re. A.R.P., evacuees, gas-masks, first-aid, air-raid shelters, Great Clifton; File re National Service; A.R.P. rally; File re messages and telegrams since the outbreak of war; Cartoon of Hitler; Order of service; Papers re disposal of refuse from military establishments; sheet music; File re control of public slaughterhouse in time of war; Memoirs of Edwin Routledge M.B.E., J.P.; Forms and orders of service; Notes in Caldbeck service register.
Farm diaries (restricted access); 2 Files re salvage of waste material; Papers re evacuation, A.R.P., fuel restriction; Personal papers of Henry Larcher; File re war service wages; File re transfer of skilled labour to war industry; File re employment of aliens in local government offices etc.; "Dig for Victory" campaign letter; Military edition Ordnance Survey sheets; O.S. Map showing War Department occupation of Ullswater and the Lake District; "Wartime Cookery in Cumberland"; Facsimile poster "Is Your Journey Really Necessary?"; Above Derwent Newsletter (for those serving in H.M. Forces); Ministry of Information circulars etc; File re War Agricultural Executive Committee; Order of Service for "National Day of Prayer", Penrith; Correspondence with the Ministry of Information; File re iron railings; Correspondence with the Ministry of Information, certificate of anti-gas training; Papers re the internment of Japanese in Carlisle; Co-operative Union War Emergency circular; File re Mutual Aid Scheme; Poster re achievement in "Wings for Victory Week"; Details of Italian POW's working for the Ministry of Supply in Cumberland forests; Article re crash of R.A.F. Lancaster bomber at Kirkby Moor, Near Crosby-on-Eden, 1943; Scrapbooks inscribed by troops convalescing at Calthwaite Hall; National Identity cards; National Registration identity cards; File re War Department's stone pier at Buttermere; Order of Service re end of evacuation of Newcastle Royal Grammar School at Penrith; Programme of Her Majesty's Theatre, Carlisle including air-raid warning device; File re naval air station, Anthorn; Files re seaplane factory at Calgarth Park, Windermere; Postcard of altar and murals made by German prisoners-of-war in the chapel at the Moota Camp, near Cockermouth; "War Illustrated", "Picture Post"; War effort of Morton Sundour, Carlisle; Q.M.A.A.C. and A.T.S. Comrades' Association, Carlisle branch; Article on weapon research tests at Lowther Castle; "B.B.C. At War"; National Savings card. 1935-73.

[1374] Cumbria Record Office. Carlisle. *World War II. The Home Front. National Service Records.*
Contents: "National Service" booklet (1939); File re National Service returns, Cockermouth (1939); File, including plans, re use of land for training troops (1940); "Facts on sex for Men" (advice for soldiers) (1940); National Service cards (c.1942); File re National Service Acts (1942-3). 1939-43.

[1375] Cumbria Record Office. Carlisle. *World War II. The Home Front. Rationing Records.*
Contents: Certificates, business records, order books, files, lists, circulars, papers, ration books, clothing books and coupons, identity cards, notes of items and other records relating to World War II rationing for the following areas: Aspatria, Carlisle, Cockermouth, Keswick, Stapleton. 1939-58.

[1376] Cumbria Record Office. Carlisle. *World War II. The Home Front. Refugees. Records.*
Contents: Papers re Czech refugees at Hawse End, Keswick (1938-42); File re refugees, Cockermouth (1940-3). 1938-42.

[1377] Cumbria Record Office. Carlisle. *World War II. The Home Front. Requisitioning of Property Records.*
Contents: Files and papers relating to the requisitioning of the following properties: Cecil Street School, Carlisle; Brampton Sunday School; Workington Assembly Hall; Carlisle Airport; Keswick and Cockermouth properties. 1938-53.

[1378] Cumbria Record Office. Carlisle. *World War II. The Home Front. Territorial Army Records. Minute Book of the Territorial and Auxiliary Forces Association for the counties of Cumberland and Westmorland.* 1939-45.

[1379] Cumbria Record Office. Carlisle. *World War II. The Home Front. War Charities Records.*
Contents: Papers, files, catalogues, books, minute books, letters and other records relating to war charities for the following areas: Carlisle, Cockermouth, Keswick, Kirklinton, Maryport, Millom, Penrith, Wigton. 1938-47.

[1380] Cumbria Record Office. Carlisle. *World War II. The Home Front. War Damage Records.*
Contents: Files, papers, circulars, receipts and records for war damage in the following areas: Carlisle, Cockermouth, Ennerdale etc. 1939-44.

[1381] --- *World War II. Peace and Postwar. Charities Records.* Contents: Minutes of the Keswick Industrial Co-op's War Appreciation Fund Effort Committee; Papers re the distribution of food gifts, Carlisle; Files re Keswick War Service Appreciation Fund. 1945-1952.

[1382] --- *World War II. Peace and Postwar. Peace Celebrations. Records.*
Contents: File re peace celebrations, Carlisle; Minute book of the Cummersdale "Welcome Home" committee; File re Peace celebrations, Penrith; Financial statement re Ivegill "Welcome Home" Fund; Files re Thanksgiving Week, Keswick; File re peace celebrations, Workington; Minute book and cash book of the Carleton Peace celebrations and Memorial Fund Committee; File re Welcome Home for H.M. Forces after the war, Penrith. 1944-1962.

[1383] --- *World War II. Peace and Postwar. Reconstruction Records.*
Contents: Files, reports, papers and reports relating to post-World War II reconstruction for the following areas: Carlisle, Cockermouth, Cumberland, Keswick, Maryport, Workington. 1941-58.

[1384] --- *World War II. Peace and Postwar. Rolls of Honour.*
Contents: Rolls of honour (or files, notices, registers etc.) for the following areas: Beaumont, Carlisle, Dalston, Grinsdale, Kirkandrews-on-Eden, Warwick, Whitehaven, Workington. 1915-55.

[1385] --- *World War II. Peace and Postwar. Victory Celebrations. Records.*
Contents: Cumberland News, V.E. Day edition; Newspapers commemorating the end of the war in Europe and the Far East; Accounts and papers re Kirklinton Victory celebrations; "Thanksgiving for Victory" (leaflet); Victory postmark; Files re Victory celebrations, Keswick and Penrith; Printed "Victory" message from George VI to schoolchildren; Account book, bank book and account book of the Carleton Victory Memorial Committee. 1945-62.

[1386] --- *World War II. Peace and Postwar. War Memorials. Records.*
Contents: Files, designs, papers, plans, minutes, accounts, orders of service and other records for World War II war memorials for the following areas: Allhallows, Aspatria, Carlisle, Crosthwaite, Cumwhinton, Great Clifton, Lazonby, Newlands, Penrith, Scaleby, Skelton, Soulby, Westnewton. 1945-53.

Farnworth Library

[1387] Farnworth. "War Weapons" Week. *Farnworth and Kearsley National Savings Campaign. Programmes and Posters 1943/4.* 1943-44.

[1388] Farnworth. "Wings for Victory Week". *Farnworth and Kearsley National Savings Campaign. Programmes and Posters 1943/4.* 1943-44.

Haslingden Library

[1389] Haslingden, Borough of. *Scheme prepared in accordance with Appendix B of the Consolidated Instructions to Invasion Committees, issued by the Regional Commissioner on the authority of the Ministry of Home Security.* [n.d.]

Lancashire County Library

[1390] Blackburn. Diocese. *The Home-coming: report of the Bishop's Committee on the return home of men and women from war service.* 1945.

[1391] Lancashire County Library. *Military Awards to Blackpool men and women: miscellaneous items.* [n.d.]

[1392] Lancashire Library. *Blackpool in the Second World War: miscellaneous items.* 194-.

[1393] Militargeographische Einzelangaben uber England. Objektbilder zu den militargeographischen Objecktkarten. 1:250000 und 1:100000,, 4: Nord-Wales und Manchester. 1942.

Lancashire Record Office

[1394] Lancashire Record Office. *Blackpool Old Contemptibles: minutes 1961-74, accounts 1939-76.* 1939-76.

[1395] --- *Burnley: Royal British Legion, branch records 20th Century.* 19--.

[1396] --- *Papers relating to work of fire guard in Fulwood 1941-44.* 1941-44.

[1397] --- *World War Two Records*:
Contents:
Urban District Council of Barnoldswick wartime records including premises compensation register, 1939-1951.

Correspondence relating to Cotton Control received by the Blackburn and District Cotton Manufacturers' Association from the Ministry of Supply, 30 Aug. 1940-25 Apr. 1941.
Minutes of the Blackburn Advisory Panel to the Blackburn and District Cotton Manufacturers' Association re the drafting of cotton industry employees, 30 Mar. 1942-7 Dec. 1945.
Blackpool Civil Defence Records, 1938-1973.
Volume including Brierfield Urban District Council Air Raid Precautions Committee minutes, 11 May 1939-2 Jan. 1945.
Clayton-le-Moors Urban District Council Air Raid Precautions file, 1939-1943.
Church Urban District Council register of accommodation, 1939-1945, and register of fire prevention arrangements, Jun. 1941-Sep. 1944.
German aerial photographs, target plans and flying instructions for raid on Flookburgh, Formby and Warton (Amounderness), 1942, 1943.
Correspondence concerning appointment and resignation of Deputy Food Executive Officer for the Preston Rural Area, with the Food Control Office, 3 Sep.1939-Apr.1945.
Skelmersdale Urban District Council Air Raid Precautions Committee, 4 Mar.1936-19 Apr.1939.
Stretford Metropolitan Borough Council record of civilian deaths due to war operations and files of related forms and papers, 1939-1945.
Thornton Cleveleys Urban District Council Air Raid Precautions letter books, 25 May 1940-31 May 1946.
Trawden Urban District Council Emergency Committee minute book, 19 Oct. 1939-19 Feb. 1940
Trawden Urban District Council's "war comforts" records, 1939-1948.
Walton-le-Dale Urban District Council War records including fire brigade and war damage, evacuation and billeting, air raid precautions and Civil Defence records, 1939-1968.
Lancashire County Council Air Raid Precautions Committee minute books, joint accounts minute books, home office circulars, ministry of health circulars, and miscellaneous memoranda, pamphlets (index) booklets, 1939-1949.
1939-73.

[1398] Lancashire Record Office. *World War Two Records*.
Contents:
Roll of men from Longton serving in the armed forces, 1940.
Municipal Borough of Nelson list of air-raid shelters provided for local schools, c.1940.
Ormskirk Urban District Council Army Social Welfare Committee minute book, 2 Apr. 1940-27 Jan. 1950.
"Salute the Soldier" week in Ormskirk: photographs of the Inaugural ceremony and parade, 3-10 Jun. 1944.
Padiham Urban District Council wartime records including Air Raid Precautions and air raid shelter records, 1938-1954.
Poulton-le-Fylde Urban District Council Air Raid Precautions, 5 Nov. 1937-7 Jul. 1939.
Preston County Borough Air Raid Precautions Committee minutes, 13 Jan.1939-17 Oct.1945.
Preston Rural District Council evacuation records, 1939-1945.
Preston County Borough Committee for the Relief of Distress by War minutes, 1914-1940.
File of Preston Home Guard and Civil Defence circulars, orders, instructions and certificates concerning courses and exercises, 1944, 1949-1955.
OS 6" town map of Preston comprising parts of sheets 61 and 69, 1933 ed., overwritten with Home Guard defence dispositions, c.1940.
List of addresses and telephone numbers in connection with air raid precautions, food

control etc., in the rural district of Preston, 20 Feb. 1941.
Fulwood Urban District Council Air Raid Precautions committee minutes and records including photographic album of activities, 1939-1945.
Garstang Rural District Council wartime records including files (219), 1939-1945.
Haslingden Municipal Borough Council Air Raid Precautions and Wartime Records, 1938-1945.
Huyton Urban District Council air raid warnings and messages, 10 Nov.1939-30 Sep.1944.
Hyndburn Borough Council plans of Air Raid Precautions, c.1938-1945.
Handbill: visit of King's Scouts, decorated for bravery in blitzes, to Lancaster, 7 Nov.1942.
Leyland Urban District Council National Savings Movement records, 1940-1956.
Lord Mayor of London's National Air Raid Distress Fund, relating to Littleborough Urban District Council, 1941.
Little Lever Constabulary register of special constables 1936-1946 and Register of Air Raid Precautions wardens, 1938-1942. 1939-73.

[1399] Lancashire Record Office. *World War Two Records*.
Contents:
Lancashire County Council Education Committee Air raid precautions sub-committee minute books, 19 Sep.1938 - 4 May 1942.
Records of a number of County of Lancaster Battalions of Home Guard, 1940-1945.
Lancashire County Control Centre records, including unexploded bombs record book, Air Raid Precautions key maps showing positions of incidents, files relating to gas bomb cemeteries, record books of persons doing Fire Guard duties at the County Offices, incident report books and message books, 1939-1945.
Letters and photographs of bomb damage at Atherton, Bury, Eccles, Warton, Freckleton, Horwich, Litherland, Prestwich, Ramsbottom and Walton-le-Dale, 1944.
Lancashire County Council War Charities Act Committee minute book, 9 Sep.1940-17 Feb.1947.
Police Headquarters "Confidential Security Scheme" memorandum books, 15 Jun.1939-27 Aug.1942.
Home Office circulars issued by the Ministry of Home Security, 4 Jan.1939-9 Jan.1946.
Air Raid Precautions memoranda, 9 Aug. 1935-6 Mar.1943.
Fire Brigade memorandum books, 30 Nov.1938-14 Jan.1942.
Police Headquarters Wartime memorandum books, 24 May 1939-6 Jul. 1940.
Volume containing copies of Special Constable's order 1923, Police & Firemen War Services Act, 1939, Police War reserve rules 1945, Women's Auxiliary Police Corps rules 1945.
Diaries of Thomas Hope Floyd of Chorlton-cum-Hardy who served as a lieutenant in the Gloucester Regiment on Home Defence in the Bristol Channel area, 1940-1942, and as a full-time fire watcher, 1943-1945, in a Manchester business house, 22 Aug.1939-20 Aug. 1945.
Letters written home by Thomas Hope Floyd during his service in the Gloucester Regiment, 11 May 1940-6 Sep.1942.
Letters to Thomas Hope Floyd (1903-1973), containing many letters written both during and after the war by comrades.
Documents, letters re service in War, R.A.F.VR. (Civilian employee), Army, 1938-1942.
Bundle of war-time information publications, 1938-1943.
A Guide to National Service, 1939.
Certificate qualifying J. Almond for admission to the "Air Raid Precautions Auxiliary Reserve" of the St. John Ambulance Brigade, 28 Oct.1939.

Correspondence concerning J. Almond's application for petrol coupons, with the Divisional Petroleum Office, 1940-1941.
Civil Defence card, 1 Jun.1942.
Correspondence and notes concerning appointment as a part-time street Party leader by the Fire Prevention Services, 1943.
"Rhymes of the War", poems by Joan Pomfret, c.1945.
Books, (2), of clothing coupons, 1946-1948.
Envelope containing agenda, minutes, 2 circular letters, circular regarding Women's Voluntary Services for Air Raid Precautions, 20 May-28 Oct.1938. (closed to public until 1999).
Wartime service documents of W.J. Blake Esq., of Walton-le-Dale- Pay Book, Release Book, Grade Card, Record of Service and Certificate of Transfer to the Army Reserve, 1940-1945.
File containing address by Councillor H. Brabin, J.P., to the Urban District Councils' Association of Lancashire on post-war problems of local government; pamphlet entitled *The Outbreak of War* issued by the Ministry of Information; and memoranda, circulars, papers and schedules issued by the Board of Education and the Ministry of Education, 22 Aug.1939-26 Jan.1945. 1939-73.

Lancaster Library

[1400]   Lancaster. Air Raid Precautions. *Minute Book of the A.R.P. Guard House, Salyard Street, Lancaster, 1940-1945.* 1940-45.

[1401]   Lancaster. Home Guard. 44th County of Lancaster Battalion. *Local Defence Volunteers: D Group, E Company*

[1402]   Lancaster. World War II. *Fire Watching Book, 1943-44.* 1943-44.

[1403]   West Lancashire Territorial Army and Air Force Association. *Home Guard Stores ledger of West Lancashire Territorial Army and Air Force Association, September 1943 to December 1944.* 1944.

Liverpool Libraries and Information Services, Record Office and Local History Department

[1404]   Civil Defence Emergency Committee. "ARP Work Since the Commencement of the War: a review." *Liverpool City Council Proceedings*, 2015-2037. 1938-9.

[1405]   --- *Community Catering in Liverpool.* 1942.

[1406]   --- *Reports, No.1-82, 84-94.* 1939-47.

[1407]   Liverpool Libraries and Information Services, Record Office and Local History Department. *Citations from the "London Gazette": awards to Liverpool people, 1939-1945.* 2 vols., 1939-45.

[1408]   --- "Defence of Merseyside against air raids." *Liverpolitan* 7.11 (November 1938) 31-40.

[1409]   --- *Evacuation from Liverpool during the Great War 1939-45, also Liverpool as a reception area.* [n.d.]

[1410]   --- *Liverpool: Military Decorations, World War, 1939-1945: rewards for gallantry.* 1939-45.

[1411] --- *May Blitz 1941.* [n.d.]

[1412] --- *Military Affairs: Newspaper Cuttings, 1929-1958.* 2 vols., 1929-58.

[1413] --- *Newspaper Cuttings.* 9 vols., [n.d.]

[1414] Liverpool University Department of Social Science. *Preliminary report on the problems of evacuation.* Liverpool: The University, 1939.

Manx National Heritage

[1415] British Legion. Isle of Man. *Scrapbook of items relating to the local British Legion including appeals, a list of war dead and programmes of events, c.1920-1947.* 1947.

Merseyside Record Office

[1416] *Sir Douglas Crawford Collection.* Crawford's records relate to the 59th (4th West Lancs) Division in the Second World War. The collection consists of 16 volumes, including 236 Battery Diaries, correspondence, despatch documents, photographs, maps, official records, operational records etc. 1939-45.

National Army Museum

[1417] National Army Museum Archives. *Order of Service for the dedication of Chindits' colours, Liverpool Cathedral 14 March 1948.* 1948.

[1418] --- "Outbreak of War with Germany." *Bolton Evening News* (3 September 1939).

[1419] --- *Programme, Far East Prisoners of War Club 27th Annual Renuion and Service of Remembrance, London 6 October 1979.* 1979.

Salford Archives Centre

[1420] *Records of Military Service.*
Contents:
Leslie Dawson: exercise books containing attached typed copies of his reminiscences of the Royal Engineers from 1940-2. 1. "Middle East Roundabout," "Book One. Arrival in India" and "Book Two. Syrian Interlude", describing experiences in India, Egypt, Syria and Palestine in 1940 and 1941 (with photographs). 2. Fortress Tobruk...by 1986431 L/Cpl Leslie Dawson, R.E., describing his experiences at Tobruk, Libya, during 1940-42 (with poems and photographs, 1 exercise book). 3. "Fortress Tobruk. By Leslie Dawson." (Slightly different from above). 4. "Book Four. Sojourn in India" describing his experiences in India and Iraq apparently in 1942 (with photographs).
Other Records: records of an army officer on the Western Front, 1916, 1918-19, [n.d.] and of an R.A.F. officer during the Second World War, 1940-45; letters on loss in action of R.A.F. Sergeant in action in 1941; Commission as Adjutant in the Third Dragoon Guards. 1859-1919.

Salford Local Studies Library

[1421] Lancashire Fusiliers. *The Ceremony of Honouring the Lancashire Fusiliers, 18th October 1947.*

Tameside Local Studies Library

[1422] Brooks, J., and L. Brooks, (eds.). *Evacuation records for FJC High School Fallowfield, Seymour Road School, Clayton, and Ravensbury Road School, Clayton, 1939. Indexed by*

J. and L. Brooks. 1988.

[1423] Wilde, S. *Notes on the production of radar and direction-finding equipment at Joseph Adamson and Co. Ltd. during World War II*. 1989.

Trafford Local Studies Library

[1424] Ministry of Food. *Copy of ration book and shopping card of Barbara Knight, Davyhulme Hall Farm*. [n.d.]

[1425] Ministry of Power. *Motor Fuel Ration Book*. [n.d.]

[1426] Urmston War Comforts Committee. *Letters from servicemen thanking UWCC for parcels*. 12 vols. 1939-45.

Wigan Heritage Service. History Shop

[1427] --- *Twenty-sixth Lancashire Battalion "A" Company Dispositions of troops and weapons March 1943*. 1943.

[1428] --- *Various papers about the Home Guard in Ashton in Makerfield*. [n.d.]

[1429] --- *Wigan German War 1939-45 Wigan Roll of Honour Draft list of the names of the men and women of Wigan who lost their lives in the war*. 1939-45.

[1430] Wigan. World War II. *Wigan War Weapons Week Nov 30-Dec 7 1940 (two albums of photographs)*. 1940.

Wirral Libraries

[1431] Birkenhead. *World War 1939-1945 Roll of Honour-list of members of H.M. Forces and Merchant Navy who lost their lives*. 1939-45.

[1432] Pike, Arnold Norman. *The non-combatant- personal reminiscences (one-time Private 106002 R.A.M.C.)*. [n.d.]

[1433] Wilkinson, J. *In Memoriam List, Bolton Men Killed in World War II: details of three local servicemen buried in foreign cemeteries*. 1992.

[1434] Wirral Libraries. Photographs. *Photographs of prisoners of war (Mr Williams of 34 Patten Street, Birkenhead)*. 1985.

ADDRESSES

Readers intending to research military history in the region are advised to contact archivists and curators before visiting. Researchers should be reminded that whilst they are welcomed at repositories, hours of opening may be limited and are liable to change.

Public Library services, whilst mostly providing a free service, should also be contacted as hours of opening and terms of access to lending and reference materials may vary considerably depending upon the individual authority.

RECORD OFFICES

See also under Libraries: Bolton, Liverpool, St. Helens and Wigan have integrated archives and local studies centres.

Bury Archives, 1st Floor, Derby Hall Annexe, Edwin Street (off Crompton Street), Bury, Lancashire BL9 0AS

Cheshire Record Office, Duke Street, Chester, Cheshire CH1 1RL

Chester City Record Office, Town Hall, Chester, Cheshire CH1 2HJ

Cumbria Record Office (Barrow), 140 Duke Street, Barrow-in-Furness, Cumbria LA14 1XW

Cumbria Record Office (Carlisle), The Castle, Carlisle, Cumbria CA3 8UR

Cumbria Record Office (Kendal), County Offices, Stricklandgate, Kendal, Cumbria LA9 4RQ

Greater Manchester County Record Office, 56 Marshall Street, New Cross, Manchester M4 5FU

Lancashire Record Office, Bow Lane, Preston, Lancashire PR1 2RE

Merseyside Record Office, 4th Floor, Cunard Building, Pier Head, Liverpool L3 1EG

Public Record Office, Chancery Lane, London WC2 1LR

Salford Archives Centre, 658-662 Liverpool Road, Irlam, Manchester M30 5AD

MUSEUMS

Blackburn Museum and Art Gallery, Museum Street, Blackburn, Lancashire BB1 7AJ

Bolton Museum and Art Gallery, Le Mans Crescent, Bolton, Lancashire BL1 1SE

Cheshire Military Museum, The Castle, Chester, Cheshire CH1 2DN

Grosvenor Museum, 27 Grosvenor Street, Chester CH1 2DD

Imperial War Museum, Lambeth Road, London SE1 6HZ

Keele University Air Photo Library, The Archivist, Air Photo Library, Department of Geography, University of Keele, Staffordshire ST5 5BG

King's Own Royal Regiment (Lancaster) Museum, Lancaster City Museum, Market Square, Lancaster LA1 1HT

King's Regiment Museum and Archives, Liverpool, National Museums and Galleries on Merseyside. The Museum is currently housed in Liverpool Museum, William Brown Street, Liverpool, until October 1994. A new museum and display will be opened at the Liverpool Life Museum, Albert Dock, Liverpool in 1996. The archives are housed in a separate site, at Dale Street, Liverpool.

Lancashire County and Regimental Museum, Stanley Street, Preston PR1 4YP

Lancashire Fusiliers Regimental Museum, Wellington Barracks, Bolton Road, Bury, Lancashire BL8 2PL

Liddell Hart Centre for Military Archives, The Library, King's College London, Strand, London WC2R 2LS

Liverpool Scottish Regimental Museum, Forbes House, Score Lane, Childwall, Liverpool L16 6AN

Manx National Heritage, Douglas, Isle of Man.

Merseyside Maritime Museum, National Museums and Galleries on Merseyside, Albert Dock, Liverpool L3 4AA

Museum of the Manchesters, Ashton Town Hall, The Market Place, Ashton-under-Lyne, Manchester OL6 6DL

National Army Museum, Royal Hospital Road, Chelsea, London SW3 4HT

National Maritime Museum, Romney Road, Greenwich, London SE10 9NF

Royal Air Force Museum, Grahame Park Way, Hendon, London, NW9 5LL

Royal Armoured Corps Tank Museum and Royal Tank Regiment Museum, Royal Armoured Corps Centre, Bovington, Wareham Dorset BH20 6JG

Royal Artillery Historical Trust, The Royal Artillery Institution, Old Royal Military Academy, Woolwich, London SE18 4DN

Royal Engineers Corps Library, Brompton Barracks, Chatham, Kent ME4 4UG

Royal Naval Museum, H.M. Naval Base, Portsmouth, Hampshire PO1 3LR

Royal Signals Museum, Blandford Camp, Blandford Forum, Dorset DT11 8RH

Townley Hall Art Gallery, Townley Park, Burnley, Lancashire BB11 3RQ

LIBRARIES

Bolton Archive and Local Studies Service, Central Library, Le Mans Crescent, Bolton, Lancashire BL1 1SE

Bury Reference Library Local Studies Section, Central Library, Manchester Road, Bury, Lancashire, BL9 0DG

Cheshire Libraries, Arts and Archives, 91 Hoole Road, Chester, Cheshire CH2 3NG   see also Cheshire Record Office above

Chetham's Library, Long Millgate, Manchester M3 1SB

Cumbria County Library HQ, Arroyo Block, The Castle, Carlisle CA3 8XF

Douglas Public Library, Ridgeway Street, Douglas, Isle of Man.

Knowsley Library Service, Central Library, Derby Road, Huyton, Merseyside L35 9UJ

Lancashire County Library, Local Studies Department, 143 Corporation Street, Preston, Lancashire PR1 2UQ

Lancaster University Library, University of Lancaster, Lancaster, Lancashire LA1 4YH

Liverpool Libraries and Information Services, Record Office and Local History Department, Central Library, William Brown Street, Liverpool L3 8EW

Liverpool University, PO Box 123, Liverpool L69 3DA
Harold Cohen Library
Sydney Jones Library
Archives

Manchester Metropolitan University, All Saints Library, All Saints Building, Grosvenor Square, Manchester M15 6BH

Manchester Public Libraries, Central Library, St. Peter's Square, Manchester M2 5PD

Manchester University, John Rylands University Library of Manchester, Oxford Road, Manchester M13 9PP

Oldham Local Studies Library, 84 Union Street, Oldham, Lancashire OL1 1DN

Rochdale Libraries and Arts Department, Wheatsheaf Library, Wheatsheaf Centre, Baillie Street, Rochdale OL16 1JZ

St. Helens Local History and Archives Library, Central Library, Gamble Institute, Victoria Square, St. Helens, Merseyside WA10 1DY

Salford Local History Library, Peel Park, Salford M5 4WU

Salford University Library, Academic Information Services (Library), Salford M5 4WT

Sefton Library Services (Local History)
North Area: Southport Library, Lord Street, Southport PR8 1DJ
South Area: Crosby Library, Crosby Road North, Waterloo L22 0LQ

Stockport Local Heritage Library, Central Library, Wellington Road South, Stockport SK1 3RS

Tameside Local Studies Library, Stalybridge Library, Trinity Street, Stalybridge, Cheshire SK15 2BN

Trafford Local Studies Centre, Sale Public Library, Tatton Road, Sale, Manchester M33 1YH

University of Central Lancashire, The Library, Preston, Lancashire PR1 2HE

Wigan Heritage Service
Archives, Leigh Town Hall, Leigh, Lancashire WN7 2DY
History Shop, Rodney Street, Wigan, Lancashire WN1 1DQ
Local History Library, Turnpike Centre, Civic Square, Leigh WN7 1EB

Wirral Libraries, Central Library, Borough Road, Birkenhead, Wirral L41 2XB

AUTHOR INDEX

The numbers cited refer to bibliographical entries.

4th Royal Lancashire Militia 585
7th Cumberland Rifle Volunteers 808
8th Hussars 1002
13th Lancashire Battalion 816
156 Merseyside and Greater Manchester Transport Regiment 817
613 Squadron 850

Ablett, H. Kellett 502
Accrington. New Jerusalem Church 1007
Ackers, James 627
Adams, W. H. Davenport 268
Adelphi Lads Club 1008
Air Training Corps 851-5
Allen, Frank 363
Allen, Madeline 1009
Allinson, Sidney 1010
Allison, J.E. 1141
Almond, S. 1283
Anderson, J.J. 487
Anderson, William Hastings 57
Andrew, Samuel 628
Andrews, Albert Williams 410
Andrews, Charles Ferdinand 1194
Anon. (Hulme Barracks) 948
Antrobus family 116
Appleton, Francis M. 542, 753
Argyle, M. A. 241
Armitage, John Basil 1011
Ascoli, David 1
Ashton, W. 906
Ashton-under-Lyne Volunteers 629
Ashurst, George 308
Ashworth, George 1168
Association of Naval Ex-Servicemen 907
Atherton, James Grenville 1195
Athletes Volunteer Force 1012
Atkinson, Robert 940
Axon, William 949
Ayers, Pat 1196
Aytoun, James 120

Bacon, G. 1158
Bacup Home Guard "B" Company 1332-3
Bacup Library 1145, 1338
Bainbrigge, Philip 309
Baker, Arnold 925
Bamford, P. G. 310
Bancroft, James W. 950, 1197
Bancroft, T. 630
Bannatyne, Neil 121
Bannerman, Alastair 1198
Barber, Eric S. 1199
Bardgett, Colin 242
Barker, John 711
Barlow, Clement Anderson Montague 311
Barlow, Frederick Watkins 312
Barlow, L. 712
Barnes, Robert Money 2
Barnes, Wally 818
Barrow Borough Council 1161
Barrow, Harry 269
Barton, B. T. 631
Barton, John 313
Bastick, J. Desmond 713
Bayliss, Gwyn 3
Beckett, Norman 1200
Beet, W. Ernest 411
Behrend, Arthur 122, 1013
Bell, Archibald Colquhoun 412
Bell, Ernest W. 1014
Bell, James 1004
Bell, Martin 492
Benson, J. 931
Bent, Spencer John 156
Berkeley, R. H. 364
Bigland, Editha Blanche Hinde 270
Bigwood, George 819-20
Billings, G. M. 856
Billings, John 1015
Birkenhead, Borough of 1016
Birkenhead News 1017
Birkenhead, World War II 1431-2
Birtill, George 1201
Blackburn, C. J. 1018
Blackburn and District Discharged Sailors and Soldiers Association 1019
Blackburn Athletes' Volunteer Force 1012,

1146-50
Blackburn County Borough 123
Blackburn Diocese 1390
Blackburn Hundred 610
Blackburn Library 174-5, 610, 1146-50, 1339-41
Blackburn, Witton 754
Blackburn, Witton Park 124
Blackpool, Arnold School for Boys 1020
Blackpool, Borough Council 1202
Blackpool, Civil Defence Department 1203
Blackpool County Borough 1204-5
Blackpool Herald 1021
Blackpool. World War I 1022
Blake, W.J. 1399
Blundell, William 1158
Boderke, David 1023
Bolton, George 810
Bolton, Joseph 502
Bolton, Peter 502
Bolton
  Air Raids 1343
  Lancashire Lieutenancy Records 696
  Militia 611
  World War I 899, 982-3, 1151
Bolton Artillery 503
Bolton County Borough 1024
Bolton Evening News 1025-7, 1206, 1343-5
Bolton Journal 1025-6
Bolton Museum and Art Gallery 315, 1028
Bolton Public Libraries 984, 1152-3, 1342-51
Bolton Regiments 976
Bolton, World War I 1029-30, 1151-3
Bolton, World War II 1342-50
Bonner, Robert 413
Border Regiment *see* King's Own Border Regiment
Border Regiment Association 243
Borron, John Arthur 632
Bowdin, Tom 1031
Bowers, Maunsell 951
Boyce, Joan 1207
Boyd, Violet 58
Brack, Alan 1032, 1208
Bradshaw, Brian 1033
Bradshaw, James 492
Bradshaw, John 618
Braham, John Randle Daniel 857
Branigan, D. P. 908

Brereton, J.M. 4
Brereton, Wallace 1209
British Legion 1415
British Limbless Ex-Servicemen's Association 1034
Broad, Richard 1210
Broadfoot, William 492
Broadhurst, Jonathan 492
Brockbank, John 941
Brooks, J. 1421
Brooks, L. 1421
Brophey, John 623
Brotherton, General Sir Thomas 972
Brown, James 995
Bruce, Anthony 5, 6
Bruckshaw, Horace 1036
Brunskill, Keith R. 858
Bryant, G. J. 1037
Buchan, G. H. 1211
Bucher, H. Ernst 407
Buckton, J. D. 544
Bull, Stephen 755
Bulloch, J.M. 365
Burden, G. W. P. N. 125
Burges-Short, George 9
Burke-Gaffney, John Joseph 186
Burne, Richard Vernon Higgins 1038
Burnley and District Association of Ex-Servicemen 1212, 1352
Burnley Barracks 985
Burnley Corporation 126
Burnley Express 1039
Burnley Lancashire Rifle Volunteers 756
Burton, Fred H. 859
Bury Archives 358-61, 987, 1154-5, 1353-8
Bury County Borough 315
Bury Loyal Association 952
Butler, Philip Henry 860

Campbell, G. L. 414-15
Campbell, W.H. 237
Cantwell, John D. 7
Capleton, E. W. 504
Carew, Tim 8
Carter, D. P. 587
Cartmell, Harry 1040
Carver, R. M. P. 1213
Catling, Robert 492
Cauldwell, A. H. 1005
Chadwick, Vince 1214

Chalmers, W. S. 909
Chartres, John 861
Chavasse, F. J. 1041
Cheshire Artillery Volunteers 535
Cheshire County Council 612, 1215-18
Cheshire Herb Committee 1217-18
Cheshire, Home Guard 1219
Cheshire Military Museum 113
Cheshire Record Office 613-14, 697, 746, 988, 1156, 1359
Cheshire Regiment 57-119
Cheshire Rifle Volunteers 807
Cheshire Territorial and Auxiliary Forces Association 822, 846
Cheshire, Victoria Cross 1042
Cheshire Volunteer Corps (Wilmslow) 807
Cheshire Volunteer Regiment 1157
Cheshire Wardens 1336-7
Cheshire Yeomanry Cavalry 746
Chester City Record Office 73, 111, 112, 613-14, 698-9, 900, 989, 1157
Chester Volunteers 588
Chester, Western Command 74
Chevasse twins 187, 237
Chichester, Henry M 9
Chichester-Constable, Cecil 1076
Cholmondeley, George Hugh 1220
Churton, William A. V. 75
Civic Service League 1043
Clague, Curwen 505
Clarke, David A. 1044
Clarkson, Herbert G. 584
Clay, Charles Butler 534
Clay, J. G. 1000
Claye, Herbert Sandford 633
Clemesha, Henry Wordsworth 1045
Clitheroe Home Guard 1361
Clitheroe Local Studies Library 1158, 1360-2
Cochrane, D. B. 945
Colley, T. 714
Colne and Nelson Times 1046-7
Colne Library 178, 937, 991-2, 1159-60, 1363-4
Colne, Red Lion Inn 991
Colne, World War I 1159-60
Commonwealth War Graves Commission 1221
Congleton Borough Council 76
Connell, A. 1048
Connellan, J. H. 757

Connon, Peter 862
Cook, A. L. Michael 823
Cooke, John H. 715
Coop, J. O. 1049-50
Cooper, G. 316
Cooper, Ian 1236
Cooper, Julia 1222
Cooper, W. 995
Coopley, John 944
Copland, D. 1015
Coward, B. 953
Cowden, James E. 1223
Cowell, Clement W. 416
Cowper, J. M. 272
Cowper, Lionel Ilfred 271-2
Cox, Bernard William 954
Craig, Hardin 10
Crawford, Sir Douglas 1416
Crompton, Walter 758
Crook, H. T. 538
Crookenden, Arthur 77-81
Cross Fleury 273
Crossland, A. 1224
Cumberland and Westmorland Joint Territorial Force Association 825
Cumbria Record Office. Barrow 938, 1161, 1357, 1365
Cumbria Record Office. Carlisle 265, 615, 701, 747, 993-4, 1162, 1366-86
Cuppage, R. Jackson 970
Currie, James 955

Darlington, Henry 417
Davidson, J.R. 237
Davies, Brian L 11
Davies, T. R. 539, 1225
Dawson, Leslie 1420
Dawson, Thomas H. 1051
Dawson-Greene, Captain 995
Deakin, Thomas 1005
Dean, Charles Graham Troughton 366
Dean, Percy T. 1082
De Curzon, Alfred 955
Delaney, William 492
Derby, Lord 589, 796
Derbyshire, George 849, 1190
De Trafford, E.F. 1168
Dewhurst, Roger 990
Dickinson, G.F. 236
Disbrowe, Ernest John Welbourn 759, 1052

Dobson, B. Palin 506
Dorning, H. 82
Duchess of Connaught's Own Irish Rangers 1178
Duke of Lancaster's Own Yeomanry Cavalry 716-21, 740
Dumbell, H.C. 237
Dupuy, Richard E. 12
Dupuy, Trevor N. 12
Durtnell, C.S. 83

Earl of Chester's Regiment of Yeomanry Cavalry 722, 748
Earle, Thomas Algernon 723
East Lancashire Division 127, 826
East Lancashire Regiment 120-85
East Lancashire Royal Engineers 540
East Lancashire Territorial and Auxiliary Forces 827, 848
Eastwood, Stuart A. 274
Eccles Volunteers 760
Eckersley, Nathaniel 1006
Edwards, Thomas J. 13
Egerton family 702
Elletson, S. C. B. 367
Elliot, George H. 14
Elliott, James 492
Ellis, A. E. 1053
Ellison, Norman Frederick 1054
Engels, Friedrich 761
England, Volunteers 762
An Englishman (pseud) 956
Enser, A.G.S. 15-17
Entract, J. P. N. 150
Evans, Horace Carlton 418
Evans, Thomas 236

Fairtlough, James 492
Fallows, James 1055
Falls, Cyril 18
Fantom, William 84, 114
Farnworth Borough Council 1226-7
Farnworth Library 1387-8
Farnworth Urban District Council 1058-9
Farnworth Journal 1056-7
Farren, Sir Richard 407
Farrow, John 957
Fell, Alfred 958
Ferguson, Aldon Patrick 863-8

Ferguson, Ion 1228
Ferguson, Lionel 237
Fielding, J. H. 724
Finch, Hugh Knightly 113
Fisher, Charles A. 1060
Fisher, P. J. 1061
Fleming, Michael 996
Fleming, Suzie 988, 1210
Flixton, Parish of 1062
Flixton, World War II 1229
Floyd, Thomas Hope 317, 1399
Forde, Frank 1230
Forshaw, C. F. 763
Foulger, L. E. 1064
Fowler, Simon 19
Francis, Alfred E. F. 1065
Fraser-Tytler, Neil 419
Frederick, John B.M. 20
Freeman, Raymond 947
French, Gilbert J. 368
Funk, A.L. 21
Fusiliers' Association (Lancashire) 318
Fytton, Francis 85

Gander, Terry 22
Garnett family 704
Garratt, Stanley Reginald 319-20
Garvock, Sir J. 966
Garwood, John M. 151
Gaskell, Paul 369
German Air Force, World War II. 1231
Gibbon, Frederick P. 1066
Gibson, Jeremy 23
Gladdern, Norman 491
Gleave, John 86
Glenn, Edward 113
Gordon, L.L. 24
Goulding, Frank 1232
Graham, C. A. L. 507
Grant, Robert 115
Great Britain, government
  Ministry of Food 1424
  Ministry of Munitions 1183
  Ministry of Power 1425
Green, Alan 244
Green, F. C. 545
Green, Howard 25, 275
Greenhalgh, Joseph Dodson 990
Greenwood, Jack 1233
Grey de Wilton, Baron 635

Grieves, Keith 1067-8
Griffin, David 26
Grimbaldston, William H. 1082
Grime, Harold Riley 1234
Grimshaw, N. 636
Groom, Graham 869
Gummer, Selwyn 187

Hall, Jasper 276
Hall, Samuel 637
Hallam, John McQ. 321
Hallows, Ian S. 27
Hamilton, J. J. 625
Hampson, C. G. 1235
Hanlon, Robert 943
Hanson, Joseph (pseud: An Advocate for the Truth) 589, 638-41, 956
Hardy, Clive 1236
Hargreaves, Percy 725
Harington, Charles 236
Harland, John 642
Harrer, H. 1237
Harris, G. H. 1238
Harris, W. H. 277
Harris, William A. 764
Harrison, H. C. Vaughan 508
Haslingden, Borough of 1069, 1389
Haslingden Auxiliary Military Hospital 1164
Hastie, Robert 531
Hawkes, Arthur J. 1239
Hayhurst, Thomas H. 765
Haythornthwaite, Philip J. 1070
Hesketh, W. T. 766
Hides, Margaret 1241
Higham, Don 643
Higham, Robin 28
Higson, James 1006
Hitchins, H.W.E. 492
H.M.S. Colne 937
H.M. S. Janus 947
H.M.S. Lancaster 942
H.M.S. Penelope 910
Hobson, William 492
Hochland, Henry 1236
Hodge, R. J. 1242
Hodgkinson, Albert 278
Hodgson, J. E. G. 870
Holcroft, Fred 959
Holding, Norman 29

Holt, Alfred & Co. 921
Hollis, B. 898
Hope, Maurice 1071
Hopkinson, Edward Campbell 152
Hopwood, Harry 488-9, 1003, 1175
Horsfall, Jack 509
Horton, Max 909, 932
Houghton, A. T. 370
Hovis Ltd., Macclesfield 1243
Hoyle, John Baldwin 546
Huckle, Eileen 153
Huckle, John 153
Hugh, James 87-8, 510-12, 541, 828, 831, 871
Hughes, D.J. 1322
Hughes, John 1244
Hulme Volunteers 644
Hulton of Hulton 939
Hurst, Gerald Berkeley 420
Hutchings, W.H. 1156
Hutchinson, Geoffrey Lord Ilford 987, 1154-5
Hutchinson, John Richard 987
Hyde, C.H.R. 492
Hyde, Borough of 1074
Hyde Tipperary League 1072
Hyde, World War I 1073
Hyndburn Borough Council 154

Illidge, Richard 590-1
Imperial War Graves Commission 1075, 1245
Imperial War Museum 30
Irby WEA Local History Class 1246
Irwin, Francis 1076
Isle of Man
    Great War 1077
    Light Anti-Aircraft Regiment 501, 513
    Military Service Local Tribunal 1247

Jack, J.A. 236
Jackson, Aubrey Joseph 1248-9
Jackson, T. 1078
Jager, Harold 1250
James, A. H. 1079
James, Edward 872
James, Francis M. 155
James, Lieutenant-Colonel 421
Jarvis, Samuel P. 547

Jarvis, Rupert C. 592
Jebens, F. 548
Jenkinson, John 645
JHW 89
Johnson, Barry 90
Johnson, James 492
Johnson, Louis H. 726
Johnston, Harrison 91
Jolley, Thomas 727
Jones, Audrey 1251
Jones, Bill 1252
Jones, Helga 1253
Jones, Herbert 492
Jones, Louise 1254
Jones, Todger 1117
Jordan, Gerald 31

Kearsley Urban District Council 1227
Kellie, Harry Francis 92
Kemp, Paul 911
Kemp, Philip L. 1171
Kempster, F. 422-3
Kendrick, James 646
Kennedy, W. B. 1080
Kennish, William 912
Kersal Moor 960
Kerslake, W. B. 93
Keymer, Ronald W. 1174
Kidney, Ralph 1185-6
King, Hugh Lionel 32-3
King-Clark, R. 424
King's Cheshire Volunteer Legion 647
King's Lancashire Convalescent Hospital 1081
King's Liverpool Regiment 188-221, 238-40
King's Own Border Regiment 245-55, 265-7, 728
King's Own Royal Lancaster Regiment 268-99, 300-07
  Regimental Museum 300
King's Regiment *see* King's Liverpool Regiment
Kinnear, Sandy 1255
Kipling, Arthur Lawrence 32-33
Kirby, Henry L. 156-7, 961, 1082
Kissack, P. D. 1256
Kitzmiller, John II 34
Knapp, G.W.W. 492
Kniveton, Gordon N. 873
Knowles, Robert 962

Koenig, W.J. 41

Lancashire and Cheshire Regiments 963
Lancashire and Cheshire Volunteer 771
Lancashire Artillery Volunteer Corps 767-9
  8th, 813
Lancashire County Constabulary 1351
Lancashire County Library 180-2, 901, 1164-7, 1390-3
Lancashire County Regimental Museum 748, 1084
Lancashire Family History Society 1083
Lancashire Fusiliers 308-62, 1421
Lancashire Fusiliers Association Band 340
Lancashire Fusiliers Regimental Museum 362
Lancashire Lad 371
Lancashire Library 617-21, 1164, 1392
Lancashire Lieutenancy Records 982
Lancashire Military Musters 770
Lancashire Museum Service. County and Regimental Museum *see* Lancashire County Regimental Museum
Lancashire Record Office 529, 616, 704, 902, 939, 995, 1168, 1394-9
Lancashire Rifle Volunteers 772-8
  17th, 756
  39th (Welsh), 811
Lancashire: Voluntary Territorial Army Units 832, 1257
Lancashire Volunteer and Yeomanry Regiments 648
Lancashire Volunteer Regiment 1085-6
Lancaster, 10th Rifle Corps 780
Lancaster, Air Raid Precautions 1400, 1402
Lancaster, Army and Navy 997
Lancaster, Commissioners 964
Lancaster Corporation 289-908, 1258
Lancaster Home Guard 1259, 1401
Lancaster Library 303-7, 940-4
Lancaster Royal Grammar School 1260
Lancaster War Memorial 1087
Lancaster, World War II 1400-3
Lancastrian Volunteers 779
Lane, Tony 913
Langley, Michael 372
Lappin, J. P. 1261
Laskier, Frank 1262
Latter, John Cecil 342
Lattimer, Amy 1088

Law, Derek 35
Lawson, Cecil C.P. 36
Leadbetter, Thomas Harold 237
Leary, Frederick 729
Lee, John A. 1089
Leech, Joseph 216
Leech, T. 373
Lees, John 593
Leigh Borough 874
Leslie, J.H. 37
Lever, Ashton 594
Lever Brothers Ltd. 1090
Lewis, Adrian S. 158
Lewis, Peter 38
Linney, Peter 1263
Litchfield, Norman E. H. 39
Little, Eddie 1264
Littlewoods Mail Order Stores Ltd. 1265-6
Liverpool, Civil Defence Emergency Committee 1404-7
Liverpool Daily Post 1267
Liverpool Daily Post and Echo 1268
Liverpool Echo 1269-70
Liverpool Fusiliers 965
Liverpool, Home Guard Units 1271-3
Liverpool Libraries and Information Services, Record Office and Local History Department 238, 622, 705, 999, 1169-70, 1404-14
Liverpool. Munitions of War Committee 1169
Liverpool Record Office 159,
Liverpool Rifles Association 812, 833-6
Liverpool Scottish Museum 237
Liverpool Scottish Regiment 237
Liverpool University 1091, 1171, 1414
Liverpool Volunteers 649, 781, 1230
Liverpool, World War I 1092
Liverpool, World War II 1274-7
Lloyd, Ian 1278-9
Lomas, A.D. 837
Longbottom, F. W. 1093
Longbottom, J. C. 549
Long Preston. St Mary the Virgin 1094
Loyal Association of Manchester 595
Loyal Bolton Volunteers 650
Loyal North Lancashire Regiment 363-409

McCaffery, P. 407
McCann, John 343-4, 1280

Macardle, Kenneth C. 425
McCauley, John 1095, 1172
McFall, A.W.C. 581
MacFie, R.A.S. 237
McGilchrist, A. M. 222
McGuffie, T. H. 671
McGuinness, J. H. 94
Machell, P.W. 256
McInnes, I. 467
Mackenzie, B. S. 493
McKenzie-Annand, A. 966
McKinnell, Bryden 237
Maclean, Lorraine 237
Maddocks, Graham 223-4
Mainwaring, George Ernest 40
Makepeace, Chris 1281
Manchester 1st Battalion 651
Manchester and Salford Independent Volunteer Rifle Regiment 657
Manchester and Salford Light Horse Volunteers 658-62
Manchester and Salford Royal Volunteers 663
Manchester and Salford Volunteer Corps of Infantry 664-5
Manchester and Salford Volunteers 666-8
Manchester and Salford Yeomanry Cavalry 730
Manchester City Art Galleries 426
Manchester Evening News 1282
Manchester, Grand Review of Troops 967
Manchester Military Association 597-9
Manchester, Navy 914
Manchester Regiment 427-64, 490
Manchester Rifle Volunteers 782-3
Manchester Royal Artillery 514
Manchester, Royal Manchester Volunteers 656
Manchester, Royal Marines 968
Manchester, Scottish Volunteers 669
Manchester, St. Mary's Collegiate Church 465
Manchester Volunteers 652-5, 670
Mansfield, William 113
Manx National Heritage 1172-3, 1415
Marden, Arthur William 466
Margerison, Russell 876
Marples, D.A.B. 237
Marriott, Sydney 236
Marsh, B. J. 1283
Marshall, William 160

Mason, Ernest Mitchelson 877
Mason, George 291
Massey, Victoria 1284
Mather & Platt Ltd. 1096
Mather, P. R. 515
Mather, Tom 396
May, Ralph Keogh 257-9, 292
Mayer, Joseph 969
Mayer, S.L. 41
Medlycott, Mervyn 23
"Meannee" (pseudonym) 95
Mellersh, Harold Edward Leslie 161
Melly, George 529
Mersey Docks and Harbour Board 1285
Merseyside Maritime Museum 946, 1174
Merseyside Record Office 1416
Merseyside Volunteer Infantry Brigade 814
Miers, R. D. M. C. 225
Miles (pseud.) 96-9, 516, 838-9, 878
Militargeographische Einzelangaben uber England 1393
Miller, John Christie 784
Milne, Samuel M. 42
Mitchinson, K. W. 467
Moffatt, James W.S. 492
Moorhouse, Geoffrey 1097
Morecambe Corporation 1098
Morison, J. P. 1184
Morten, J. C. 1099
Mount, Kevin 1286
Mullaly, B. R. 550-1
Munn, Lieutenant-Colonel 785
Mursell, Arthur 786
Musgrove, W. 1100
Myers, William 617

Nabarro, Derrick 1287
Napier, Sir Charles 113
Nash, Thomas 468
National Army Museum 114-17, 239-40, 408-9, 488-90, 184-7, 581-4, 624-6, 749, 1000-04, 1175-7, 1417-19,
National Association of Discharged Sailors and Soldiers 1101
National Publishing Company 1102-3
National Registration Act 1187
Nayler, J. 1104
Naylor, Bill 1288
Neligan, T. 552
Nelson Borough Council 1105

Nelson Leader 1106
Newbigging, William Patrick Eric 466
Newnham, Maurice 879
Newton-in-Makerfield Local Militia 787
Nicholson, Lothian 162
Nield, James 788
Northern Air Division 880
North West Sound Archive 1107
Northwich Hundred 969
Northwich War Memorial 1108

Oatts, Louis Balfour 553
O'Dell, Audrey 1289
Ogle, Henry 1109
Oldham Chronicle 815, 1110
Oldham Corporation 469
   Tramways Department 1111
Oldham, County Borough of 824
Oldham Local Studies Library 491, 1178-9
Oldham Metropolitan Borough 1112
Oldham Recruits and Local Heroes 1171
Oldham Regiment of Local Militia 600
Oldham Troop Yeomanry Cavalry 731
Ormerod, George 700

Packman, John B. 361
Palin, B. 517
Parachute Regiment, 13th Lancashire Battalion, T. A. 816
Parachute Training School, Ringway 9032
Parker, Rev Canon 970
Parkin, Betty C. 1290
Parr, John 352
Parry, William Augustus 470
Partridge, Joseph 971
Pendlebury, J. W. 163
Pendleton Volunteers 672
Pennington, Thomas Edward 471
Perrett, Bryan 972, 1291
Pertwee, Jon 915
Peters, H. 973
Philips, Francis 732
Phillips, Shakespear 601
Phoenix, J. P. 1292
Pike, Arnold Norman 1432
Pitts, James 1082
Pizer, R. 1171
Polish Air Force 881-2
Polish Artillery (Manchester) 1293

Pomeroy, Ralph Legge 733
Pomfret, Joan 1399
Poole, John 602-4, 673
Potter, C. H. 345
Pownall, Thomas 998
Preece, Geoff 472
Preston, Henry 974
Preston, Thomas 184-5, 789
Preston, T. H. 184
Preston, W.J. 492
Preston Catholic College 1294
Preston Corporation 397
Preston Guardian 1113
Preston Sailors and Soldiers Free Buffet 1166
Preston Volunteer Training Corps 790
Preston War Memorial 1114
Preston, World War I 1115-16
Primitive Methodist School, Waterhead 1327
Prince of Wales' Regiment of Dragoon Guards 734-8
Prince of Wales's Volunteers (South Lancashire Regiment) *see* South Lancashire Regiment
Princess Charlotte of Wales's Regiment of Dragoon Guards 739
Prisoners of War Packing Centre 1295
Pronay, Nicholas 49
Prosser, George 492
Public Record Office 43
Pugh, N. R. 916-17
Purdon, H. G. 399-400

Queen's Lancashire Regiment 494-9
Quincey, Sylvia 1296

Radcliffe, Leslie N. 883-4, 1117
R.A.F. Padgate 885
Rainford, R. W. B. 886
Rawstorne, John George 605
Ray, Cyril 346-7
Read, Fergus 740
Reeves, D. 791-2
Regiment of Body Guards 975
Regimental Museum, Preston 183, 409, 584
Renison, J.D.W. 235
Richardson, Arthur Johnstone 582-3
Richardson, Neil 1118

Richardson, Sue 473, 1080, 1118
Ridgway, E. 1297
Rigby, Bernard 100-101
Riley, C. O. L. 793
Ringway Airport 875
Roberts, Enos Herbert Glynne 226
Roberts, Gilbert 924
Roberts, W. 1172
Robertson, G. W. 517
Robertson, J. C. 227
Robertson, Terence 918
Robinson, Brian R. 887
Robinson, G. 474
Robinson, H. A. 919
Robinson, Jack 1298
Robinson, William 995
Rochdale, Bolton and Stockport Volunteers 674
Rochdale Observer 1180
Rochdale Times 1181
Rocke, Joan 1299
Roe, Tom 401
Roeder, Charles 920
Rogan, John 1112
Rogers, H. 403
Rose, R. B. 794
Rosens, J.P. 237
Roskill, Stephen Wentworth 921
Rossendale Society for Genealogy and Heraldry 1119-20, 1160, 1167, 1300
Rowbottom, Lever Robert 480
Rowland, Stan 1301
Royal Air Force 901
Royal Air Forces Association 888-90
Royal Army Medical Corps War Memorial Fund 1302
Royal Artillery Association 518-19
Royal Artillery Historical Trust Archives 533-5
Royal Auxiliary Air Force 610 (County of Chester Squadron) 900
Royal British Legion 164
Royal Engineers
  1st Cheshire Royal Engineers 536
  Corps of Royal Engineers 537
Royal Field Artillery
  2nd West Lancashire Brigade 532
  "A" Battery, 330th Brigade 530, 1168
Royal Lancashire Militia 617. 621, 626
  Hospital 619
Royal Lancashire Volunteers 675, 666,

702, 704
Royal Lancaster Militia 620-1
Royal Manchester and Salford Volunteers 677
Royal Manchester Regiment 678
Royal Manchester Volunteers 679-83, 702
Royal Regiment of Fusiliers 348
Royal Welsh Volunteers 684
Royal Westmorland Battalion of Militia 606-7
Royd, Captain 708
Rutter, David 685

St. Annes-on-Sea 1121
St. George's Volunteers 686, 706-7
Sale Moor 687
Salford Archives Centre 1005, 1182, 1420
Salford Volunteers 688
Sanderson, Thomas 1152
Sargeaunt, Bertram Edward 976-7, 1122
Scarlett, James Yorke 970, 978, 986
Scarth, Alan J. 922
Scheepers, Commandant 584
Schofield, John 1082
Scotch Brigade 689
Scott, Daniel 741
Seager, Edward 1002
Sharp, C. Martin 1304
Sharp, John R. 891
Shaw, Frank 1305
Shaw, T. P. 349
Shears, Philip J. 260
Shepperd, Gilbert Alan 228
Short, Walter 1123
Sidebotham, Randal 1124
Silvester, J. 690
Simpson, Alexander William 520
Simpson, Frank 102-106, 795
Skinner 107
Slack, James 475
Smith, Charles 108
Smith, David J. 892-4
Smith, Leslie 1125
Smith, Myron J. 44
Smith, Peter J. C. 1126, 1306-7
Smith, Robert Jeffrey 712
Smith, Sam D. 978
Smith, Thomas 492
Smyth, Benjamin 350-2
Smythies, Raymond Henry R. 554-5

Sotheby's 923
South Lancashire Regiment (Prince of Wales' Volunteers) 556-77,
Southport Royal Naval Artillery 924
Spalding, Hilton 237
Spence, J. C. 1308
Spencer, Julie 109
Spiers, Edward M. 45
Spooner, Tony 1309
Sprenger, Cyril H. 1310
Spring, Howard 925
Stanley, Earls of 995
Stanley, Ferdinand Charles 229
Stanley of Alderley 796
Starkey, Pat 1311-12
Starkie, Thomas 608
Stedman, Michael 353
Stephenson, William Henry 521
Stephenson, W. H. 840
Stewart-Brown, R. 926
Stitt, J.C. 522
Stockport Corps of Riflemen 709
Stockport Independent Cavalry 691
Stockport Loyal Volunteers 697
Stockport Museums and Art Gallery Service 1313
Stockport Volunteers 692
Stockport Yeomanry 742, 750-1
Stourton, Marmaduke 492
Strachan, Hew 46
Stuart, George Henderson 424
Stubbs, Herbert Molyneux 1174
Stubbs, S. 1127
Summerfield, Anne 1314
Surtees, George 354-5
Sutherland, Douglas 261-2
Swinson, Arthur 47
Synge, Laurence Millington 523
Synge, W. A. J. 235

Tallon, J. 927
Tameside Local Studies Library 492, 1183- 4, 1315, 1422-3
Tameside. World Wars I & II 1316
Tapley 1128
Tatham, William 928
Taunton, Book of 1129
Taylor, Edward Lyon 797
Taylor, F.A.J. 1130
Taylor, H. 1153

Taylor, H.S. 237
Taylor, James 1131
Tempest, R. 999
Territorial, Auxiliary and Volunteer Reserve Association for the North West and The Isle of Man 841
Terry, Astley 798
Thomas, Garth 48
Thomas, J. J. 230
Thomas, L. J. 743
Thomas Pownall's Troop of Dragoons 998
Thompson, George 1132, 1317
Thompson, M. 1141
Thompson, William 492
Thomson, J. 895
Thorne, A. D. 293
Thornycroft, C. M. 476
Thorpe, Frances 49
Threlfall, T. R. 231
Thurot, Francois 920
Tildsley, Dorothy 1318
Titherington, Arthur 1319
Toc. H. Rossendale Group 1145
Tomkinson, William 988
Tottington Rifle Corps 806
Towneley Hall Art Gallery and Museum 979
Townend, Michael S. 1320
Travis, Arthur 929
Trescatheric, Bryn 1321-2
Turner, William 165-8, 236

Ulverston Volunteer Infantry 634, 693
Urmston Library 1188
Urmston Urban District Council 1323
Urmston War Comforts Committee 1426
Usher, H. Y. 799
Uttley family 152

Valentine, H. 492
Vane, Francis 1189
Vardon, John 969
Vernon, A. 306-7
Vaughan, Edward 492
Venn, George 758
Verdin, Richard 744
Veysey, Arthur Geoffrey 1324
Vickers Ltd. 938
A Volunteer pseud (see Hanson, Joseph)

Volunteer Journal 800

Wade, Beryl 1325
Wadham, W. F. A. 294-5
Wadsworth, W. W. 524, 1133
Walker, Frederick John 918
Walls, William 1190
Walsh, George 896
Walsh, Jean M. 505
Walsh, Philip J. 609
Walsh, R. Raymond 156-7, 500, 1082, 1326
Walton, D. 694
Ward, C. H. 1134
Ward, H. 1135
Ward, Ron 1127
Wardle, Arthur C. 930
Warre, William 117, 1001
Warren, C. E. T. 931
Waterhead Primitive Methodist School 1327
Watson, Campbell 236-7
Watson, H.M. 237
Webb, Harold 1136
Webb, Raymond John 897
Weir and District War Memorial 1137
Welsh and Midland Command 111, 989
Wemyss, David Edward Gillespie 932
Werrell, Len 1328
West, Margery 1139
Westall, R. 1329
Western Command 111, 989
Westhoughton Roll of Honour 1140
West Lancashire Division 842, 1138, 1170
West Lancashire Division Territorial Forces Association 843-4
West Lancashire Medium Regiment 525-6
West Lancashire Territorial Army and Air Force Association 1403
Westmore, A.W. 1141
Westmorland and Cumberland Yeomanry 747
Westmorland Volunteer Forces 703
Westropp, Henry Charles Edward 422-3, 428, 477
Whalley, Joseph Lawson 296-7, 809-10, 980
Whalley-Kelly, H. 578
Whalley, Lancashire 1142
Wheeler, John, 944
Wheeler, Kenneth 356

Whelan, Peter 169-71
Whiston, Harold W. 1143
Whiston, W.M. & Sons Ltd. 1143
White, Arthur Sharpin 50
White, D. F. 403
Whittaker, L. B. 51
Whittington-Egan, Richard 1330
Whitton, Frederick Ernest 579
Whitworth, R. A. 1331
Whitworth, Rodney 1332
Whyte, Wolmer 478
Wickes, H. L. 52
Widditt, John 695
Wigan and District Volunteer Rifles 801
Wigan Armed Association 710
Wigan County Borough 1192-3
Wigan Drill Hall 802
Wigan Heritage Service
   Archives 710, 752, 947, 1006, 1190
   History Shop 998, 1191, 1427-30
Wigan Loyal Volunteers 710
Wigan Territorials 479
Wigan Volunteer Light Horse 710, 745
Wigan Volunteers 480
Wigan Yeomanry Cavalry 752
Wilbraham, Richard 988
Wilde, Herbert 481
Wilde, S. 1423
Wilkinson, Eric 263, 803
Wilkinson, J. 1433
Wilkinson, James 1176
Williams, Ellis 298
Williams, Jack 933
Williams, John 492
Williams, Mark 934
Williams, W.D. 1333
Williams, W. R. 232
Williamson, Ralph John Thomas 299
Willis, Steve 898
Wilson, Eunice 53
Wilson, Frank 54
Wilson, J. 404
Wilson, S. J. 482
Winder, Eric 804
Wingfield, A. J. 527
Winton, John 935
Wirral Libraries 905, 1431-5
Wise, Terence 55
Wolff, Anne S. 110
Women's Junior Air Corps 902, 904
Wood, Brian 1334

Wood, Ernest 483
Wood, F. W. 172-3
Wood, Richard 936
Wood, Walter 233, 357
Woodcock & Sons 359
Wright, John 981
Wright, Simon 1335
Wurtzburg, C. E. 234
Wylly, Harold C. 264, 405-6, 484-7
Wyrall, Everard 235

Yarwood, Derek 805
Young, Henry & Sons Ltd. 1144
Young, William 156

Ziegler, Janet 56

SUBJECT INDEX

The numbers cited refer to the bibliographical entries.

5th Princess Charlotte of Wales's Dragoon Guards 733, 739, 951
7th Armoured Division 1213
41st (Oldham) Royal Tank Regiment 824
53rd (Welsh) Division 1134
156 (Merseyside and Greater Manchester) Transport Regiment 817

Accrington 153, 159, 165-171, 1007
Adamson, Joseph & Co., Ltd. 1423
Airfields, military 892-3, 898
Air Raid Precautions 1237, 1264, 1274, 1277, 1300, 1336-7, 1351, 1360, 1367, 1369, 1373, 1397-9, 1400, 1404, 1408
Air Raids 1027, 1126, 1151-3, 1204, 1239, 1342
Altcar 823
Appleton 1064
Army, British,
  Bibliographies 5, 6
  General guides 1
Art 1314
Ashton-in-Makerfield 1428
Ashton-under-Lyne 974
  munitions explosion 1015, 1183-4
Audenshaw 1068
Audlem 1359
Avro Aircraft 1248

Bacup 1338
Bamber Bridge 1328
Bands, regimental 515
Bantams 1010
Barnoldswick 1397
Barnston, Roger, Volunteer Corps 698
Barrow-in-Furness 1161, 1321-2
Battlefields 24-5
Birkenhead 1016-17, 1245, 1431
Blackburn 1019, 1082, 1101, 1339-41, 1397
Blackburn Athletes' Volunteer Force 1012, 1146-50
Blacko 1031
Blackpool 1020-2, 1060, 1070, 1165, 1202-5, 1233, 1301, 1392, 1394
  Old Contemptibles 1394
Blitz 1231, 1252, 1261, 1268, 1282, 1303, 1329-32, 1335, 1368, 1411
Boer War 72, 715, 720, 726, 959, 992-3
Bolton 962, 1024-30, 1033, 1037, 1053, 1176, 1206, 1342-51, 1434
  World War I archives 1151-3
Bolton Artillery 503-6, 527
Bolton Loyal Volunteer Corps 630-1, 650, 674
Bootle 1282
Border Regiment 241-267
Borneo Bough 59
Bramhall 1240
Brierfield 1397
British Legion 164, 1395
Bucklow 612
Burma 859
Burnley 907, 981, 1037, 1320, 1352, 1395
Burnley Barracks 995
Burtonwood Airbase 818, 856, 863, 867
Bury 1097, 1154-5, 1353-8
Bury Loyal Association 952
Bury Volunteer Movement 765

Cavalry
  Bibliographies 14
Chadderton 1129
Cheshire, Royal Auxiliary Air Force 871, 878
Cheshire Home Guard 1219, 1308
Cheshire Militia 613-4, 624
Cheshire Regiment 57-119
  Arabia 89
  Archives 111-119
  Boer War 72
  Periodicals 60, 66, 67

159

Public Health records 111
Territorial Army 87-88, 97-99
World War I 61, 63, 69, 70, 75, 78, 82, 90, 104-105, 108, 110
World War II 64, 71, 79, 83
Cheshire Rifle Volunteers 798, 807
Cheshire Royal Engineers 1225
Cheshire Territorial and Auxiliary Forces 822, 828-31, 838-9, 845-6
Cheshire Volunteer Regiment 112, 759, 1157
Cheshire Yeomanry 715, 734-6, 744, 746
Chester 1093, 1299
Chester Volunteers 535, 588, 795
Chorley 150
Chorlton-cum-Hardy 1399
Church 1397
Civil defence 1369
Clayton 1422
Clayton-le-Moors 1397
Clitheroe 1360-2
Clwyd 1324
Colne 992, 1046-7, 1119-20, 1159-60, 1167, 1363-4
Colours 42
Commonwealth War Graves Commission 1221
Conscientious objection 1312, 1370
Cotton Manufacturers' Association 1397
Crimean War 276, 949-50, 961, 970, 978, 981, 988, 994
Cumberland and Westmorland Joint Territorial Force Association 825, 847
Cumberland Rifle Volunteers 808
Cumberland Volunteers 701

Darwen 869
Davyhulme 1224
De Havilland 1249, 1304
Diaries
  Personal 84, 91, 110, 113, 236-237, 361-362, 492, 995, 1151-3, 1172, 1195
  War 108, 111, 216, 236, 300, 362, 492, 535, 1133
Dictionaries 10
"Doodlebugs" 1306-7
Duchess of Connaught's Own Irish Rangers 1178
Duke of Lancaster's Own Light Infantry Militia 569
Duke of Lancaster's Own Yeomanry 711-13, 716-17, 720-1, 726, 740, 743, 748
Dunkirk 1220, 1305

Earl of Chester's Regiment of Yeomanry Cavalry 722, 729, 744, 749
East Lancashire Association Territorial Force 848
East Lancashire Division 127, 826, 1066, 1080
East Lancashire Field Ambulance 1065
East Lancashire Regiment 120-85
  XXX Regiment 140
  Archives 174-175
  Gallipoli 122
  Lilywhites 143, 155, 157
  Periodicals 134-7, 143, 149
  World War I 122, 130-2, 138, 141, 147, 150-1, 157, 162, 165-71, 173
  World War II 125, 133, 142, 160, 162
Eccles Volunteers 760
Encyclopedias 10, 12, 22
Evacuation 1207, 1241, 1251, 1253, 1372, 1409, 1414, 1422
Exercises 59, 93

Fallowfield 1422
Family history, army records 19
Farnworth 1056-9, 1118, 1226-7, 1387-8
Fencibles 48
Film 1009
Fleetwood 973
Flixton 1062, 1229
Food Control 1045
Formby 1177
Fulwood 1396, 1398
Fulwood Barracks, Preston 380, 408, 496
Furness 958

Gallipoli 132, 820, 1097
Garstang 1398
German Air Force 1231

Haslingden, 1069, 1100, 1164, 1389,

1398
Hazel Grove 1240
Heaton Park, R.A.F. 891
H.M.S. Chester 908
H.M.S. Colne 937
H.M.S. Janus 947
H.M.S. Lancaster 942
H.M.S. Penelope 910, 933
H.M.S. Thetis 931
H.M.S. Thunderbolt 931
H.M.Y. Eradne 917
Home Guard 48, 51, 1219, 1235, 1250, 1256, 1259, 1271-3, 1308, 1338, 1340, 1359, 1361-3, 1398, 1401, 1428
Horwich 381, 1398
Hospitals, military 1081, 1142, 1164, 1168
Hovis Ltd. 1243
Hulme Barracks 948
Hulme Volunteers 644
Huyton 1398
Hyde 1072-4, 1124
Hyndburn 1398

Imperial War Graves Commission 1075
Imperial War Museum 30
India 371, 387
Inniskilling Dragoon Guards
Isle of Man 206, 501, 513, 873, 920, 976-7, 1018, 1077, 1095, 1122, 1139, 1172, 1247, 1415

Kearsley 1118, 1226-7
Kersal Moor 960

King's Liverpool Regiment 186-240
   Archives 236-40
   Liverpool Pals 223-224
   Liverpool Scottish 217-22, 237
   Periodicals 199, 202, 210, 220-1
   Rifle Battalion 190, 200
   World War I 204, 208-209, 216, 222-24, 226, 229, 234-5
   World War II
King's Own Border Regiment 241-67
   Archives 265-7
   Pals Battalion 263
   Periodicals 249, 251-2
   World War I 241-2, 254, 261, 263-4
   World War II 244
King's Own Royal Regiment Lancaster 268-307
   Archives 300-07
   Boer War 273, 302-07
   Periodicals 284-5
   World War I 270, 283, 287, 294
   World War II 282
Kohima 1283
Knutsford 1038

Lancashire Artillery Volunteer Corps 767-9, 809, 813
Lancashire Fusiliers 308-62, 1421
   Archives 358-362
   Boer War 321
   Kohima 343-344
   Periodicals 318, 324-6, 329, 332
   Salford Pals 353
   World War I 308, 311, 316, 325, 327, 332, 336-7, 342, 345, 356
   World War II 321, 333
Lancashire Hussars Yeomanry 723
Lancashire Light Horse Volunteers 799
Lancashire Militia 625-6
Lancashire Mounted Rifle Volunteers 799
Lancashire Rifle Volunteers 230, 544, 755-7, 772-80, 785, 811
Lancashire Territorial Army 832
Lancashire Volunteers 648
Lancashire Yeomanry Cavalry 751
Lancaster 928, 1400-2
Lancaster Home Guard 1259, 1401
Leigh, prisoner-of-war camp 1125
Leyland 1398
Lieutenancy, Lancashire 953, 982
Lifeboats 1177
Little Lever 1398
Littlewoods 1266-7
Liverpool 762, 911, 922, 926, 930, 955, 1041, 1043, 1048-9, 1132, 1196, 1206, 1237, 1242, 1244, 1261, 1265-77, 1291-2, 1325, 1329-32, 1404-14
   Airport, 860
   Dock Battalion 1067
   Military Education Committee 1171
   Munitions Committee 1169
   Port 1285, 1317, 1333
Liverpool Battery 971

Liverpool Fusiliers 965
Liverpool Independent Rifle Corps 705
Liverpool Irish Volunteers 1230
Liverpool Rifles Association 812, 833-6
Liverpool Scottish 217-22
Liverpool, University of 1091
  Officers Training Corps 1171
Liverpool Volunteers 643, 649, 781, 791-2, 794
Loyal Lincoln Volunteers 402
Loyal North Lancashire Regiment 363-409
  Archives 407-9
  Boer War 399
  Crime 380, 408
  Periodicals 376, 382-3, 398
  World War I 369-70, 373, 379, 381, 384, 388, 390, 394, 406
  World War II 385-6, 396, 401

Macclesfield 1143, 1243
Macclesfield Volunteers 633
Malaya 86, 363
Manchester 1103, 1236, 1393
  World War I 1008
  World War II 1236, 1280-1
Manchester and Salford Independent Volunteer Rifle Regiment 589, 638-41, 657
Manchester and Salford Light Horse Volunteers 658-62
Manchester and Salford Royal Volunteers 663, 671, 677-83
Manchester and Salford Volunteers 627, 637, 663-8, 690
Manchester and Salford Yeomanry Cavalry 730, 732
Manchester, aviation 887
Manchester City Council 1264
Manchester Corps of Marines 628, 967
Manchester Corps, Yeomanry 725
Manchester, Port of 945
Manchester Regiment 410-92, 1175
  Archives 488-92
  Ardwick Battalions 413, 436
  Boer War 434, 438, 445, 466, 470, 474, 489
  Oldham Comrades 463, 467, 481, 483, 491
  Periodicals 433, 439-42, 444, 449-50, 454-5, 458-9, 462
  World War I 410, 414-15, 419, 420-3, 425, 428, 435, 444, 455-9, 463, 471, 473, 477, 481-3, 488, 490
Manchester Rifle Volunteers 766, 782-3
Manchester Scottish Volunteers 669
Manchester Volunteers 642, 645, 651-6, 670-1
Manchester Loyal Association 595
Manchester Military Association 597-9
Manchester Militia 601-4
Meannee 113
Marton 609
Medals 11, 24, 923, 980, 983, 1042, 1055, 1191, 1197, 1391, 1410
Medical services 1065, 1141, 1142, 1151, 1217-18, 1289
Merchant Navy 1174
Mersey Docks and Harbour Board 1285, 1817
Merseyside Volunteer Infantry Brigade 814
Military History, Bibliography 1-56
Military tribunals 1068, 1151-3
Militia 48, 585-626
  Archives 610-26
  Lists 22, 37
Morecambe 1098
Museums 55, 100, 257, 301, 314, 472, 979
Musters 23

Napier, Charles 113
National Service Records 1374
Nelson 1105-6, 398
Newton-in-Makerfield Local Militia 787
Northwich 969, 1108, 1211

Oldham 957, 1110-12, 1178-9
Oldham Horse Association 724
Oldham Regiment of Local Militia 593, 600
Oldham Troop Yeomanry Cavalry 724, 731
Oldham Volunteers 815
Orders, regimental 111
Ormskirk 1398

Padgate Airbase 872, 885
Padiham 1398
Pals 150, 153, 165-171, 223-4, 263, 353, 410, 463, 467
Parachute Regiment 816, 879
Peace celebrations 1382, 1385
Pendle 1286, 1320
Pendleton Volunteers 672
Perch Rock 1071
Polish Air Force Association 881-2
Polish Artillery 1293
Port Sunlight 1090
Poulton-le-Fylde 1398
Prescot Militia 612
Preston 961, 1051, 1113-16, 1166, 1168, 1397-8
Preston Royal Air Force 888-90
Preston Volunteer Infantry 636, 790, 793
Prince of Wales' Regiment of Dragoon Guards 734-8, 954
Prince of Wales's Volunteers *see* South Lancashire Regiment
Prince Regent's Own Regiment of Royal Lancashire Militia 596
Prisoner of War camps 1125, 1127, 1224, 1287
Prisoners of War 1131, 1295, 1319, 1365-6, 1434
Property, requisitioning of 1377
Public Record Office 7, 19, 43, 48

Queen's Lancashire Regiment 493-500

Radar 1423
Rationing 1375, 1424-5
Reconstruction 1383
Red Cross Society 1035
Refugees 1376
Regiments
 Badges 9, 13, 32, 33
 Bibliographies 2, 4, 26, 27, 34, 50, 52
 British Army
 Lancashire and Cheshire 963
 Lineage 20, 47
 Nicknames 8
 Records 9
Rifle Volunteers 48, 753-815
 Archives 806-15
Ringway Airport 875, 897, 903

Rochdale 1180-1
Rochdale Rifle Volunteers 772
Rochdale Volunteers 674, 797
Rock Ferry 919
Rolls-Royce 1278-9
Rossendale 1145
Roundheads
Royal Air Force 38, 53, 850-905
 Air Training Corps 851-55
 Archives 899-905
 Manchester Squadron 850
Royal Artillery 175, 501-35
 Archives 528-535
 World War I 509, 524
 World War II 504-5, 525
Royal Auxiliary Air Force 150, 871
Royal Engineers 536-541
 Cheshire Royal Engineers 539, 1225
 East Lancashire Engineers 538, 540
Royal Lancashire Militia 362, 585, 605, 617, 619-21, 625-6
Royal Lancashire Volunteer Regiment 635, 675-6, 704
Royal Lancaster Volunteers 635, 675-6, 695, 702, 810
Royal Manchester Volunteers 700
Royal Navy 349, 906-47, 1174, 1261, 1269
 Archives 937-47
 Bibliography 35, 40
Royal Welsh Volunteers 684
Royal Westmorland Militia 606-7

Saar 128, 177
Saddleworth 906
St Annes On The Sea 1121
St George's Regiment of Volunteers 686, 706
Salford 1096, 1102, 1136, 1182, 1335
Salford Volunteers 688
Scotch Brigade 689
Sealand 866
Singapore 461
Skelmersdale 1397
Somme, Battle of 132, 1014
South Lancashire Regiment (Prince of Wales's Volunteers) 542-84, 1155
 Archives 580-4
 Boer War 542, 552, 573
 Periodicals 566-7, 575

163

World War I 546, 558, 571-2
Southport 924
Stockport Corps of Riflemen 697, 709
Stockport Independent Cavalry 691
Stockport, King's Cheshire Volunteer Legion 647
Stockport Rifle Volunteers 763, 784
Stockport Volunteers 670, 692, 694, 697,
Stockport Yeomanry 742, 750
Stonyhurst 1076
Stonyhurst College 1326
Stretford 1195, 1397
Swinton 1318

Tatton 1216
Taunton, Massachusetts 1129
Territorial Army 520-1, 816-49, 1257, 1378
Territorial Artillery 39
Territorial Force 816-49
   Archives 844-9
Thornton Cleveleys 1397
Toc H. 1145
Tockholes 1128
Todmorden 1089
Tottington Home Guard 1235
Tottington Rifle Corps 806
Trafford Local Studies Library 118
Trawden 1397

Ulverston Volunteers 634, 685, 693
Uniforms 2, 11, 32, 33, 36, 211, 954
Urmston 1323

Vickers Ltd. 938, 1194
Vimy Ridge 90
Volunteers 627-710, 1052
   Archives 696-710

Walton-le-Dale 1397
War charities 1379, 1381
War comforts 1426
War damage 1380
War Memorials 129, 198, 286, 378-9, 961, 1016, 1024, 1031, 1064, 1069, 1083, 1087, 1108, 1114-15, 1119-21, 1137, 1151, 1159-60, 1167, 1192, 1205, 1258, 1260, 1300, 1302, 1353, 1355, 1357, 1364, 1386
Warrington Rifle Volunteers 753, 758
Warrington Volunteers 586, 632, 646
Waterhead 1327
West Lancashire Field Ambulance 1141
West Lancashire Brigade 1133
West Lancashire Division 1050, 1138, 1170
West Lancashire Territorial and Auxiliary Forces Association 837, 840, 842-4
Westhoughton 929, 1140
Westmorland and Cumberland Yeomanry 728, 741, 747
Westmorland Volunteers 701
Whitton 754
Wigan 802, 849, 1192-3, 1427-30
Wigan and District Volunteer Rifles 801
Wigan Armed Association 710
Wigan Loyal Volunteers 710
Wigan Volunteer Light Horse 745
Wigan Yeomanry 752
Winwick 1232
Wirral 119, 968
World War II 1246
Women 1196, 1276, 1313
Woodford 1214
Woodvale Airbase 864-865, 868
World War I 1007-1193
   Bibliographies 15, 18, 41
World War II 1194-1434
   Bibliographies 3, 7, 16, 17, 21, 44, 56
   Film 49

Yeomanry 48, 711-52
   Archives 746-52
Ypres 317, 1063, 1170